HIDDEN TREASURE TALES
FROM 'BLACKWOOD'

HIDDEN TREASURE TALES

from

' BLACKWOOD '

WILLIAM BLACKWOOD

EDINBURGH AND LONDON

1969

© 1969

WILLIAM BLACKWOOD & SONS LTD
45 GEORGE STREET
EDINBURGH 2

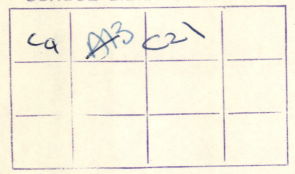
PRINTED AT THE PRESS OF THE PUBLISHER
WILLIAM BLACKWOOD & SONS LTD, EDINBURGH

SBN 85158 018 1

CONTENTS

Continued overleaf

These stories first appeared in *Blackwood's Magazine*
on the dates indicated

1

THE LOST SECRET OF THE COCOS GROUP

J. Jebb

Those of my readers who some years back were fortunate enough to see Bierstadt's ' Storm in the Rocky Mountains ' will remember the lake—or rather lakes, for there are two of them—which form so prominent a feature in the middle distance. They are called the Chicago lakes, and for a certain wild grandeur of surrounding scenery are perhaps unrivalled in the world.

On the north-western shore of the upper of these lakes is a narrow bay or inlet almost entirely shut in by vast dykes of rock, half hidden by a thick growth of stately but storm-worn pines, which find roothold in the interstices of the crags, and grow thickly above on the shoulder of the gulch. Enclosed in this natural amphitheatre, and sloping slightly upwards from the lake shore, is a small open space covered with thick and velvety turf. Here, during the fall of '65, on the evening of which I write, were camped a party of explorers, seven in number—four being white men, whilst the remainder were Indians of the Ute tribe, who had been engaged as guides and hunters to the expedition. Of the white men two were Western Americans, tall sinewy men, the very beau idéals of the frontiersman ;

the third was of mixed nationality—an Irish American, not of the vile Fenian type, now, alas, so prevalent, but a wild, hearty good fellow, who, impelled by the national ' demon of unrest ', had spent the last ten years of his life in wandering through America from the St Lawrence to the San Juan, sometimes doctor, sometimes, as now, miner, and generally Ishmaelite. Amongst his friends he is generally known as ' the Doc ', though for the outside world he bears the name of O'Brien.

The four explorers, or ' prospectors ', as they are there called, had started from Denver—then a mere camp— about a fortnight previously, and working up Clear creek to its junction with Chicago creek, had followed the latter stream up to the lakes from which it takes its name, and had now for several days been camped on the spot already roughly described, which, being naturally so secluded, offered a capital camping-ground in a district where the Indians, though then nominally friendly, were rightly considered neighbours to be, if possible, avoided. The days, varied by an occasional bear-hunt, had been passed in carefully ' prospecting ' for indications of the precious metals, which were then supposed to exist in the spurs of Grey's Peak. Hitherto the search had not been very successful, but the explorers were full of hope and energy, and forgetting yesterday, always thought of tomorrow. The evenings were occupied with the usual routine of camp-life : supper being cooked and disposed of, arms and accoutrements carefully looked to and cleaned, a small ration of grog would be served out, and, seated round the cheery crackling fire, and soothed by the ever-to-be-commended evening pipe, the hours would rapidly pass in social chat, varied now and then by some tale of wild adventure, in which the narrator was generally a witness, if not indeed a participator, till, tired with the day's work, or warned by the night chill of the lateness of the hour, one and all, with feet turned towards the fire, drop asleep, each rolled in his blanket or buffalo-robe, trusting the safety of the camp to the watchfulness of two gaunt dogs, whose quickness of ear, however, would scarcely be surpassed by that possessed by the Indian braves, who sleep, or appear to sleep, equally soundly with their white allies. Such the scene and such the actors whom the writer would introduce to you.

" It must have been in '55 or '56," began the Doctor, pushing with the toe of his boot a log farther into the fire, and hurling after it the stump of his cigar, " when I made my first voyage as ship's surgeon. I was only a young shaver then, and knew no more about surgery than I had picked up at home in the old country, where my old dad kept a druggist's store. I could bleed with a penknife, and draw a tooth with a bullet mould, make a real stinging mustard-plaster, or tie up a broken head (I learned to do that same at the Galway elections); and to that last accomplishment I owed my first rise in life, and in the medical profession. It happened in this way: I was one fine morning wandering about the quays at Boston, looking at the ships, and wondering which of them came from old Ireland. I was jingling in my pocket the last three dimes I had in the world, and thinking, maybe, that I had better just take a drink for luck, when what should I see coming towards me on the side walk but a couple of men, discoursing away like a brace of half-boiled lobsters. Well, naturally I pulled up to see the fun. One was a big red-faced pimply young man in black, the other a lathy individual in a broad Panama hat, and otherwise dressed like a ship's skipper. When just as they came abreast of me, the pimply-faced chap, who seemed the cussiest of the two, let fly, and hit the skipper an all-rounder under the ear, which sent him staggering. In a moment, however, he recovered himself, and whipping out a bowie went at the other; but the black and purple boy was too quick for him, and seeing the knife, picked up a broken stave of an old cask, which was handy, and let the skipper have it straight on the top of his head as he rushed in; down he went all in a heap in the mud, and no wonder, for it was as illigant a rap as I had seen given in the country. I felt quite kindly to the big man when I saw it, and would not have minded taking a drink with him; but I fancy he thought he had killed the skipper outright, for, after one look at him, he took to his heels, and I never saw him again.

"Well, I lifted up the dead man as well as I could, and two or three sailors helping, we carried him on board a barque which lay alongside, and which chanced to be his own command. We carried him down to the cabin.

"'Where's the Doc?' sings out the chief mate, who came up from the hold just as we laid him out on the table.

"'Doc be durned,' says one of the men; 'it was him as gived old demijohn that crack on the sconce. I seed him.'

"Now, thought I, here's my chance.

"'No need of *another* medical man, my boys,' remarked I (splashing some water in the skipper's face). 'I am a medical man myself, and will attend to the case.'

"I don't think they quite believed me; but they did as I told them, and brought me some more water, a basin, and a pair of scissors. I soon had the hair clipped away (the barrel stave had made a baddish cut), and set to work to dress the wound.

" ' Now,' said I, ' bring me some whisky.' The steward did so, and I poured a little into the cut (for there is nothing like spirits for a broken head) ; but I didn't waste much on him, but drank off the rest myself, and a tidy drop it was.

" ' Guess that 'ere Doc was raised where they make good medicine,' grumbled the mate, ' shouldn't mind being a bit ill myself.'

" I finished dressing the wound, and was beginning to feel rather scared, for the skipper had been insensible for wellnigh half an hour ; and I was just settling in my mind that it would be as well to bleed him and put a mustard-poultice on his stomach, when he began to come to, and opened his eyes. After a bit he seemed to know where he was, and asked for a drink. This I gave him,—whisky as before—only this time inside of his head instead of out ; then we put him into his bunk, and he went to sleep. As it was clearly my duty under these critical circumstances to keep an eye on my patient, I decided not to leave the ship. I called the steward and explained to him that, as the captain might awake at any moment and require my services, I would risk leaving my other patients unvisited for the day, and remain with him. I fancy the steward did not quite believe in my patients, but he got me some dinner, and that was the main point.

" Towards three o'clock the skipper awoke, and called the steward, with whom I left him. He soon tumbled out of his bunk and joined me in the saloon. ' Good morning, sir. The steward tells me that you are the doctor who fixed up my head a while ago, and helped to carry me in when that all-fired villain had nearly murdered me.' I bowed, and replied that I had had that pleasure. There was a bit of a pause, during which I felt that the skipper was taking my measure, then he broke in : ' Now, you'll be Irish ? '

" ' I am, sir ; county Kildare.'

" ' And you'll not have been long in the States ? '

" ' Four months only,' I replied.

" ' Well, and what air you agoing to do ? You have done me a good turn, and I shall be glad to do you one if I can.'

" This rather put me on my guard, as I fancied I saw an intention to defraud me of (as I considered) my well-earned fee. ' Well,' said I, ' I am at present practising as a surgeon.' (That, you see, was safe enough ; for hadn't I dressed his head not three hours before ?)

" ' That won't pay,' answered he ; ' you'll find there are a sight too many docs in this location for a free country, and there are some of 'em we could very well do without, I guess ' (this he hissed through his teeth, evidently having a lively recollection of some of his latest transactions with a member of the medical staff). Then he continued : ' Now, you'll not find dollars very plentiful here away, I'll be bound.' I admitted that I had not yet made that discovery. ' Have you been to sea ? ' I reminded him that the over-land route to America from Ireland was not as yet much used.

" Though vague, this answer seemed to satisfy him, for he came to the point at once. ' Say, now, stranger, will the surgeon's berth of this 'ere barque suit you ? 'coz I'm bound to sail tomorrow, and it is not likely that I shall set eyes on that durned doc of mine again ; if I do ' (and he whistled softly). I was expressing my willingness to accept of his offer, when he added carelessly (at the same time giving me a sharp glance)—' You have your papers all correct, stranger, of course ? '

" I had to admit that I had not—had left them in Ireland.

This statement the worthy skipper received with another whistle of very different tone.

" ' You have passed your examination, though ? '

" ' Sure and I have,' said I, boldly. That again was *thrue* as gospel, for hadn't I passed last in my class for English composition, and didn't I remember that same well, by rayson that my dad gave me such a larruping that evening, when I came home and told him, that I had run away before the rest of the examinations came on ; for what between bateing at school and bateing at home, I wouldn't have had a sound bone in my body to sit down upon by the end of the week.

" ' Now, young man,' said the skipper, reaching down two tumblers from a shelf, ' I think we can do business. Owing to the *loss* of your papers, you see I can't well give you the surgeon's berth or pay, but I *can* take you as surgeon's assistant. I sail for Colon tomorrow, and so, if you fancy the trip, I'll give thirty dollars and board you ; for you see I'd like to do you a good turn, *I* would.'

" I didn't long hesitate, for the offer, though not much, was better than a ' poke in the eye with a tarry stick ', and in a couple of minutes I walked out of the cabin the better by a glass of old rye, and a slip of paper appointing me surgeon's assistant to the barque *Flying Cloud* of Boston, U.S., Captain Jackson. (I afterwards found out that that cute old sea-dog had represented me to the owners as an experienced surgeon *en route* to Lima, whom he had engaged for the trip at 180 dollars, and free passage, thus clearing a bonus for himself of 150 dollars.)

" I found the *Flying Cloud* a roomy barque of some 850 tons, her cargo consisting almost entirely of railway plant ; and in addition to the regular crew and officers, he had on board about a dozen passengers, mostly all clerks and employees of the Panama Railway Company. Nothing of importance occurred during the voyage except the death of one of the seamen. I don't know what the poor fellow died of, but I did my best for him, bleeding him every morning, and putting a mustard-plaster on his stomach every night; but he would die in spite of all I could do, just before we reached Aspinwall. When we got in, the skipper and I fell out, so much so that I swore I would never enter his ship again. He told me to be off at once, and be thankful that he didn't hand me over to the police for an impostor; for, says he, ' Young man, I guess you're no doc at all, and know no more about surgery than the vet ' down east ', who knew no more about horse-flesh than how to fix up a Colt's revolver, and I shouldn't be doing my duty to my owners if I didn't withhold your pay, for durn me if you have earned a red cent of it.'

" I confess this made me uncommon wrathy. Still, un-luckily for me, I didn't feel quite safe as to my treatment of the poor fellow who died, and I think old Jackson knew I daren't say much; so I had to cave in, and the skipper fingered my 30 dollars, and landed me and my bag on the wharf at Aspinwall, without a dime to buy a drink with. So I reckon the old man cleared 180 dollars, and got him-self and crew doctored for nothing, all in return for his generosity in giving me assistant-surgeon's berth.

" Well, as I was saying, I contrived to keep my joints hanging together (and that was about all), till at length I was lucky enough to catch a real hot typhus fever, and was taken to hospital. That fever saved my life, I guess, for I was fed and taken care of there; so as I got my strength again and got stout a bit, I began to make myself useful to the other patients, and by being always ready to bear a hand, I got noticed by the medicos, and when I

8

was almost ready to leave, the head-surgeon offered me the post of hospital dresser and attendant. This I gladly accepted, thinking, as I did so, that evidently nature meant me for an M.D.; still I thought it wiser to tell the chief nothing about my having before been in the medical line. I had been in hospital for maybe three or four months, when a case was brought into my ward (they always brought the English and Americans, and, in fact, foreigners generally, to mine, as none of the other attendants could understand them; always excepting one other employed in the hospital, an English doctor or rather a Scotchman, and indeed he had more to do with the gold-hunting than I had).

"As I was saying, a case was brought in (we always called them cases, and numbered them, you know—this was No 13). He was an old man, with hair as white as cotton, but a face as swarthy as a Jack Spaniard's. He was American, though, or at least they said so; but he was a remarkable-looking cuss, of whatever nation he was. He had been put ashore from a San Francisco schooner coasting it down to Valparaiso. He had come as passenger with another chap, a common sailor, along with him. They brought in his sea chest, a big one, and stowed it at the foot of his bed. I didn't quite know what to make of him at first, except that he was stark staring mad; but when Dr M'Gill saw him, he settled the question at once. Inflammation of the brain, he said; but I suppose he meant d.t. The sailor chap who came along with him tried mighty hard to be allowed to stay in hospital with him; but when he found he couldn't, as that was of course against rules, he actually wanted to take him away again; but that couldn't be, so he had to content himself with the regular visiting days—twice a week. It struck me at the time that it was queer that he should take such

9

a fancy for staying with the patient; but as neither of them had a figure-head that you would suspect to see come off a bishop, I guessed that the sailor was afraid of his mate telling too much—and I wasn't far out in my guess, you bet.

"I was sitting out in the veranda when he was brought in, and they put him down in the bed nearest to the window where I was; then I first heard his voice, very weak and broken it was, but clear enough for me to catch what he was saying: 'Lat., 5° 27′ N., lon. 87° 15′ W. Steady, boy—keep her full—three days more if this breeze lasts. Yes, yes, I shan't forget—lat. 5° 27′ N., lon. 87° 15′ W. I shouldn't do, for *I* took the sights. Call the captain—he knows too—so does Rowley, and Don Pedro the nigger; but the Doc's dead, and he won't share—ho, ho!'

"By this time I was by his side, and was assisting to undress him. The sailor was there too, and I just heard him whisper in the sick man's ear, 'Keep still, damn you —you'll blow it all.' But the patient paid no attention to him or to any of us, and kept on chuckling and talking to himself, always, after a bit, coming back to lat. 5° 27′ N., lon. 87° 15′ W. Dr M'Gill came and saw him, prescribed, and he was put into the usual course—his head shaved and blistered, and some blood taken from him. This seemed to ease him, and the first night he slept a little by snatches like; but as I passed his bed, going my last rounds, I could hear him still muttering in his sleep, 'Lat. 5° 27′ N., lon. 87° 15′ W.'

"For several days he kept much in the same state; for though the delirium and fever seemed to get less violent, his strength declined in proportion. Still he talked, though hardly above a hard whisper. He had evidently been a sailor, and perhaps an officer, as he was constantly giving orders as to a ship's course, making or shortening sail, and once I heard him growl, 'We might as well heave the long tom, and the barkers, overboard, for we shall never want them again, and then we might put into Bahia with clean decks.' At first I took no notice of his rambling talk, thinking it merely the effect of delirium; but the one constantly recurring topic at last riveted my attention. Lat. 5° 27′ N., lon. 87° 15′ W. ended everything, but beyond that he gave no sign. Some power greater even than delirium seemed to tie his tongue. Sometimes he spoke of going shares with Rowley and Don Pedro. Shares in what? Money, no doubt; but how, what, and where? 'Lat. 5° 27′ N., lon. 87° 15′ W.,' whispered the sick man's voice.

"My curiosity was more and more excited, the more I thought over the matter. I borrowed an atlas, and there, just at the point indicated, I found marked down in mid-ocean a solitary group of islands. This discovery roused in me the strongest anxiety to find out more; for now I entertained no doubt but that the sick man's ravings pointed to some hidden secret, the value of which I could not guess, but that it was of immense value I felt no doubt. One other in the hospital, I began to fancy, shared my idea. Dr M'Gill. I noticed that he now came to visit the patient oftener than formerly, and would, instead of asking a few questions and passing on, sit by his bedside listening to his rambling talk, and twice I saw him making a note in his casebook, I supposed of what fell from the patient in his raving. It was, I think, on the eighth day after his admission that he recovered consciousness; he had slept for an hour or two, and I noticed that when he opened his eyes he lay quiet, without speaking. I went up to his bed, and in a moment saw that he was sensible.

He looked steadily at me for a few moments, and after an ineffectual effort to raise himself, asked :

"'Where am I?'

"'In the hospital at Panama ; but you must keep quiet now.'

"He gave a sort of groan, and then, after a pause, said :

"'Where's Bill?'

"'I'll send for him if you like.'

"'Yes, be quick.'

"I sent for him, and in half an hour he was by the sick man's bedside ; but he was sleeping again, and when he awoke later in the afternoon he was wandering. Sorely against his will, Bill the sailor had to leave the hospital at the usual hour. I thought at the time that the rule might have been waived, for I felt certain that No 13 (that was his number) would sink in the night. But Dr M'Gill would not allow it, and, of course, I had nothing to say in the matter. At about 8 P.M., M'Gill made his usual round, and stayed for some time by No 13. He was now evidently sinking fast, and in all probability would never again recover consciousness.

"The Doctor, when he left, told some of the attendants to put the black screens round the bed, which is always done in hospitals when a patient is near his last. Half an hour later M'Gill sent for me to his private room. I was rather surprised, as he had never done so before. When I entered I found him sitting at a table, before him some books and papers and a chart rolled up. He looked up quickly as I came in, and motioned me to a seat opposite to him. After a moment's pause he began :

"'You have been in charge of No 13, I believe. What do you think of the case?'

"'Very bad, sir ; he'll hardly live through the night.'

" ' I know that well enough,' replied M'Gill; ' but I mean, have you noticed anything peculiar—*very* peculiar— about the case?'

" I did not care about telling him all I thought, so I hesitated a little, trying to think of an answer. I saw, too, that M'Gill was getting nervous and excited.

" ' I understand your hesitation, Mr O'Brien, but there is no occasion for it; our interests in this matter are identical. I don't think you know much more than I do; but by comparing what we each know, we may render quite clear certain points which neither of us entirely understand. You have, no doubt, observed the extraordinary amount of sameness which his ramblings have always had.'

" ' Lat 5° 27′ N., lon. 87° 15′ W.,' remarked I.

" ' Yes, precisely so; and do you know to what that refers?'

" ' The Cocos group,' I replied.

" ' Right,' said the Doc, ' here they are ' (opening the chart and laying his finger on a particular point)—' here they are. The Cocos Islands, lat. 5° 27′ N., lon. 87° 15′ W.'

" ' Well, and what do you deduce from that?'

" ' That No 13 knows some secret (a valuable one perhaps) connected with those islands.'

" ' And do you know what that secret is?'

" ' I can guess—buried treasure of some kind!'

" ' Exactly my idea; and neither you nor I have as yet the key to the secret.'

" ' No.'

" For nearly a minute the Doctor paused, his head resting on his hands and his eyes fixed on the chart. Then, rising quickly from his chair, like a man whose mind is quite made up, he came round the table to where I was sitting. I rose, too, and we stood facing each other, looking into each other's eyes.

"'O'Brien, if there is anything to be done in this matter we must trust each other entirely.'

"I nodded assent.

"'I tell you frankly that I would do without you if I could; but chance has placed a great secret equally within your reach and mine; if we can find the means by which to render ourselves masters of the key to that secret, our fortunes are made—of that I am morally convinced; and working together as allies that key we shall find. Now I will tell you what I know already, and what I deduce from my knowledge, then what I propose to do. As you may have noticed, I have spent a considerable amount of time by the bedside of No 13, and have now and then taken notes of various rambling statements and hints, all of which have reference, more or less, to the subject we have in hand. You doubtless have also heard and may remember many things severally unimportant, but which collectively, or when taken together with what I have heard, may be most valuable. Let us now see to what deduction your data added to mine will bring us.'

"I willingly agreed, and for the next half-hour we were busily employed in putting together a mass of facts and conclusions from which we deduced this theory: that No 13 was in possession of the secret of the exact locality of an immensely valuable hidden treasure; that he himself was one of those who originally buried it; that it had been accumulated by unlawful means, probably by piracy; and that it was still left where it was originally buried—on an island in the Cocos group, lat. 5° 27' N., long. 87° 15' W.

"'To my mind,' pursued M'Gill, 'these deductions are as clear and exact as possible. But one thing puzzles me, and that is this,—it is so long since anything like a real

14

pirate has been on these coasts that, granting No 13 to have been connected with these gentry, it must have been when he was quite young. How comes it, then, that for all these years neither he nor his former comrades have returned to recover the treasure ? He must, I fancy, have had some good reason for believing that it has remained undisturbed till now, or he would hardly have come here to look for it after such a lapse of time.'

" ' Possibly,' said I, ' his mates were all hanged, and he on account of his youth escaped.'

" ' Ah, I see what you mean—transportation for life. Yes, that may be it, but I trust we shall know more soon. Now I will tell you what I mean to do. In the first place, I take it for granted that, chance having placed this secret within our reach, we are perfectly justified in making what use of it we can. Certainly we are more entitled to it than the Government, who, if they got scent of the affair, would not leave us a dollar ; and as for our piratical friend No 13, he can't last out the night. And even if he should recover by a miracle, I doubt if he could substantiate any legal claim ; and as for his sailor friend, I look upon him as merely an accomplice. Now you know that by the rules, after the death of any foreign patient I shall have to make an inventory of his belongings, and hand them over to the governor, who gives them in charge of the consul pending inquiries. I need not repeat that should there be amongst them any plans or papers by which the police might be able to obtain the clue to this secret, our chance would be gone for ever. So what I propose is this,—you must sit up with No 13, and, when necessary, have me called. You understand me ? '

" ' Yes.'

" ' Then when all is over we will make a private search

in his chest, and whatever is useful we can retain; for, as I have said before, we have as good or a better right to this information than the beggarly Government, or that consequential ass the consul, who, you may swear, would make a good thing of it.'

"I objected that we could not take away any of the papers, as, if we were found out, that would get us into trouble.

"'Perhaps you are right,' said the Doctor. 'But we can make copies; and as far as destroying a link or two in the chain, a few drops of aquafortis will do all we require.'

"Then we parted, and I returned to my ward, and to the bedside of No 13. He was much quieter now, poor fellow. I confess I had several qualms of conscience—I had some of that left then—about the business; but I was so excited at the thought of becoming a rich man, that all the ten commandments would not have stopped me. Even the short time I had been away in M'Gill's room had made a marked alteration in the patient. He was evidently sinking fast, and was quite still and insensible: before ten o'clock, longer and longer became the intervals between each breath; and by midnight it was all over.

"I at once sent for M'Gill, without, however, telling the messenger that No 13 was dead, and in about ten minutes he was with me. He looked pale, and a trifle nervous, I thought; and, to tell the truth, I did not feel comfortable myself. After satisfying himself that the patient was really dead, M'Gill selected from a small box at the bed-head—in which all articles found on the persons of patients were always put, and the key of which was kept by the surgeon—the key of the sea-chest at the foot of the bed. This we opened, after first making sure that the black screen entirely hid us from view. We carefully examined its contents one by one. There was nothing differing much from the usual run of articles comprised in a sailor's kit, till we came to near the bottom ; there, carefully rolled up in a piece of oiled cloth, we found a black-leather case secured with a strap. In a moment the Doc pounced on it, and with trembling hands spread out its contents on the lid of the chest which was opened back on the foot of the bed. He knelt at one side and I at the other. I remember the queer turn it gave me as I saw that the lid rested on and was a little tilted up by the dead man's feet ; but the Doc didn't notice it, and I was too excited to mind much.

" Silently we divided the packet, and by the faint light of the night-lamp began to search for what we required. At first we merely glanced over the papers, putting aside those which appeared to have reference to observations, charts, etc., and then began again with these, making a careful examination of each. One after another was put away as useless ; some related to stores, some to harbour matters, rations, etc. I was just trying to decipher the almost illegible characters scrawled on what appeared to be some leaves roughly torn from the log-book of some ship, when a sort of choking sound which I can hardly describe, caused me to look across at M'Gill. Never in a few moments was human face so changed. In place of the hard passionless lineaments I knew so well, every feature was altered and expressive of the most intense excitement ; his face was as pale as that of the corpse, and beads of perspiration were standing on his brow. In a moment I was by his side, and was reading the paper, which with trembling hands he held stretched out on the lid of the chest.

" Now, boys, I'm not going to tell you what those figures

totted up to. Firstly, because you wouldn't believe me, and next, because I'm sworn not to tell; but this I can say, that there ain't a placer here—no, nor yet in California —that would be a circumstance to the pile we had the certainty of handling. No, sir; I can see that list now— thousands and thousands of Mexican dollars, dozens of bars of pure gold, case after case of precious stones; yes, and gold crucifixes and candlesticks, and suchlike; piles of them,—for there was the loot of more than one Spanish town there. And with this list, water-stained and yellow with age, was another paper, or rather two: one was calculations, figures, and measurements, and all that; the other was a rough sketch of an island—a curious-shaped island it was, long and pretty flat all but two peaks connected by a ridge, near the middle of it, and in the side of one of them was a crag shaped just like the spire of a church —not these square-topped things they have down New Mexico way, but like what I remember the village spire was at home in the old country, so steep that none of us boys could ever climb it; and when the old weathercock came down one windy night, the parson couldn't find a man in the parish who could put it up again.

"Well, I reckon, I'll cut the yarn short, for it's getting late. You know at first we only meant to copy whatever papers we found, but that good intention wasn't carried out, you bet. No; we kept all we could find that related in any way to the plunder, and the Doc touched up some of the rest with some chemical stuff he had, which took all the colour out of 'em right away, and spoilt 'em for ever. I was kneeling by the box helping the Doc to fix the papers and, feeling a bit stiff, just raised myself for a stretch. Somehow, instinctively my eyes sought the bed,— and I tell you, boys, it's true—never but once since have

I felt the fearful cold start that seemed to fly through me and root me to the spot. Now, mind, this is true, boys, and you needn't snigger, for you would have been scared too, I guess. You know, when M'Gill had done examining the body, it was dead—dead as could be; there warn't no manner of doubt on it. Well, we had done what always is done—that is, drawn the sheet over his face and closed his eyes. And what do you think I saw when I looked up? Why, as sure as I now live, the sheet was drawn down again, and there he was, his eyes wide open and staring hard into mine, and on the face was a cold mocking sneer which I can't forget, and never shall. Those eyes have haunted me for ten years, and will till I go under, I guess.

"M'Gill jumped up in a hurry and sprang to him, thinking he had come round; but no, he was dead and cold enough. Well, hurriedly we repacked the chest, locked it, and put the key back, and then woke up one of the attendants. (I mind well how M'Gill went at him for being asleep.) Next day No 13's friend the sailor came as usual, and precious odd he looked when he found that his mate had slipped his cable in the night. However, he made application through the consul to have the effects, which were given over to him; and that was the last we heard of him, except that, a week later, I found that he had taken a passage back to 'Frisco. The papers M'Gill and I had secured, when we came to examine them closely, seemed to give all we wanted—the exact locality of the island, with the sketch of it to make sure, the bearings and observations taken from different points (from the foot of that steeple-rock for one), and the measurements to the very spot where, years ago, the treasure had been hid. From the papers, too, we found that No 13 had been the sailing-master of the schooner (her name was never mentioned), and had shared with four other officers in the plunder, which they themselves had hidden, the crew having buried their share at some other place.

"Now there were stories in Panama which everyone had heard of some years previous. The west coast cities, from San Francisco to Lima, had been flooded with old Spanish coin; and it was generally reported and believed that a great treasure had been found or recovered by a party of foreign sailors who had about that time chartered a small schooner from Panama, and after a month's cruise, no one knew where, had put in at the Gulf of Fonseca, sent the schooner back to Panama, and dispersed, no one knew whither. Now we argued that these men (all strangers in Panama) were some of the crew of the very vessel that No 13 had been sailing-master of, and that after years of absence (possibly in prison) they had returned and recovered their booty. We knew that the officers had taken the greatest precautions to keep the secret of their *cache*; as on the drawing, at a point from which the harbour was visible, we found a mark, and under it, in faded writing, ' The point where the Don stood sentinel to watch the schooner.'

" Within a fortnight the Doc and I got leave, and started in a fishing-boat, with four Negroes for crew. The Doc understood taking sights, and suchlike, and was gay sure he could make the island, which wasn't 300 miles off; but we got into a gale which all but swamped us, and, as it was, drove us altogether out of our course, and back again into the coast, 100 miles south of Panama. Our provisions were all spoilt with salt water, and one of the blacks had his arm broken, and both M'Gill and I were dead beat; so we coasted back to Panama to refit. We had delay after delay; and finally, when we were nearly ready for a second start, I was struck down with ' them cussed shakes '. Yes, you may laugh, Goldey; but I tell you, chills and fevers in Louisiana ain't a circumstance to the regular Panama shakes. No, sir. So, when I couldn't stir from my bed, M'Gill came and swore to me he would treat me fair, but that he meant to try alone. I couldn't help myself; so he went.

"Never shall I forget the anxiety of that fortnight; and when, one morning, I chanced to hear that the Doc was back, the attendants had to hold me down, weak as I was, I was so wild to get to him. In a little time he came in, and I saw in a moment he had failed. He looked worn to death, his eyes were as red as beef-steaks, and he could hardly walk. When he was about again next day he told me all. He had sighted the island—got close to it, near enough to see the very cliff from which the measurements had been made, and recognised the bluffs and bays on the coast which were marked in the sketch; but just when he thought himself certain of success, his crew—four blacks as before—who had shown symptoms of discontent for the last twenty-four hours, came to him, and refused to proceed or to land. Two of them were old pearl-divers, and they said that the island was ' debbil island '—that no one lived there, and no one who had ever landed there had ever come back, and finally flatly refused to go ashore. M'Gill tried entreaty, threats, everything; and at last tried force. The four then rushed on him with their knives, and he was obliged to shoot down the leader in self-defence. This cowed the rest; but he recognised the impossibility of doing anything, as, had he landed alone, the blacks would certainly have carried the boat off and left him; and he could do nothing with them on shore. So, reluctantly he turned the head of the boat towards Panama.

" A fearful voyage he had. The three blacks sulked in the bows of the boat, ready at any moment to rush on him ; so he dared not sleep, but sat night and day for two whole nights and three days steering with one hand, the other hand grasping his revolver. Several times he was almost overpowered by sleep, but roused himself in time to see the three blacks glaring at him each with his machette in his hand, and on the point of springing aft upon him. Sullenly, as he instinctively raised his pistol, they crouched back into their former positions, and sat there muttering to each other in their own language. He knew that to sleep was to die ; but it was a fearful struggle ; and no wonder that he was more dead than alive when at last he reached Panama. If he hadn't luckily had a fair breeze back it would have been all up with him ; as it was, his sufferings under that burning sun must have been fearful.

" By the time we were both about again, the calms had set in, and a sailing-boat would be no use to us. Besides, cash was running short ; so, after many consultations, we decided to take in some partners. We had to be very careful in choosing our men ; and every one, before he was told a word, was sworn to secrecy. But there was no lack of ' bully boys ' in Panama then, who had plenty of shiners always ready for a spree, and this one suited them exactly. In about a month we had fourteen in our party, and £5,000 actually subscribed. With this money we chartered a small steamer that chanced to be lying idle in port ; and one dark night we cleared for Tetuantapec—all fourteen of us on board, and a crew of ten hands, chiefly firemen. Every mother's son of them was searched as he came on board, and not so much as a knife left ; for you see we couldn't trust them. We were all armed—well, too, you may bet. To hide our track effectually as we left the harbour, we put her head to the northward and steamed up the coast. The lights of Panama were reflected a thousand times on the dancing water astern of us, then one by one they sank and faded out, till those at the pierhead alone were visible, and broad on the quarter, the lights of the mail-steamer lying at anchor under the lee of the islands. In another hour these too disappeared.

"Then the helm was put hard down, full steam ahead was the order, and we shot out from the dark shadow of the land, and headed direct to sea. An hour later we had made a good offing, and her head was put S. by W. $\frac{1}{2}$ S., and without a light showing, we steamed past the islands again, leaving them on the port hand, and held our course. Not till then did we leave the deck, for the Doc and I had bargained that, until we were fairly at sea, the exact measurements, observations, and plans should remain in our keeping and secret. The crew were all sent forward. One of our party took the wheel, whilst another stood sentry at the head of the cabin-stairs. The rest of us crowded round the small table. There was a dead silence as one by one M'Gill spread out the worn and yellow papers, and his voice seemed hushed and trembled as he read out to the rest the great secret. Then one by one the papers were closely examined, and the observations and measurements compared; and then as, finally, M'Gill placed his finger on a particular spot in the map, and remarked, ' It's just thereabouts, gentlemen ', there rang out such a cheer, such a wild exulting shout, that I verily believe you might have heard it here from Denver.

"Down rushed the guard we had left on duty, and the man who was steering, unable to remain longer on deck. We had quite forgotten them ; and as some of us tumbled up to take their places, we saw the crew, engineers and all, clustered together forward, and looking half-scared, as if they thought themselves in a floating mad ship. There was not much sleep that night, you bet; and morning still found us grouped aft talking over our chances and 'counting our piles'. The steamer was a fast little boat, and towards the afternoon we sighted land ahead. What a scurry there was. Every glass in the ship was pointed at the two blue cones we could just make out rising apparently from the water.

"Higher and higher grew the blue cones, and hour by hour the outline of the sharp broken ridges connecting them became more distinct; down went the sun like a ball of blazing gold; and I mind how eagerly, whilst there was a ray of light left, we scanned the mysterious island, and tried to locate the spot where our treasure lay hidden.

"By ten o'clock we were close in with the land, and had to lay to till morning. The boats were launched and provisioned; instruments, spades, picks, and tools were stowed beneath the thwarts; and as soon as the first symptom of dawn appeared, the oars fell into the water, and we started for the land, some two miles off. M'Gill was in the bows of the launch and I in the whale-boat— he leading, as he knew the coast. The island had been a volcano one time, I guess, for the shore was steep and rocky all but one spot where there was a little sandy bay; and in front of this, as if to guard it, some four hundred yards out was a reef, over which the rollers thundered and dashed, throwing up clouds of spray. As we neared it there seemed to be no break in the belt of foam, and some of us thought M'Gill must have gone mad or lost his bearings as he went for it; but we followed half a dozen lengths astern, and I guess we'd have rowed over Niagara if it had been in our way. But M'Gill knew what he was about, for sure enough there was a channel just where the old chart said; and as the launch seemed almost in the white water, down went the helm, and she shot into the gap. Narrow enough it was; for as we followed there seemed hardly room enough to use the oars as a big sea slid from under us, and the grey sharp-pointed rocks seemed to rise on each side as if by magic. With a thunder and a roar the next huge roller came in; and, catching the whale-boat on the quarter, half-filled her, and lifting her like a feather, carried her clear over the rocks that a moment before seemed ten feet above us. It seemed but a couple of seconds, but in those two seconds I experienced what it was to be nearer death than ever I was before; for apart from being smashed and drowned in that hell of water, a man has no chance where the sharks are as plentiful as fish in the lake here.

"Well, all we got for our scare was a shout of laughter from the boys in the Doctor's boat, who had pulled through without a splash; but we took the shine out of them in the race to the beach; for though they had a good start, we reached it with them, and ran our boat half her length up on the sand. Then such a cheer! We had won our goal at last. They had been watching us from the steamer, and above the hoarse roar of the breakers we could hear the boom of her gun as she saluted. *Viva*, boys; but my heart felt big then I tell you. From the little strip of sand at the landing there was a steep pull up a dry water-course some two hundred feet or so, till you came to the woods: woods!—I tell you, boys, there's no such woods in the five republics, nor yet in the Amazonas, to equal them. Why, the mangrove-swamp down to Realejo isn't a circumstance to them—big trees, little trees, vines, tree-ferns, creepers—every kind of green thing that grows was there, I guess, and all matted and tangled together, so that a snake could hardly get through. I never saw such an undergrowth in my life—never. Well, we took the bearings of the steeple-rock from the point where we first landed, and found, sure enough, it was just as the old chart gave it. That put us in high spirits, and we set to work with axe and machette to cut a trail through the bush. What a job that was !

"Night came on, and we had only just reached the foot of it. We found no water, so had to return to the boats, and camp on the beach ; but there wasn't one of us who slept a wink, I reckon. The mosquitoes were downright desperate. I tell you, boys, there were so many of them, there wasn't room on all our carcases for them all to sit down at once—so they had to work by relays ; and when one million or so had got a good square meal, they would fly off to the woods, and perch on the biggest tree they could find to rest, while the next million, who had been patiently waiting all the time, would fall to by sections and subdivisions, and give us a lively time till No 3 went on duty. I tell you, it's a fact, that before morning the air all round camp was quite thick as London fog with the cusses. We got our coffee before daylight, and set to work again, and soon got our second bearing—from the foot of the steeple-rock, three hundred yards W. by $\frac{1}{2}$ S., to the jiccatybar tree.

"Now, as most of the trees were of that kind, and as the ground was all broken up with steep ravines and over-grown with scrub, you may fancy what a piece of work we had to keep the line, and get the right post at the end of it. We had to start up the side of the ridge, and as we got within a couple of hundred feet of the summit, it was as steep as the side of a house. As we got higher and the ground became steeper, there were fewer big trees, but the undergrowth got thicker than ever. It was just ten o'clock, and we were nearly at the top, when the Doctor, who was leading, gave a whoop, and scrambled up the bank in front, on all-fours ; we all followed at double-quick, and in another minute were on smooth ground again. The ridge seemed to have been broken here, making a sort of gap—the ground falling away rapidly on each side ; and then, just in the centre of the little plateau was about the biggest tree I ever saw ; it was a jiccatybar, and the one we wanted. That tree, I mind, was sixty-seven feet round, and went up straight as the mainmast of a three-decker for a good hundred and twenty feet without a branch ; then it broke off into five great arms, five or six feet thick they seemed, but all grown over, and covered with ochids and suchlike.

"There were two old macaws sitting up near the top, and croaking to each other, with their heads all on one side squinting at us ; and, it struck me, expressing their opinion that we must be a blamed set of fools anyhow, to come sweating and swearing up the mountain-side on the ground instead of by the tree-tops, like other monkeys. One of our boys fired his revolver at them, and they flew off into the woods ; and, I believe, took our luck with them. (I never saw another pair all the time I was in the island.) When we had got our breath, and taken a drink, we all fell to examining and measuring the tree.

"' What's this ? ' said Dick Gregory, pointing to a mark in the bark.

"' Looks mighty like a rifle-ball,' said I. ' Anyhow, we'll see,' and so I set to work with my bowie. Almost directly I felt something hard, and, after whittling a bit more, found on the edge of my knife a bit of stuff that shone like gold! And what do you think we found?—why, a big copper bolt, six inches long, which had been driven in years before and over which the bark had closed. Now in the old instructions it said that the *cache* was at a certain distance from this tree, measured with the deep-sea line, so many fathoms; and there round the head of the bolt and completely cased in the bark we found some strands of hemp. That old bolt had been used to fasten the measuring-line to.

" I don't think there were a dozen more pleased men in the world than us, as we rested under the shade of that big jiccatybar that morning. But we didn't spend much time in resting; we had plenty of work before us. Somewhere in the valley that sloped down from our feet was the treasure, but its exact position could only be determined by following the line of the shadow of the big tree, as projected at 6.45 A.M. on the 17th day of a certain month years before. Now in the old leaves from the log-book in which the observations had been written, the upper corner had been torn off, so that we never knew the month, though the rest of the date was clear enough; and to this slight flaw in the chain we owed all our troubles.

" We employed the afternoon in clearing away the undergrowth as nearly as we could judge in the line of our future explorations, so as to be able to get a good view of the valley from the great tree looking N.W. This we did, and before sundown sufficient timber was down to enable us to get an uninterrupted view all over the valley, and right down to the shore three or four miles off. Some of us voted to fetch up a keg of water and to camp where we were; others proposed returning to the ship for the night, none caring to face the mosquitoes and sandflies down on the beach again.

"At last it was settled that the Doc, with about half a dozen, including two who were complaining of sickness, should return to the ship, while I and four others should camp where we were. The three previous days had fagged us all, and we soon turned in; but for my part, after two or three ineffectual efforts to doze off, I quietly got up and, lighting a fresh cigar, seated myself on a rock just within the belt of black shadow cast by the great tree. Insensibly I fell into a reverie, in which the present, the past, and the future were strangely blended. From where I sat I could distinctly see the little steamer lying at anchor outside the reef: the night was so clear, the moonlight so bright, that I almost fancied I could distinguish objects on her deck. Then I began trying to picture them to myself—two or three men on watch—others lying about the deck asleep—the Doc and one or two more stretched out on chairs under the little awning aft, smoking cheroots and indulging in iced shangaree, and talking together in low tones. I could almost hear the murmur of their voices and the wash of the tiny waves rippling along the sides of the vessel and splashing under the counter, as she ever and anon rocked slightly to and fro as she felt the ground-swell or the slight power of the sea-breeze, which was just springing up and whispering softly through the tree-tops.

"Was it the tree-tops? No; the land is too far off; it must have been the light tracery of spars and rigging standing out indistinctly against the starlit sky. How they have changed the look of the boat since morning! What a rake they have given to the topmasts! Surely there were no such spare spars on board; nor had she even a sail bent. What strange madness possesses me! An icy chill seems to strike to my very bones—a vague terror possesses my very soul; but I cannot fly—a power I cannot resist seems to urge me to look: the steamer herself seems changed—a long low schooner with spars raking considerably, and appearing too big for her, her mainsail and foresail brailed up and flapping heavily in the night-breeze; an awning extending fore and aft, and protected by it from the heavy night-dew, forward of the mainmast, some fifty or sixty men—rough wild-looking men of every nationality and colour, lying about in every position, sleeping heavily.

" Forward, sitting on the heel of the bowsprit, are two men on watch. Aft, the officer on duty is slowly pacing to and fro on the small quarter-deck; four nine-pounder carronades are mounted on either side, whilst amidships is a long gun of Spanish make, profusely and grotesquely ornamented, as was the fashion fifty years ago. Below I find another group; they too are on watch. They sit silently smoking and playing cards by the light of a rude lantern. Piled up against the bulk-head behind them are heavy chests filled to the lid with broad silver dollars fresh from the mint of Mexico, rolls of valuable silks, silver-mounted pistols and swords, watches and valuables of all kinds. Aft in the cabin are still others: a dark-bearded, broad, stalwart man looks over another who is writing to the dictation of a third, who is carefully repacking in an arm-chest plunder also like that guarded by the sailors forward; but far richer—ingots of solid gold—small canvas bags filled with precious stones—golden cups and bowls and heavy plates. Opposite to this young man writing the list sits another busy with a log-book, also young, but with a face prematurely aged by guilt—a dark southern face, with piercing eyes and black hair. *I had seen the face before.*

" Wonderingly, I look back to the first writer: he has

just finished his task, and holds out to the elder man the parchment he has been writing. Heavens, it is the very one we now possess! Then the dark-faced man pushes across the log-book, on which the ink is still wet. He points to the last entry: Lat. 5° 27′ N., lon. 87° 15′ W. Ah, I know him now; he is the dead man I robbed in Panama. Yes; the same eyes, hair, and features, though now full of youth and strength, that I saw aged, worn, and dead there in the hospital six months since. The scowl in the dark fierce face changes into a mocking sneer, as he looks me straight in the eyes. That face—cold and still—but the eyes open and staring at me, and seeming alive with vengeful hate. My God, how I remember that look! I remember trying to banish the horrid vision from me, but I was held firmly entranced by horror as one is when in a nightmare. I closed my eyes to shut out the hateful face peering into mine; my senses seemed in a whirl.

"Then I *felt* there was another change, and looked again. The spectral freebooters were gone—the racks of arms and old-fashioned cabin fittings had disappeared; in their place I recognised the well-known furniture of our own little steamer. I could hear the engines working, and the rush of water along the sides of the ship. Seated round the cabin-table were five of my companions. I was about to spring forward and accost them, when an indescribable 'something' arrested me. I looked closer; the light from the cabin-lamp brightened for a moment, as it swung to and fro with the motion of the ship, and, for a few seconds, fell on the face of the one nearest to me. It was the face of a corpse. . . . With a suppressed gasp of horror I awoke, chilled to the bone and cramped; but with an intense feeling of thankfulness that it was all but a dream.

"The night had somewhat advanced, and the moon, now nearer the horizon, was throwing a broad belt of light across our camping-ground near the roots of the giant tree, leaving the spot where I sat still in deep shadow. The fire was almost quite out, nothing left but a mass of white ashes—whiter still in the moonlight—with one thin column of transparent smoke rising straight up from the centre and losing itself in the darkness of the tree-top above. I was on the point of rising to throw on some fresh branches when my attention was riveted by a glimpse I caught of some moving object projected beyond the bole of the tree. In another moment a human figure was outlined dimly against the dark starlit horizon. I knew it could not be one of my friends, for there they all four were lying sleeping in the full moonlight before me. With a noiseless step the figure approached the sleepers till it reached the edge of the belt of light; it then sank to the ground and commenced to crawl forward on hands and knees. Then, as it came into the clear light, I in a moment recognised the deadly peril that hung over one, at least, of my sleeping friends. The figure was that of a Negro, and an old man at that; but of all the big Negroes I ever saw, that one was the biggest : he must have been six feet six, and had shoulders on him like a buffalo bull. He wore no clothes but a tattered old piece of canvas ; but in his teeth he held a long narrow-bladed knife, near as long as a machette. I should say he was creeping straight towards the nearest sleeper, and his purpose was written as clearly in his face as ever a murderer's was. Such a face, too ! If ever a fiend's and a living human being's were combined, they were in that old Negro's ; but I hadn't much time to admire him, for he was within ten feet of my friends.

" Quickly I drew my pistol and sighted him. As I did so, he took the knife from between his teeth and raised it in his right hand . . . then I pulled. I never heard such a yell as he gave. He was just on the spring as I fired, or, I think, I'd have thrown him. As it was, he bounded clear over the boy nearest him, and landed in the ashes of the fire, kicking up a cloud of dust and sparks, and scattering the smouldering embers in all directions. I couldn't get another shot, as the boys sprang up between us, and before they were fairly awake, he was off into the woods. To follow him was useless ; so we stayed where we were, not knowing what was coming next—the rest not even knowing what had happened, in fact. In half a minute we heard a rock dislodged from the steep face of the hill go bounding down a little way ; so, taking the sound as a guide, we sent half a dozen rifle-balls whizzing through the trees, but nothing came of it, and not another sound was heard.

" We didn't build the fire again, you may bet, but sat there in the darkest shade at the foot of the tree, and never closed an eye all the rest of that night ; for the idea of the island being inhabited had never occurred to any of us till now, and we didn't know but what we might be attacked in force before our mates could arrive. Slowly enough the night wore on, but nothing happened ; and glad were we when, after the hour of intense darkness that succeeded the setting of the moon, the faint grey morning light began to make things visible ; and not till then, or rather till we had light enough to shoot by, did we rebuild our fire and begin to talk about breakfast. Before sunrise our friends arrived from the steamer ; and all, I think, felt more or less uncomfortable at the idea of there being others on the island besides ourselves, who might perhaps be watching us at that very moment, or might even have some inkling of our secret.

"There was another cause for anxiety. The two who had complained of sickness the day before were worse this morning, and had to be left on board, together with a third one of the crew who had exhibited the same symptoms. The Doc, however, made light of it, and expected them to be all right in a day or two; but somehow I didn't feel easy, for I remembered the five figures I had seen in my dream sitting round the cabin-table; and two out of the three now on the sick-list were certainly there.

"Impatiently we waited till the sun was high enough in the heavens to project the shadow of the great jiccatybar tree into the valley below. Slowly the minutes passed, till the nearest trees (which, standing some one hundred and fifty feet below us on the hillside, raised their topmost branches above the level on which we were standing) were touched with golden light. Then the boys cheered, and every man took to pointing out the exact spot where the shadow would fall in half an hour's time, which would give us the exact hour at which to take our observation.

"But everyone quieted down as the important moment drew near. Then the Doc stood at the foot of the tree, just in front of the spot where the copper bolt had been driven in, with the compass fixed upon a tripod, ready to get the bearing the moment the time arrived. When it did, and when the Doc had read off the exact direction, we went to work with a will—most of us hacking away with axe or machette, and others scouting out in advance and on each side of the working party, with shooting-irons ready, and eyes skinned in case of trouble; but none came; and in less than an hour we had cut a trail through the bush and measured the distance. Then we set to work with picks and crows, spades, and even knives, every man burrowing like a musk-rat. What work it was, down in that deep gulch ! The heat towards noon was stifling, and not a breath of air ; but we worked on as if our lives were staked on our work ;—and so some's were, though they didn't know it, poor boys.

" The papers told us the treasure was only buried three feet deep ; and before evening we had a dozen shafts down, each four feet good—but not a sign of the plunder. We remeasured the ground, and found our first measurement right. Then whilst some worked on deepening their shafts, others prospected about, and tried likely places a few yards farther off, and so on, but with no results. Then as evening began to close in, we silently and one by one quitted work, and came out of the gulch up to the foot of the big tree again. In the morning we had roughly thrown together some logs, so as to make a sort of cover in case of an attack ; and here eight of us were to pass the night and guard the workings, which could easily be seen in the clear moon-light. Those whose lot it was to return to the ship started about twilight, taking with them in a hammock one of the party who had been seized with the same symptoms as those the day before. He had in a few hours become quite light-headed ; and they were obliged to take away his knife and revolver, to prevent his doing some of us or himself a mischief.

" The disappointment caused by the unsuccessful day's work, coupled with the illness of our friends, and the strange encounter of the previous night, made us the reverse of a jovial party under the big jiccatybar tree that night. No one volunteered a song, and no one seemed to care to talk ; and so, a guard being set, and reliefs arranged, one by one we fell asleep. I confess the remembrance of my last nocturnal experiences kept me awake for some time; but finally I snoozed off, and did not awake till the watch aroused me to take my spell on guard. The night passed quietly—not a sound, not an indication of there being a living soul on the island but ourselves.

" Morning came, and with it a fresh supply of pluck to the whole party. We hastily finished breakfast, and hurried off to our shafts and cross-cuts, each returning to where he had left off work the night before. Hardly had I taken up my pick when a hurried call from Charley Burt brought us all to his location. He had been working in soft earth the day before, and had thrown up quite a heap of it. He was now standing in his ' claim ', stooping forward and examining this heap.

" ' Look here boys,' " says he, ' Pat was not dreaming after all. I guess there is none of you got a hoof to match that track, have you ? '

" Sure enough there, deeply impressed in the soft black soil, was the print of a human foot. I doubt if Robinson Crusoe ever examined the first footprint he found with half the eagerness we did that one ; but there was not much to be made of it beyond that it was a foot-track certain sure, and a big one at that—the biggest any of us had ever seen. I wish now we could have measured it, but it seems to me that it must have been fourteen inches long if it was one. As for following the trail on that ground, it was out of the question. At least none of our crowd was up to it, though I have known some Indians who might have ; yes, and Dyaks too—they could track a bird, I think.

" As it was, we thought we could touch on it here and there, but nothing came of our search ; and when the rest of the party came from the ship, they tried and could make nothing of it either. Bad news they brought. One of our companions had died in the night, and M'Gill had remained on board with the other three sick, one of whom seemed almost gone. I felt there was no hope for him, for his face came back dimly to me as one of the five I had seen in my dream. Doggedly and silently we worked on through all the weary hours of that day. The sun seemed to pour down all its concentrated heat into that lonely gulch—the air seemed hour by hour to become more dense and stagnant—the sun seemed to beat down into one's brain and cause fearful agony. Sick and giddy, at length I threw down my spade and staggered back to the camp. I remember hearing Seth Parker's voice speaking kindly in his rough way, and feeling some one supporting me and guiding me. Then all seemed to become indistinct, and I remember no more.

" It was near three weeks after this, as I afterwards found, that I awoke from what appeared to have been a long deep sleep. I had a faint consciousness of being deadly sick and weak, so weak that my arms felt like lead when I tried to move them. I dimly recognised the well-known hospital ward at Panama ; then I slept again. When I awoke my head was clearer, and I tried to speak to M'Gill, who was standing by my bedside ; the sight of him brought back in a confused way the events of the past up to when I gave up work that fearful afternoon. I tried to ask M'Gill what had happened, but I could hardly whisper ; and it was not till after several days that he gave me the closing scenes of our unfortunate expedition.

" It seemed that after I was taken ill, I was at once carried on board ship, where M'Gill was engaged in nursing the other three patients. We were all down with the same complaint, a jungle fever of the most deadly kind. The next day added three more to the sick list, and another death occurred. For two more days did the treasure-seekers work on literally with death in their midst; and it was not till a third of our party had sunk that the quest was for the time abandoned. During the run to Panama another sank, and one more in the hospital after landing.

"'And, O'Brien, my boy,' said M'Gill, kindly, 'for days and days I feared you would make the sixth.'

"'No, Doc, no,' muttered I. 'There were only five that night.' I was just dozing off again from weakness, I suppose, but I heard M'Gill say to the attendant, 'The laddie's wandering again, but he'll pull through.'

"It was not till some days after that M'Gill would tell me all that had happened. It was a weary tale of disappointment; and I mind feeling so heart-sick and down at the time that I heartily wished I had been one of the five, and hardly care to think of it now.

"To cut matters short, it appeared that the only explanation M'Gill and the rest could give of our failure was, that each month the shadow thrown by the big tree would fall on different ground—I don't see why it should, but they said so; and that, not knowing the month, we had gone at the wrong date. M'Gill vowed he would never give it up, if he had to make eleven more trips. But, as for me, I kinder felt I had had enough of treasure-seeking and the Cocos Islands; and then I couldn't get rid of that face, which fairly haunted me; so I concluded to try my luck at the diggings, and haven't been near Panama since.

"There, boys, that's the yarn, but it's run out longer than I reckoned. Goldey, I say! Charley!—why, if the boys ain't asleep. Thunder!"

NOTE—The story of the Lost Secret of the Cocos Group is true—that is, all the leading facts happened much as I have tried to tell them—but since several of the survivors of the party are still (to the best of my belief) alive, and being so, have certainly never for a moment given up the intention of trying again, names, dates, and localities have been, for obvious reasons, altered by the narrator.

[January 1873

2

THE TRUE STORY OF THE
TREASURE HUNT

Wilfred Pollock

Many magazine readers will remember an article in a contemporary just a year ago, entitled, ' The New Treasure Hunt '. The hunt is over for the nonce, and one of the hunters proposes to tell the tale.

Great secrecy was thought necessary as to the object of our enterprise, and it is my first duty to mention that the writer of the above-named article, and, through him, his readers, were completely deceived. It was no pirates' horde, collected from East Indiamen, that we were after, but a far more serious treasure, that of the Cathedral of Lima. Is there any one so ignorant as not to know all about Lima ? I fear most of us gentlemen-adventurers had much to learn : this is what we were told. Peru was the wealthiest of the Spanish possessions in South America, and also the last to revolt. In the early part of 1821, when the revolution was imminent, many wealthy Spaniards fled for Europe, taking with them such of their possessions as they could get on board ship : this was too good an opportunity to be missed, and several enterprising persons (it is cruel to call them pirates, seeing that they mostly sailed under the Chilean flag) became uncommonly wealthy about this period, treasure hunting being more profitable then than at the present day.

Now the Cathedral of Lima was one of the wealthiest in the world : its riches, like those of Milan, the capital of opulent Lombardy, were to be reckoned in millions, and as there was little doubt but that the Republic would secularise Church property, the authorities determined to save as much as possible ; so the more portable portions, the jewelled chalices, monstrances, and vestments, and the solid gold candlesticks, shrines, etc., were smuggled on board a vessel which was sailing for Spain. Shortly afterwards, as was so frequently the case, the treasure changed hands, and the new owners were too pleased with their booty, which they estimated at over a million sterling, to give it up to the Chilean Government. They got round the dreaded Cape Horn in safety ; but off the mouth of the Plate fell in with a *pampero* (the south-west gale for which these seas are famous), and had to beach their vessel in a sandy bay on the south-east shore of the islet Trinidada (lat. 20° 29′ S., long. 29° 32′ W.). A convenient ravine received the valuables, and they signalled the first ship which passed. To their disgust it proved to be a Spaniard, which took them to Cuba, and there hanged them, one alone, a boy of fifteen or sixteen, being spared (as is usual in all pirate stories) to tell the tale, and, many years afterwards, exhibit his faded chart of the island.

This personage, since dead, reappears in the story, after an interval of some fifty years, as mate on board a sailing-ship trading in the China seas. He was a Finn, well conducted and trustworthy, but illiterate, and getting too old for his work. One day, in a moment of confidence, he told his skipper, with whom he had sailed for several years, this tale of untold wealth only waiting to be fetched away ;

but the skipper, a practical man, made very little of it. Ten years more elapse : on his deathbed the aged sailor sends for his old captain, again he repeats the story, and hands over the plans of the island, which he had made when he escaped hanging at Cuba. Captain X seems still to have doubted ; but he arranged with a shipping firm that his son should go out in a sailing-vessel which would pass Trinidada, and that it should lie off the island for a couple of days, while young X went on shore and explored. X had to swim through the surf (we ourselves found this to be frequently the only means of landing), and on his return on board reported he had found all the marks exactly as described by his father ; but that the spot where the treasure had been buried was covered with a landslip of rocks and red earth, which it would take both time and labour to remove. This was in 1884.

The following autumn a second expedition left England —in this the X's had no share. A gentleman (whom I will call Y) connected with the shipping firm alluded to above, thought he knew sufficient of the secret to manage without them : he took out some English navvies, and arranged that the vessel should wait for him a fortnight. He did not meet with any success : for some days he was unable to land ; when he did land, he upset his boat, and lost two men and most of his stores. (We used to do this too, though fortunately we never lost any men.) The overhead sun, and the land-crabs, with which this island swarms, made these adventurers so uncomfortable that on the second day they mutinied, and refused to do any more work. Y having returned to England, fell in with Mr Knight's delightful book, *The Cruise of the Falcon*, which described a visit to Trinidada, and thinking he was a likely man to organise a new expedition, imparted to him so much of the secret as he knew, Captain X again refusing to have anything to do with it.

This, then, is the story, on the strength of which we sailed last August from Southampton; but I think it is only fair to add that the rank and file of the expedition did not hear all the details, or the somewhat underhand manner in which the information had been obtained, until Trinidada had been reached.

A definite agreement was drawn up, by which Mr Knight bound himself to find vessel, tools, and stores for the voyage out and home, and six months on shore, should the work take so long, while each of the amateur crew, except the doctor, agreed to subscribe £100, and work under Mr Knight's directions, both on board and on shore, and was to receive one-twentieth of the treasure in the event of success. Four paid hands were taken forrard, and as we totalled nine aft, and also finally sailed on a Friday, we certainly deserve the sympathy of all Thirteen Clubs in our subsequent failures.

After some difficulty a suitable boat had been found, a twenty-five-year-old racing cutter, of thirty-three tons (fifty-six yacht measurement). In her first youth, she had been to Australia and back, and her hull was still as sound as ever. Being of old-fashioned shape, she had little or no counter, a great advantage in deep-sea sailing: in fact, she was exactly the craft we wanted, except in one respect —she was miserably slow for a yacht; we had had her altered from a cutter into a yawl, and the cut-down main-sail fitted abominably, while the jib-headed mizzen was too small to hold any wind. Yachting men will wonder how the nine of us aft were accommodated with bunks: it was managed, however, without trespassing on the saloon sofas. The saloon itself was crammed with all manner of things, chief among them being five casks of thirty over-proof rum, two condenser tanks full of water, and another holding ninety gallons under the table, a quick-firing gun with its case of ammunition, also a medium-sized forge, etc.; while the ceiling was decorated with nine camp-bedsteads, nine repeating rifles, and a large collection of charts. The four paid hands in the forecastle had ample room, and were somewhat envied.

We had capital weather all through the voyage, which was uneventful; so I merely give a list of dates and approximate point to point distances:

Date	Leave	Date	Arrive	Distance Nautical miles
Aug 30th	Cowes	Sept 13th	Salvages Islands	1,900
Sept 17th	Salvages	Sept 18th	Santa Cruz (Tenerife)	130
Sept 25th	Santa Cruz	Oct 2nd	St Vincent (Cape Verde Islands)	850
Oct 9th	St Vincent	Nov 2nd	Bahia	2,000
Nov 14th	Bahia	Nov 20th	Trinidada	700
Feb 15th	Trinidada	Mar 9th	Trinidad (West Indies)	2,800
	Add Trinidada to Bahia and back (twice)			2,100
			Total	10,480

The first land we sighted after leaving England was the Great Salvage island, some one hundred and fifty miles south of Madeira. It is the largest and highest of the little-known Salvage group, the two others being named Great and Little Piton. This too is the scene of a treasure story, and as it was on our way, and we had plenty of time to explore, we had determined to see what we could make of it, if only, as one of us remarked, to get our hands in for Trinidada. The legend runs as follows :

In 1804 a treasure ship was bound to Cadiz from South America with two million dollars in silver on board : the crew mutinied, and killed their captain. At the same time they sighted some small desert islands, lying, as they supposed, some two hundred miles south of Madeira. Running their vessel into a snug little bay on the south side of the middle island, which was high, flat, and green at the top, they landed the treasure and buried it in the white sand just above high-water mark. They then placed the captain's body in the mouth of the hole, in order that, if the traces were discovered, it might be supposed to be merely a grave. Soon afterwards they were shipwrecked off the Spanish coast. A dying survivor told the secret to his comrade in hospital, an English sailor, called Christian Cruse, through whom it reached the English Admiralty, who in 1813 sent Rear-Admiral Hercules Robinson, in H.M.S. *Prometheus*, to visit the Salvages, which were undoubtedly the islands referred to. He landed and dug on the Great Salvage without any success, and reported that the centre island, the Great Piton, was quite inaccessible.

Now we had provided ourselves with the Admiralty chart of these rocks ; and having observed that the *Prometheus* only went to the north island, and did not visit the middle island, expressly mentioned by Cruse, we had decided to explore the Great Piton thoroughly.

As we coasted round the Great Salvage in order to anchor on the lee side, to our amazement we saw a rakish-looking schooner brought up in the only cove that the island possesses. It had just landed a dozen Portuguese fishermen, who for the winter months of the year desert their wives and homes in Madeira for this barren pile of rocks. They looked, however, far more like smugglers, as we watched them dragging heavy casks up a steep path to the cave in which they dwelt. On landing and making friends, we found one of these barrels did contain *aguardiente*, and another a capital dry Madeira ; but the others were merely full of salt for their fish. In the evening their vessel sailed away, amid heart-rending *adios*, not to return till spring.

The next morning five of our party sailed in the yacht's whale-boat to try and effect a landing on the centre island ; the rest had a run ashore on the Great Salvage, whence they returned laden with rabbits and fish. After dinner the yacht followed the other party, who had landed on this quite inaccessible island without much difficulty, and who indicated a bay in which to anchor the yacht. This was a snug little bay with a vengeance, sown with reefs, and no small swell running. The shore party were very pleased with themselves ; they had found what they thought a likely place for the treasure, and also considerable quantities of a black mineral, supposed to be antimony. (Months afterwards we heard from England that it was hornblende, of no commercial value.)

The Great Piton does not at all agree with the description ' high, flat, and green at the top ' : on the contrary, it is very low, and green all over, except the one high, black, rocky crag from which it derives its name. It was obvious now why Admiral Robinson had chosen the Great Salvage, for it does fulfil the conditions ; still there was no doubt but that ours was the centre island, and we landed our tents and tools, and started work in what were pronounced the most likely places. We did not experiment in either of the two sandy bays, for the master-mind of the expedition had decided that no white sand could remain so for eighty years; and for somewhat similar reasons we did not dig on the beach, but a little way inshore.

This island has no water, and is consequently uninhabited, although the fishermen from the Great Salvage apparently come over for a few days in calm weather, for we found several of their belongings, including numerous volatile insects, who stayed with us afterwards till the end of the cruise. On the third afternoon we decamped, and with a fair wind for the one hundred and thirty miles to Tenerife were at anchor in Santa Cruz harbour by 2 P.M. the next day. This is a most delightful spot, and those of us who went up into the interior of the island were amply repaid for their trouble. Everyone has heard of the fourteen thousand feet high peak, but comparatively few English know the ancient city of Laguna, once the capital of the Canaries, with its quaint cathedral and glorious forest of Mercedes. Why do so many invalids choose Portuguese Madeira, in preference to the equally salubrious and far more picturesque Spanish Canary Islands?

St Vincent, our next port of call, is a bare rocky island: though it is Portuguese, the English are the dominant residents, officials of the great coaling firms, and the Anglo-Brazilian Telegraph Company. The hospitality we experienced from these gentlemen will always be gratefully remembered. Then came our longest spin, across the Atlantic, the Doldrums, and the Line. Skirting the convict-island of Fernando Noronha, we made the Brazilian coast close to Pernambuco, and coasted down to Bahia, the second city of Brazil, and formerly the capital. Here, too, our compatriots did everything in their power to make our stay agreeable, and here, to my great regret, our first and second mates decided to abandon the enterprise, owing to the lax discipline which prevailed on board, and although we were only a few days' sail from our destination. Two other amateurs had already left, and we were now ten all told, five being paid hands ; our worthy bosun had resigned at Santa Cruz, and in his place we had two West Indian blacks, strong, plucky fellows, and always cheerful at their work, a great contrast to their white brethren.

At daybreak, on November 20th, our seventh day out from Bahia, we sighted Trinidada right ahead, its great height making it clearly visible sixty miles away : the same afternoon we were at anchor in twenty fathoms, under the lee side of the island, which is here over two thousand feet high, and very precipitous ; Treasure Bay, as we called it, being about three miles distant round a point. Opposite our anchorage is a kind of natural pier of coral-rocks, running out beyond where the surf breaks : it is consequently easy to land there, even when it is impossible in any other part of the island ; for though Trinidada is six miles long and three wide, the Atlantic swell breaks as heavily on the lee side as it does on the windward. Mr Knight, who had crossed the island from this spot on his previous visit, volunteered to do so now, in order to inspect Treasure Bay, and find the best landing-place in it ; so the morning after our arrival he and another were put ashore, and left to perform their arduous and even dangerous climb. The second morning after, when we were getting anxious about them, we dragged our anchor, and had a very narrow squeak of being wrecked : before we could get any sail to draw, we had drifted down on a rocky bluff, on which the surf was dashing to a most unpleasant height. By marvellous luck we shaved it by some forty yards, the spray falling on our decks ; then the foresail filled, and we breathed again. This was the only really anxious moment of the whole voyage. Our explorers had now returned, and were much exercised to see the yacht under way : they set the tussock-grass on fire to call our attention, and we returned, and got them on board, anchoring now about a mile from the shore in twenty fathoms of water.

Several days then elapsed before we could get our effects landed, and we began work on December 1st. Rising at dawn, we laboured from 5.30 till 9, and again in the after-noon from 4 to 6.30: after work a bathe, a splendid swim in the surf, regardless of the sharks and barracoutas ; after the bathes our two chief meals. During the hot part of the day—and it was so hot that even our blacks could not walk on the sand with their naked feet—we either lay in our tents, or went fishing. Sundays and Wednesday after-noons were holidays, and on those days the more energetic of us rambled about the island. Its rugged picturesque-ness, the millions of sea-birds of every species, which make each ravine like a vast artificial aviary, the fishes of brilliant hue which swarm in the rocky pools, the variety of wreckage of all ages which covers the windward shores, and no doubt, too, the knowledge that it is so seldom visited owing to its evil reputation, give this island a charm possibly possessed by no other. At night we used to watch for turtle, which abound here, just as they do at the kindred island of Ascen-sion ; and as they weigh from 400 to 800 pounds, the turn-ing of them was attended with considerable excitement. Fish-catching was but poor sport, they were so numerous and tame, except when a shark took the bait, and some-times hook and line as well. We had no shooting, except at bottles stuck in the sand ; for the birds could be caught with the hand or a string-lasso, and the only mammal is the common mouse.

The ravine in which we dug averaged about ten yards across, and was sufficiently deep to shade us from the sun's rays both in the morning and evening. There is no actual landslip, in the common acceptation of the word ; but the ravine is choked with large boulders which have fallen at various times from the precipices above : these are packed together with red earth, which has also silted down from above, or which has been washed down the ravine by heavy rains. We were there in the drier season, and on two occasions only during our three months' stay was the ravine flooded. Work with pick, shovel, and wheelbarrow alternated with the more familiar hauling on the rope of a watch-tackle. Owing to the steepness of the ravine, we succeeded in thus rolling down quite large rocks with comparative ease. We had also plenty of powder, but, alas, none of us knew how to use it, and the results of our experiments with it were amusingly unsuccessful. The depth to which we went varied with the locality from eight feet to even twenty feet, wherever it seemed possible that a cave might have existed. We found one especially large boulder, under which the soil had subsided, making a distinct hollow, and for a time hopes ran high. At night a calculation was made as to how much one's share (increased now to one-eighth, owing to our diminished numbers) would come ; £6,000 a year was, I remember, the lowest estimate.

Mr Knight and myself took it by turns to take charge of the yacht, with a crew of two men : this was necessary, for had a *pampero* occurred it would have been advisable to slip anchor, and ride it out in the open sea. He took the first fortnight, and I the second ; and I think I liked the life on board better than on shore. The yacht's deck was a grateful shelter from the midday heat. Owing to the constant breeze, the temperature in the cabin was never higher than 85°. On the calmer days, one could take the dinghy, and, landing at the pier, fetch off wood and water, also stones for ballast to supply the place of the tools and stores which had gone on shore. For this I had a black man and an Englishman; and it was humiliating to note the inferiority of the white, although the work was done in the cool of the day. On one occasion he had been unusually mutinous, and while doubting what to do with him, I observed the whaleboat rounding the point. Mr Knight was bringing off another white hand, who had mutinied on shore; so we exchanged prisoners to our mutual content.

We were now in imminent peril of the rum giving out, so on December 30th, Mr Knight and myself, with the three whites, started back to Bahia to fetch more stores, chiefly oatmeal and spirits, also fresh fruit. We calculated we might take three weeks, so we gave the shore party a full boat-load of provisions (which they promptly lost in the surf when landing at the bay), and bade them farewell. One of our precious crew refused to help to get up the anchor; and as we had out sixty fathoms of chain, and the windlass was old-fashioned and worn out, it took us about an hour and a half. Then we had a quick, pleasant run to Bahia. As we sailed up the famous bay, we were puzzled to see everywhere a sort of imitation American flag, consisting of four red and white stripes, with a blue corner containing a white triangle. Knight suggested it was a compliment to a Yankee frigate which we saw in the harbour; but as it was hung out from the Fort do Mar and the guardship I had my doubts. It turned out to be the colours adopted by the Republican State of

Bahia. The revolution had occurred the very day we had sailed, and was now almost forgotten.

The most exciting episode which occurred at Bahia in connection with the revolution has not, I believe, been yet narrated in England. The military, who, as will be remembered, ran the business, were not sure that the navy, as represented by the guardship, would join in; so on the famous November 14th they loaded the venerable guns in their fort with round-shot, and prepared for the worst. The navy, however, like everyone else, took things as they came. Now Bahia de Todos os Santos is famous for its piety, and on Christmas Day the Host is carried in procession through the chief streets. As it passed Fort do Mar the customary salute was fired, and a poor old Norwegian barque, which was entering the harbour, was drilled between wind and water.

Going back to Trinidada we encountered nasty weather, head-winds, and constant rain-squalls. After a week of this, when we were little more than half-way, one of the hands again mutinied, making it his third time. He had been remonstrated with for coming on watch twenty minutes late. It occurred at midnight, and after a short rough-and-tumble, the other men remaining neutral, he was tied up, and we ran back again to Bahia, and discharged him. We had now only two hands, one of whom had also mutinied, but no others were to be obtained. As soon as we were outside the bay again, the better of these two managed to scald himself so severely on both hands that he was quite useless for the whole passage. As it was blowing hard, we took two reefs down in the mainsail, and so they remained for a fortnight; for when we reached Trinidada, having been away just a month, it was a whole week before the surf would admit of the shore party launching their boat. During this time we did not anchor, but remained hove-to.

When the boat came off, they told us they had been living on the young sea-birds, which were rather tasty than nice. An English gunboat, H.M.S. *Bramble*, had passed the island, and seeing the tents had paid them a visit, and had given a very welcome supply of biscuit, in exchange for a turtle. The work had been going on steadily, and was almost finished, the whole of the corner of the ravine where Y had supposed the treasure to be, had been dug away, and several other likely spots had been tried. Then some ten days more were spent in finishing the work and fetching away tools and stores, after which we sailed for the West Indies, where the expedition broke up.

We were thus at Trinidada about three months, and I don't think any of us will entirely regret them. It is, to say the least of it, a novel experience to a jaded Londoner to be encamped on a surf-bound desert island under a tropical sun, to exchange his walking-stick for a pick and shovel, and to get up, instead of going to bed, with the dawn. It was, in fact, just the complete change that doctors are so fond of advising.

The island has much to recommend it : there are no snakes, and none of the usual tropical insects, no mosquitoes, centipedes, scorpions, or venomous spiders. The land-crabs were a little too friendly at first ; but they soon got to know their place. They are of a bright yellow colour, the largest being perhaps four inches across the back ; very soft-shelled, and so easily killed ; not a single nip was received by any one of us during our whole stay ; and they were most useful to us as scavengers. A limited company, to be called the Trinidada Turtle Importing and Canning Company, might pay a dividend, and it would probably be worth while to collect the phosphate deposited by the birds; and then, thrown in, as the dealers say, is the treasure of the Cathedral of Lima, valued at over a million sterling, only waiting to be fetched away.

We used to wonder, supposing we got the treasure, how many nations would claim it: England, who hoisted her flag at Trinidada as early as 1700; Portugal, for the Portuguese of Brazil had a settlement there about 1750; Brazil, since the island is off the Brazilian coast; Spain, to whom the treasure belonged; Peru, from whose cathedral it was taken; and of course the Roman Church.

We also discussed how we should get it into England, so as to avoid the Customs. Mr Goschen little thought the other day, when he took the duty off gold and silver plate, that we had contemplated a return to England, with the largest cargo of these commodities that has ever entered a British port.

Since returning to England, I have been told that the Salvages Islands are rented by a Portuguese gentleman, residing at Madeira, and that we were consequently trespassing on his private property.

[September 1890

3

THE NEVADA SILVER BOOM

A. I. Shand

Washoe, which was destined to have a world-wide renown, is believed to have taken its name from a wandering tribe of Indians. It is a bleak range of hills, with an average height of five thousand feet, running parallel to the Nevada on one side and to the Rockies on the other. The range is cut up in all directions by deep cañons and gullies. The cities that afterwards sprang up immediately beneath the crests enjoy perhaps the vilest climate in the States. The summers are scorching, and there is no shade. In winter, and indeed at all seasons, the gales from the north, pleasantly known as the Virginian zephyrs, and confined between two mighty mountain-ranges, burst on the treeless plateau with incredible fury, when the warmest clothes are no sort of protection. But the earlier prospectors kept to the shelter of the gullies, for it must be remembered they were still searching for gold, and had no thought of the silver-reef. In one or two of these lateral *arroyos* they struck it rich, and Gold Cañon was the magnet which drew multitudes to the camps. At first the yield was highly satisfactory. But as the washers worked up the ravines, the gold-dust visibly deteriorated. San Francisco brokers, who had been buying for twenty dollars an ounce, would now give little

55

more than half the money. The workers themselves were forced to own that the siftings were decidedly lighter in colour. Moreover, the loose auriferous gravel had been changing to sticky clay, and, with many a curse, they tossed wide 'the blue stuff', which accumulated in unregarded refuse-heaps. The ignorance was profound, and it seems almost incredible now that the evidences did not penetrate their dull intelligences. For the grey shimmer of the depreciated dust was due to the rich combination of the white metal; the execrated blue stuff was so richly impregnated with the overflow of inexhaustible silver stores, that it would have yielded them twice the profit of their gold. The hills, on the sides of which they were painfully scraping, were pregnant with their lodes of silver: everywhere interspersed through the reefs of quartz and porphyry were bonanzas of almost virgin ore.

How the existence of those wonderful silver-reefs was first realised is by no means clear, though much has been written on the subject. Comstock and others who have left records of their investigations were notorious liars, and all that is certain is that they are never to be trusted. The story of all the miners who were first concerned with the find is one of almost unchecked misfortune and bitter disappointments. All sold out for a comparative trifle and came to subsequent grief; but the fate of the men who are most plausibly credited with having struck the silver is the most tragical of all. They were two brothers of the name of Grosh, sons of a New England minister, and fairly educated. They devoted their scanty leisure to the survey of Mount Davidson, while toiling from hand to mouth as working miners. They are supposed to have transferred notes of their surveys to paper, with sketches of the ground. But they saw that capital was indispensable to work the quartz, and capital they could not command. One brother died of an accident. The other started to cross the Sierra to San Francisco in the depth of winter, with a single companion, in the intention, as it is supposed, of seeking the necessary financial assistance. He succumbed to the severity of the weather after untold sufferings. The donkey which they had loaded with their outfit, and which carried the papers, was abandoned.

Probably the secret of the mines perished with the donkey: yet there is a doubt whether some stray memoranda left behind may not have fallen into the hands of Comstock. For when Allen Grosh left the camp he handed over his stone hut with his implements to Comstock's keeping. Comstock, who claimed to be the original discoverer, and gave his name to the great treasure-lodes, was ignorant as any of his comrades; but he must have been an uncommonly sharp fellow. He has put on record that he was led to his discovery by his panning out the rich contents of a gopher-hole. It seems more likely that he was cute enough to take advantage of the find of another party. Water was indispensable to working. He claimed a convenient spring to which he had questionable pretensions, and forced himself as a partner on a little fraternity who apparently had really struck rich silver.

In those primitive times a man's asseveration, even if he were a notorious liar, seems to have passed current as a state deed or a formal mining-lease. Be that as it may, it did not matter much in the end. The silver-mining and the silver boom were fairly launched; but not a man of that group made anything solid by their transactions. Had they suspected it, they were on the verge of being enriched by potentialities beyond the wildest dream of avarice. Four out of the six sold out for a few thousand dollars, and squandered them. A fifth held on a little longer, realised a good round sum, speculated in stocks, and died a lunatic. Comstock waited just long enough to miss his chance. He sold in his turn, and went prospecting. He came back penniless to his Comstock, to work on his own ledges for an ordinary wage. After a time he threw up his pick in disgust, and ended by committing suicide.

In 1860 the rush to Mount Davidson had fairly set in : in 1863 the excitement may be said to have culminated. Before that a characteristic incident had occurred which seriously disturbed the municipal economy. A man digging in the soil of his sage-bush tenement chanced to come on a silver-vein. By miner's law he had the right to peg out a claim for a length of four hundred feet, and concede stretches of two hundred feet to any chum. Consequently all his neighbours in the adjacent streets had to quit, or trade, or shoot, as the case might be. For at that time every citizen was on the shoot, and the pistol was the ultimate court of appeal. There was a strange mingling of desperadoes with the hard-working miners, who would gladly have been peaceable had that been possible. The swaggerers, who terrorised the town, carried not only re-volvers, but, as a rule, shotguns. The miner went girded with a Colt in self-defence, and the bowie-knife was his inseparable companion.

The climate, as we have said, was unhealthy enough, yet three-fourths of the corpses borne to the quiet grave-yard had come to a violent end. The innumerable drinking-bars were the only places of recreation when a man tired of the theatre or the travelling circus. But when he dropped in for the evening gossip or drink, he knew that he took his life in his hand. A breeze blew up in a corner, and forthwith the six-shooters were out. The bar-tender's was a popular and lucrative post, but the privileges inferred corresponding liabilities. He kept his private armoury in a drawer beneath the counter. The bar was intrenched and fortified with sand-bags till it was shot-proof. At the first symptom of trouble, he dropped. The customers who were not over-excited by curiosity scuttled promptly behind full casks, left around for their accommodation, or cleared out into the street. The bars charged dear, and made good profits. But one of the heaviest drawbacks was the outlay on mirrors. The miners insisted on a grand show of plate-glass, and a pistol-shot might send a week's profits to smithereens. And naturally the stray bullets would often find billets in the bodies of disinterested and involuntary spectators.

There is much that is grimly humorous in the matter-of-course way in which the local news-sheets reported these nightly brawls. A year or two later, after an atrociously cold-blooded shooting-scene, an old resident, in his fond reminiscences, plaintively remarked that it brought back the lively times of 1860. For those Washoe camps were the most lawless of all, and only surpassed subsequently by the wilder licence in Montana. Notable bullies turned up from the Californian placers to terrorise the community : the crimes for which they had been outlawed were so many feathers in their caps, and the biggest ruffian of all arrived with the brilliant record of a baker's dozen of unjustifiable homicides. Then there were the more gentlemanly, but scarcely less bloodthirsty, professionals, who made a livelihood by gambling. Bret Harte has relieved their darker shades, for purposes of romance, by crediting them with qualities they seldom possessed ; and a certain Cherokee Bob, who hailed from Idaho, is said to have been the prototype of Mr Oakhurst and Mr Hamblin. They had the one redeeming virtue of being the most abstemious members of the society, for they could not afford to lose their heads.

Burglary, too, was good business, though the risks were proportionate to the gains. The sage-bushes of the first hovels had been replaced with boarding, as roads improved and lumber was cheapened : but the loose planking was a frail protection to buried deposits of gold, and locks and bars were of the most primitive description. As robberies grew more frequent, the prudent miners felt it was simple wisdom to squander their money. At least they had the satisfaction of spending it themselves.

The advent of ladies was a tempting opening for extravagance. At first the apparition of a woman was as rare as that of an accredited ghost. The rude celibates hungered for the sight of a feminine face. Mark Twain has a story, at any rate *ben trovato*, of how a stage with a lady passenger inside was stopped by a gang at some outlying diggings. With levelled pistols they compelled her companion to hand her out. They gathered round her ; they gazed her out of countenance ; they actually wept over her ; and then they presented her with a purse of twenty-five hundred dollars subscribed on the spot. That gives an idea of the warmth of the reception of the frail San Francisco beauties who speculated in a trip to the ironically named Virginia City. They were intoxicated with adoration and champagne, and loaded with costly gifts. Attended by trains of admirers, bedizened with jewels of price, they trailed their satins and silks through the dust and foul refuse of a city where it seldom rained. A girl of talent, who could dance, or sing, or play the piano, was engaged at twice a senator's income, to figure at some theatre booth, or bait a gambling-saloon.

The development of the subterranean industry had been

prodigious and unprecedented. In 1859 ground was broken; in 1860 the boom was well on, and sixty stamp-mills were running; in 1863 it was in fullest swing. Enormous capital had been invested in the companies. The Ophir, the Gould & Curry, and many other mines almost as widely advertised, had been marked out with fixed boundaries. Yet the border rock was often fiercely disputed, and after those sanguinary encounters below ground, the derricks would be busily at work hoisting up the dead and wounded. For each miner was personally loyal to his salt, and fought for his paymasters with feudal devotion.

Right through the mountain and under Virginia City ran the Comstock lode: from the main branch diverged innumerable lateral veins, like the fibres on a leaf or the side-creeks from a sea-channel. The main vein was from sixty to eighty feet thick, traversing walls of barren rock. Expectation was always kept upon tiptoe, by the fact of the silver being stored in bonanzas, often solid deposits of almost pure metal. Shafts had been sunk in all directions; tunnels and adits were branching away in gloomy labyrinths on both sides of the main gallery. That transept for the length of nearly two miles was loftier than the roof of the noblest cathedral, and, like the cathedral, it was reared upon stately columns. Pillars of the rock had been left; but they could not be trusted, and were supplemented by massive supports of timber, where the tree-trunks, as thick as the body of a man, were bratticed and riveted by strong clamps of iron. They bore up a network of ponderous cross-beams and rafters. Yet not infrequently, and in spite of all precautions, rock and timber succumbed to the pressure of the hill, burying a gang of workers under a stone avalanche.

The Spaniards, who had their own experience of mining, say that it needs a gold-mine to run a silver-mine, and there never was a truer proverb. That colossal timbering cost infinitely more than the marbles and sculpturing of many splendid fanes. Each tree had been felled in some distant forest, dragged laboriously over snow or rutted tracks by interminable teams of oxen, hauled up the steep slopes of Mount Davidson, and painfully lowered by huge derricks. And, apropos the derricks, it must be remembered that all the machinery was transported from San Francisco. Before the erection of the mills, when the first tons of valuable ore were sent to California for crushing, the freights had swallowed five-sixths of the profits. And a continuance of that excessive outlay was the history of all the mines : when the best were making enormous yields, perhaps not a tenth might be distributed in dividends. The quick-silver alone was an enormous item.

Never was more powerful pumping-machinery erected than on the Comstock. At one time the pumps were lifting about ten million gallons a day; yet they were too feeble to cope with the flooding of the lower levels when the shafts had only gone down to four hundred or five hundred feet. That was one of the chief reasons for the protection of the Sutro tunnel.

> 'Water, water, everywhere,
> Nor any drop to drink,'

sang Coleridge in ' The Ancient Mariner '. When the miner ran a fair chance of being drowned below, above he had the choice between slow poisoning and perishing of thirst. Water there was, though in no great profusion, but it was impregnated with alkali, or even tainted with arsenic ; and that, perhaps, was the best excuse for the hard drinking. Afterwards, when the first fever of the silver-chase had calmed down, the community came forward in a public-spirited manner, fetching the pure element from distant lakes in channels and long aqueducts worthy of the Romans.

As for the Sutro tunnel, it is not only one of the most stupendous achievements of modern engineering, but one of the grandest monuments to individual determination. Sutro, by sheer indomitable strength of will, actually forced it upon the hostile capitalists it was to benefit. He was a young man with no influential connections, who owned a small quartz-mill on the Carson river. His ambition was as aspiring as his means were small. He set himself to solve the drainage and ventilation problems, so that the mines might be worked profitably, and more or less salubriously, at the deepest levels. He was no man for half-measures. He proposed to pierce the mountain at the depth of two thousand feet : with lateral branches his tunnel was to be six miles in length : and though the estimates fluctuated as conditions changed, the ultimate cost was a million sterling.

The tale of his trials and disappointments is a long one. At first his hopes were high, and everything ran in his favour. He had obtained the signed support of all the leading owners. He obtained Acts conferring certain privileges from the State Legislature and from Congress. Then the Bank of California, which was all-powerful on the Comstock, took alarm, and induced the owners to repudiate their pledges. Most men would have given up in despair. Sutro, by selling himself up, cleared a sufficiency of dollars to pay his expenses to Washington. His trip was successful, for Congress confirmed its grant, and, moreover, he got some substantial financial assistance. He came back to make burning appeals to the miners of the Comstock, by explaining to them that they were missing their sole chance of relief from discomfort and immunity from accidents.

The fierce agitation put pressure on the capitalists. Next he crossed the Atlantic to stump France and England : there he raised sums by subscription which were swelled on his return, till the funds were secured for commencing the enterprise.

When the financial difficulties were overcome, the engineering troubles had to be surmounted. We have heard something of similar troubles from the St Gothard works ; but the Swiss engineers benefited by the Sutro experiences. We cannot enter into details, but the labour was carried through in face of fire and water. The vertical shafts sunk from above were flooded by the drain from the porous rock, and the labourers, whose shifts were changed every two hours, were drawing their breaths in the blasts of a burning furnace. Notwithstanding the use of all scientific appliances, the temperature, towards the end of the work, had risen to 114°. The strongest men would drop asphyxiated, and the mules refused to face the heat. Human endurance had wellnigh reached its limit when the final wall of partition was breached and free ventilation established with the cooler drift on the other side, in a drift of dust and debris that nearly suffocated the exhausted pioneers.

Going back to the spring of 1860, Virginia City was already in a hot fit of speculation. Never was seen such strange gambling : it was all for counters, with no cash. The ready money was planked down in the gambling-dens or on the drinking-bars. No one had any credit, yet any number of sales were effected without even the formality of setting them down on paper.

But as genuine lodes yielded real profits, and exaggerated reports of the results reached San Francisco, transactions became serious. The Californian capitalists were beset in the passes of the Sierra by penniless prospectors, offering the most tempting bargains. When they got to Virginia the shrewdest of them saw that the reefs were quite good enough to gamble on. Now and again a shaft struck a bonanza which showed the value of the prizes to be gained. The simple enormity of the sums nominally paid for claims sufficed to float a prospectus and rig a market: 500 dollars per mining foot was no extraordinary price, and as much as 2,000 dollars had been given.

The formation of new companies, the shares of which were readily subscribed, went on with unexampled rapidity. In two or three years they were to be numbered by the hundred: some had a more or less fictitious capital of a million sterling. A regular Stock Exchange had been established in Virginia, and in San Francisco from three rival board-rooms the buyers and sellers overflowed into the adjacent streets. It was a case of Law's South Sea Bubble over again, and with more universal excitement. For everybody, without exception, was trafficking in stocks, from the state governor and the mayors to the bootblack at the block corner. Yet still, and for long, the claims were only held by right of occupation; important transactions were carried out without the execution of title-deeds, which was to give the primitive law courts excessive occupation, and enrich a class of legal specialists. One mine, the Ophir, went in for nearly thirty lawsuits in three years: there was such a rush on the services of one popular pleader that for a single fee he had 160,000 dollars. That litigation, by the way, was responsible for a large proportion of the crime.

A Galway sessions in the beginning of the century was a scene of millenium peace compared to the proceedings of a Virginia tribunal. The judge, like he of the *Bon Gaultier Ballads*, backed up his judgments with his Colt; the litigants took shots at the opposing counsel, and subsequently argued the questions out among themselves, when they drew and fired over their whisky-skins.

The capitalists who came to the front would never have become millionaires had they made much pretence of playing fair. It was the small investors who went to the wall : as one was beggared another came in ; and the great object was to tempt them, and then squeeze them out. If small holders refused to be scared, irresistible pressure was put upon them by increasing the calls for the development of the mine. They failed to pay up, and their shares were forfeited. So each speculation, whether good or bad, was at the mercy of the innermost circle who controlled it. It was such a commanding position which enabled the Bank of California, holding large interests either in property or on mortgage, nearly to balk the gigantic enterprise of Sutro, when success seemed practically within his grasp.

Reticence was of the essence of that shady speculation. The gloom of the deepest recess of the Comstock was not so dark as the ideal secrecy observed in the working of a favourite quartz-mine. Surprises of one kind or another were always to be sprung, and the shareholders had any amount of sensation for their money. No outsider was admitted to the workings on any pretext. The superintendent and foremen were well paid to be silent, and only a chosen few of the miners were engaged for ' the secret shifts '. One company tried the plan of imprisoning their people in the works at proportionate wages, but the plan did not answer. The free-born Americans refused to be enslaved. Yet it is astonishing how staunchly the employed stood in with the employers, and how seldom important revelations were made. For the surface swarmed with spies of the speculators, who had *carte blanche* to bribe to any amount, and who stood drinks in the saloons that they might worm out invaluable confidences.

But when there was no authentic intelligence, reports were invented, and being accredited by the sales of leading banks and brokers, they served pretty much the same purpose. At length, after crying wolf time after time, a Nemesis overtook the largest operators. In 1864 the inflation suddenly collapsed, when Gould & Curry burst up. The owners had bought it for a trifle from Gould, who wandered off to get a livelihood by lumbering. It had paid three million dollars in a couple of years, and now it was said to have given out. There was a simultaneous fall in other stocks: the panic spread : the small shareholders went bankrupt: no calls could be enforced : the pumps ceased to work, and the lower adits were drowned : the mills were abandoned : buildings and timbering fell into decay, and temporarily the Comstock was a solitude. The ruin was universal, yet it was a false alarm, for ten years afterwards the biggest bonanza of all was discovered. When industries and speculation were resumed with redoubled vigour, the victims of that unreasoning scare had sad cause to repent their precipitation.

For a time there was consternation and general perturbation. The fever of speculation was succeeded by a cold fit, and many thousands of immigrants saw their subsidiary occupations threatened. Not to speak of the actual workers in the mines, for three years the three hundred miles of mountain and valley from the coast to Washoe had been overcrowded with ever-increasing traffic. The teamsters who brought machinery and provided supplies were to be numbered by the thousand. Lumbering camps doing lively business had been set up in the lonely forests of the Sierras. Now the Stock Exchanges were deserted, there was a stoppage in the passes, and the axe of the woodman was thrown aside. But the momentary set-back proved a blessing in disguise.

In 1864 the mining activity of the West was still severed from the settled States to the eastward by dreary expanses of unpeopled territory. The collapse at Washoe made adventurous men desperate, and sent forth a lost legion of prospectors, who had to choose between discovery and starvation. Reckless as they were, they argued reasonably that the wealth of Washoe could be no isolated phenomenon. Nor were they without material proof of the theory, for the year before, in another district of Nevada, fresh ground had been broken at the promising diggings of the Reese river. There was a scattering rush from east to west, and new treasure-troves lured on the advance-guards of the army. On the Reese river they struck it gold- and silver-rich, beyond the most sanguine hopes of the prospectors. Oregon ledge ran a good second to the Comstock lode.

Austin City sprang up in a couple of years, from two to twenty thousand inhabitants. Again at Austin there was the sharp pinch of famine, when flour was fetching two shillings the pound ; again the constraining force of hunger opened up regular communications, and with the trains of wagons setting in from Washoe there mingled picturesque strings of camels, who found themselves at home in the sandy wastes, and breathed freely in the sulphurous atmosphere. Again adventurers had to endure the tortures of Tantalus. There was wealth at will, but it cost dear to realise it. Remoteness from sea and rivers made the outlay almost prohibitive. Timber brought from a distance fetched a dollar for the two feet. But the chief trouble was the cost of the smelting : ore which would have paid well at Virginia, at Austin was barely worth the taking. Never-

theless the settlements flourished, and made another start
with the approach of the eastern railways.

Then gold placers, which were always the preludes to
the silver finds, were discovered in the Black Hills, the
Mauvaise Terres of Dakota. That unkindly and repulsive
region began to be colonised, and the prospectors had
pioneered the way for the ranchers. Next the tide of exploration swelled up in Montana, where at the euphoniously
named Silver Bow, and round ' Granite Mountain ', richest
of all the Montana mines, it reached high-water mark.
Thence it overflowed into Idaho, and the more remote
territory of Washington was not unsuccessfully *exploité*.
We do not say that the prospectors were disappointed, but
more systematic investigations were indefinitely deferred.

But the second stage of the great boom was the revival
of enthusiasm over Washoe. In the first, the expenditure
had been lavish to extravagance : the new era was to be
characterised by economy and retrenchment, for the speculators were wise enough to profit by experience. We have
alluded to the opposition offered by the Bank of California
to the Sutro tunnel. The bank had become an autocratic
power. It was fortunate in a manager of remarkable
shrewdness and foresight. Sharon had still faith in the
Washoe future : he could not believe that the silver had
been worked out, though the sinkers had got down to a
barren stratum. He knew well that it was a question
whether the suspended mines were worth anything or
nothing ; but he had the eloquence to persuade a group
of financiers to play *le tout pour le tout*. It needed all his
eloquence and iron determination to keep his confederates
up to the mark through a time of prolonged and intense
discouragement. Under his prompting the bank had been
making the most of its opportunities. As shares had been

flung on the market, as its mortgagers got hard pressed, and as stockholders backed out of their assessments, it had been buying cheap or confiscating, until it owned or controlled many mines and mills. Under its auspices and the direction of Sharon, the Mill and Mining Company was launched, to resume prospecting operations on a large scale. On the Crown Mine, one of its numerous investments, it bored down for nearly a thousand feet. Nothing but barrenness was the invariable report. The financiers were in despair, and even Sharon felt dubious. Then the workers came on a shimmering of metal. It led them straight down to the second biggest of the bonanzas : San Francisco and Virginia were in a hotter fever than ever, and there was a rise of fifty million dollars in Comstocks.

In the meantime another small group had gone quietly to work under the shadow of the great monopoly. Very different they were from the strong capitalists who were backing Sharon. All were men of the smallest means, but all were cool and sagacious, and the leaders were practical miners. These were the famous bonanza kings. Mackay is the best known ; but in his friend Fair he had a colleague at least as capable. Mackay had drifted west from a clerk's stool in Broadway to do a little placer-mining on the Sacramento. Having saved a few hundred dollars, he tramped into Virginia City in 1860. When that money was gone, he engaged as a common miner. He was fortunate enough to come across Fair, whose previous history was very similar : they were prompt to appreciate their common qualities, and thenceforth the two were in closest partnership. From labourers they rose to be overseers, and could lay by. They practised severe economy to form a joint fund. Mackay had the miner's ambition in excess. He would often say afterwards, that from the beginning he had devoted himself to becoming the greatest mine-master in the world.

The Man of Destiny moved steadily onward; but he had his fluctuations and his anxieties like Sharon. Yet most of his little ventures had succeeded, and each gain was shrewdly invested in mines, as a stepping-stone to something further. Sharon had secured all that was supposed best; but these outsiders could pick and choose among abandoned properties, and Fair had the scent of a sleuth-hound in puzzling out signs of metal. The partners, who had already accumulated a moderate fortune, decided to break ground on a tract of the hill comparatively neglected. Fair pronounced that it had a likely look, and the purchase-money was a trifle. Performance seemed to belie the promise. When they had sunk to a depth of twelve hundred feet, they had nearly touched their bottom dollar, and the big Californians were chuckling over their discomfiture.

Then came one of the most wonderful turns on record of the capricious wheel of Fortune. For weeks Fair had been growing more gloomy and more anxious. One day when Mackay met him at the mouth of the shaft there was a smile on his worn face. At last they had broken through the barren quartz to rock that showed distinctly metalliferous. Next morning they had picked up the thread of a tiny silver vein. They followed it: they lost it when Fair had broken down under the strain: they harked back, and they found it again. Tunnelling along it for two hundred and fifty feet from the bottom of the shaft, it brought them out upon the upper floor of the Comstock bonanza *par excellence*. Foot by foot, as the new shaft went down, the bonanza steadily increased in richness. They tested its width by cutting transverse drifts, and nowhere did they strike indications of poverty. In fact, with the silver sparkling from the sides in the lamplight, they might have fancied themselves in some fabled treasure-cave of the gnomes.

Almost as surprising as the rare richness of the find was the comparative secrecy in which it was shrouded. Sharon and his Californians obstinately refused to give credence to the reports till the yields of the ore made unbelief impossible. In truth, the little syndicate was literally a close corporation. Mackay and his partners kept the mine in their own hands : there were no shares to be rigged on fluttering markets. He always held to the principle he avowed, of sticking to mining and never speculating in stocks. In the course of some seven years their bonanzas had paid the partners nearly fourteen millions sterling in dividends. They had made their piles and should have been well satisfied, when, after a sudden and swift decline, all the bonanzas had simultaneously given out. They sold the reversions for what they would fetch : they retired from business, and when Mackay the millionaire was being fêted in the Old World as the bonanza king, many of the adventurers who had taken over his property were filing their schedules of bankruptcy.

[April 1899

4

THE MYSTERY OF THE TOBERMORY GALLEON REVEALED

Andrew Lang

Few readers need a description of the Sound of Mull, and few tourists, as their steamer passes Duart, and Mingarry, and Ardtornish castles :

> ' Each on its own dark cape reclined,
> And listening to its own wild wind,'

think of the strange tragedies which these crumbling keeps have witnessed. To my fancy the Sound is peopled with ghosts of galleys flying through tempest, or clashing in battle, or crowding into the strait entrance of Loch Aline at the fatal call of the Lord of the Isles. ' They went to the wars but they always fell.' Galleys of Clan Gilzean, Clan Donald, Clan Diarmaid, the Sound has been your Salamis, and nowhere should wrecks and bones and weapons of dead men lie thicker than in that still and quiet harbour to which a victory of Angus Og of the Isles gave the name of ' Bloody Bay '.

As readers of the newspapers know, within a long stone's cast of Tobermory pier, and even closer to the northern horn of the harbour, sleep the soldiers and crew of a Spanish galleon, a lost ship of the Armada,

> 'Out of sight she passed, out of hearing,'

like Odysseus the Wanderer. She was rediscovered, and many strange and pleasing relics of 'that great fleet invincible' were brought to upper air in 1906 to 1910 by gentlemen adventurers styled 'The Pieces of Eight Company'. But they could not find 'the King's treasure', with which the galleon is naturally endowed by legends based on the hopes of kings and chiefs, princes, earls, and the one Marquis of Argyll, in times long enough agone. A new company has been formed, to succeed, if it can, where so many bold adventurers have failed.

A most lively and readable pamphlet, well illustrated, written by Colonel Foss for 'The Tobermory Galleon Salvage', came lately into my hands. It is not a stock-jobbing affair, it appeals to the love of romance, to curiosity concerning an old secret of the sea, to the hope of finding works of Renaissance art,—and there is the off-chance of treasure. Treasure or no treasure, I owe to Colonel Foss the joys of the chase, the search for the secret of that galleon,—for a galleon it is—through the English, Scottish, French, Irish, and Spanish papers on the Armada. No treasure-hunter by sea or land has had more exciting moments than myself, more alternations of hope and despair. Luckier than they who seek for diamonds and rubies, gold and plate, I have found what I wanted, THE SECRET OF THE GALLEON. The reader, if he will, may now share at ease in what to me were the toils of 'the longest and sorest chase'. I must give my references, 'as a proof of *bona fides*'. Some papers were deciphered by the skill of Miss E. M. Thompson from the charred fragments of Sir

Robert Cotton's manuscripts.

To begin with,—*What is the name of the galleon?* Here I am constrained to differ in opinion from the Duke of Argyll, the owner of the vessel and of most important manuscripts ; and from Colonel Foss, who has also studied the subject, and has most kindly supplied me with references to old printed books.

Perhaps the earliest printed English reference to the nationality of the ship is that given by Archbishop Spottiswoode, writing about 1636. He speaks of ' a ship of Florence burned by certain Highlanders '. This is vague indeed. Tuscany had more than one ship in the Armada. On August 2nd (Spanish style, which I shall follow), ' The Florentine galleon *San Medel* greatly distinguished herself ', says Pedro Coco Calderon (chief accountant on the Armada, and a most entertaining character), writing at Havre de Grâce on September 24th. But it is not the *San Medel*, it is another Tuscan ship, the *Florencia*, or ' the Great Galleon of the Duke of Tuscany ', that is recognised by the Duke of Argyll and by Colonel Foss as the ship of Tobermory Bay. At Lisbon, where the Armada dallied long, the *Florencia* (961 tons, 52 guns, 400 soldiers) was (May 9th) in the squadron of the Commander-General, the Duke of Medina Sidonia. On July 13th, at Corunna, she was with the Levantine or Italian squadron, and had but 294 soldiers. The Duke of Medina Sidonia, commander-in-chief, reports the gallantry of the *Florencia* on August 1st, and on August 2nd she and the *San Juan Bautista* (a vessel contributed by Sicily) pursued the English flagship ' with sails and oars ', but, says Purser Coco, she ' left them as if they were standing still '. They wanted to grapple and board ; she had the heels of them and riddled them with her guns from afar.

After that, silence about the *Florencia* till September 11th. Then the sole survivor of the *Nuestra Señora de la Rosa* of the Guipuzcoan squadron, wrecked on the Irish coast on September 9th, gives his information to English officials. ' He saith the Florentine ship is gone with the Duke ' (of Medina Sidonia). ' He saith where he left the Duke he knoweth not, but it was in the North Seas.'

As we all know, the mass of the Spanish ships fled north round the Orkneys, and down the west coast, smitten by Atlantic storms, and losing many a vessel on the shores of Argyll and Ireland and the Faroes.

This witness was John Antonio of Padua, the son of the pilot of the *Nuestra Señora de la Rosa*. A Spanish officer shot the pilot for treachery, when the vessel ran on the rock ; the boy alone escaped on broken pieces of the ship—which, by the way, had four shots clean through her.

After that, no more about the *Florencia*. She is not in a Spanish list of vessels lost, of which Captain Fernandez Duro, the historian of the Armada, publishes a copy. She is not in a list, more copious, of the losses on the Irish coast, examined by Major Hume. Sir John Knox Laughton has found nothing about her loss. In a Spanish manuscript list she is reported as having reached a Spanish port.

In support of the *Florencia* the Duke of Argyll adduces the long beautiful bronze gun, with the salamanders and ' F's ' of François I, which is now at Inveraray Castle, having been salved from the wreck ' in 1670 '. The gun was among those lost by François I at Pavia in 1525, and the Duke quotes ' the records ' (Tuscan ?) for the fact that some of the French King's guns ' were put on a vessel contributed to the Armada by the State of Tuscany '. Also from ' the records ', the ship was the *Florencia*, and at Vigo took on board a Portuguese captain, Pereira, and crew.

No doubt all this of the Portuguese crew is correct as regards the *Florencia*. But ' on board ' the *Florencia*, and in command, were Gaspar de Sousa, Colonel of a regiment, and Manuel de la Vega. As to Pereira and Sousa, what the Spanish records say is that they were to levy Portuguese soldiers, two thousand if possible, and Gaspar de Sousa commanded in the *Florencia*. The recognition of the Pereira shield on a plate recovered from the galleon in 1906 is of no avail. The bearing is a saltire, which the noble family of Pereira bore—but were not alone in bearing.

Meanwhile there is no hint to be found of the loss of the *Florencia*.

Nobody suggests that *two* Armada vessels were burned in *two* Scottish harbours. Therefore if I can show on good evidence that a famous Armada vessel, not the *Florencia*, was burned in a haven of Scotland, I have nearly solved the problem of the identity of the Tobermory ship.

I call as witness Captain Marolin de Juan, Pilot-General of the Armada. We know that the *San Calderon* hulk, with Chief Purser Coco Calderon, reached Havre de Grâce on September 23rd, ' and all spoiled ships drift thither, and all disastrous things ', through the late autumn and early winter. The Pilot-General was there, when, on December 26th, some Scottish vessels brought thirty-two Spanish soldiers and certain sailors, waifs of the great Venetian vessel the *Valencera*, (1,100 tons, Don Alonzo de Luzon commanding, Colonel of the *tercio* of Naples). On September 14th she was wrecked on the Irish coast, off the Blasquets. How infamously the English betrayed, robbed, and slaughtered many officers and men may be read in the examination of her commander, Don Alonzo

77

de Luzon.

There is a much more full and vivid description of the sufferings by Juan de Nova. 'A savage gentleman, O'Cahan' (O'Callaghan?), with his people, harboured one hundred men who escaped—'feeding them and waiting on them hand and foot.' O'Callaghan was a blinded papist. He forwarded his guests to another ' savage gentleman '— Sorley Macdonnell of Dunluce, who kept them for three weeks, and sent eighty soldiers in boats ' to an island off Scotland, which is only ten miles off'. Sorley, defying the Lord-Lieutenant of Ireland, also sent to Scotland the rest of the men, where they had the comfort of meeting ' a savage who spoke Latin ' (probably the parish minister). They were all harboured and passed on by Scottish gentleman to Scottish gentleman, were clothed and fed at Edinburgh by gentle King Jamie (or rather by the town at his orders), Lord Claude Hamilton, and Sir John Seton, and finally the King sent them to France in four Scottish ships. Among these waifs of the crew and soldiers of the *Valencera* were the thirty-two Spanish soldiers and the sailors who, coming to Havre de Grâce on December 26th, gave their Scottish news to the Pilot-General of the Armada. In that news was the secret of Tobermory Bay ; in the words of the Pilot-General (December 27th) : ' The Ship *San Juan Bautista* of Ragusa, 800 tons, was burned in a Scottish port with Don Diego Manrique on board. They say that the only persons who escaped were fifteen who were on shore at the time.'

Now no Spanish vessel was ' burned in a Scottish port ' except the galleon burned in Tobermory Bay. The bringers of the news had been both among the savage gentlemen who spoke Latin on the west Scottish coast, and also for a month, at least, in Edinburgh. They knew the talk of the day. They said not a word of the *Florencia*, but only of the *San Juan Bautista* of Ragusa (800 tons), burned in a Scottish harbour. They mentioned Don Diego Manrique as 'on board', but while three of his surname were in Ireland, and one, Antonio, reached Scotland, I find but one Diego Manrique who came back to Spain, and think that Don Diego Enrique or Enriquez is intended, for he, while he lived, commanded the *San Juan Bautista* of 800 tons.

Now, what do we know of the *San Juan Bautista* of 800 tons, doubtless the *San Juan* burned in Tobermory Bay, according to the old tradition of Mull?

Our ship is the *San Juan Bautista* of Sicily, 800 tons, two hundred and seventy-nine soldiers, which was in the Levantine squadron at Lisbon on May 9th. On July 13th she was at Corunna (two hundred and thirty-eight soldiers), and was with the Guipuzcoan squadron under Admiral Pedro de Valdes. On July 31st, in a fight off the English coast, the flagship of Valdes, *Nuestra Señora del Rosario*, broke her bowsprit and her foremast in a collision with the *Santa Catalina*, could not be extricated, and was captured,—Valdes, pay-chest (52,000 ducats), soldiers, sailors, and all.

On August 2nd the Duke of Medina Sidonia placed Don Diego Tellez Enriquez in command of the *San Juan Bautista* of Sicily, and on 'the galleon *San Juan*' he put 'Don Diego Enriquez, son of the Viceroy of Peru'. According to Purser Coco, and Medina Sidonia himself, the Duke also gave the command of the whole of Valdes' squadron to 'Don Diego Enriquez, son of the Viceroy of Peru'. On August 8th both the Enriquez commanders were engaged, and displayed great valour, while, on board the *San Juan Bautista* of Sicily, Don Pedro, the brother

79

of Diego Tellez Enriquez, ' had a hand shot away '.

Now let us clearly distinguish the two Diego Enriquez and their two ships of the same name, *San Juan Bautista*. The position is this : Don Diego Enriquez, son of the Governor of Peru, in a *San Juan Bautista* of the squadron of Diego Flores, on August 2nd takes over command of the squadron of Valdes, who, with pay-chest and flagship, is a prisoner in English hands.

Meanwhile Don Diego Tellez Enriquez, son of the Commandant of Alcantara, commands the *San Juan Bautista* of Sicily, a ship in the squadron which Valdes had led before his capture. Don Diego Enriquez, son of the Viceroy of Peru, was lost off the coast of Ireland.

Thus we are left with Diego Tellez Enriquez, commanding the *San Juan Bautista* of Sicily, in Valdes' squadron. Of her we read that, fighting gallantly on August 8th, ' she suffered to such an extent that every one of her sails had to be replaced '. On August 19th, in the dim seas vexed with mists of the North, some sixteen ships collected ; but, says Purser Coco, ' we looked anxiously for the *San Juan Bautista* of Sicily, on board of which was Don Diego Tellez Enriquez, who had fought so bravely. She had been so much damaged that not a spar of her sails was serviceable ' (though we have just learned that they ' had to be replaced '). ' It is feared she may be lost.' I have identified in her the Tobermory galleon.

True, Captain Marolin de Juan calls her ' of Ragusa '. But, even in 1588, the Tobermory galleon was described, we shall see, as ' Venetian ' ; and Ragusa was Venetian. Sicily probably chartered or bought the ship as her contribution to the Armada. Again, the Pilot-General speaks of the commanding officer on board her (*en que iba* Don Diego) as ' Don Diego de Manrique ', not ' Enrique '. But between error of his informants (not eye-witnesses), the transcriber of his letter, and the compositors, ' Enriquez ' might easily become ' Manrique ', and I find no Don Diego Manrique in the Armada, save one who came home.

Finally, while correcting the proof-sheets of this paper I receive the following extract from a letter (undated by Duro) of Mendoza, the Spanish Ambassador in Paris, to Philip II :

> ' *La* San Juan Bautista, *en que iba Don Diego Manrique, entro en el puerto de Tobermory, de la isla Mull, en Escocia; los naturales la incendiaron sin que escaparon mas de quince personas.*'

That does not need to be translated. The ' Diego Manrique ' is manifestly ' Diego Enriquez ', and evidence of 1588, 1589, proves that many more than fifteen persons escaped with their lives.

Sic transit Florencia !

Escaping from the storm of mid-September, which strewed the Irish shore with wrecks, the *San Juan Bautista* arrived at Islay, whence, with a native pilot, she could sail up the Sound of Jura into the Sound of Mull. Lauchlan Maclean of Duart sent the news to James VI., and Asheby, of the English Embassy to Scotland, apprised Walsingham thus :

W. ASHEBY TO [WALSINGHAM]

' EDINB., 23 *Sept.* '88.

' [*Postscript*]—As I had writt this lettre Sr William Kith sent me wourd that MackCleiden [*sic*] an Irishe Lord writ to the K. that on Fridaie the 13 of September there arrived a greate ship of Spayne of 1400 tuns, having 800 soldiours and there commanders; at an Iland called Ila on the west part of Scotland, thether driven by wether, thei thinke that the rest of the Fleet is driven on the north part of Ireland; I will make further inquirie and presentlie certifie yor hono^r with speed: thei reporte this ship to be fournished with 80 brasse pieces, she beaten with shotes and wether.'

Walsingham, who received this news (the size of the ship and numbers of men and guns are much exaggerated), was the astute head of Elizabeth's Secret Service; everywhere he had his agents and spies: it was he who deliberately led Mary Stuart into the conspiracy with Babington. To destroy the Spanish ship was his object, and in John Smollett, a burgess of Dumbarton, and ancestor of Tobias Smollett the novelist, he found a miscreant who worked his will on the *San Juan Bautista*. This I proceed to prove. Here my evidence is that of William Asheby of the English Embassy to Holyrood. Writing to Walsingham on November 6th, he says that ' a great ship of Spain' has been for some six weeks on the west coast, is now off Mull in Maclean's country, is unable to sail, is supplied by ' those Yrishe people with victuals, but they are not able to possess her, for she is well furnished with shott and men. If there be anie (English) shippes of warr in Ireland they might have a great praie of this ship, *for she is thought to be verie riche* '. Here began the rumour of the wealth of the vessel. Next week, November 13th, Asheby writes : ' The Spanish ship . . . is burnt, as it is here reported by the treachery of the Yrishes, and almost all the men within is consumed by fire; it is thought to be one of the principalle shippes, and some one of great account within, for he was always, as they say, served in silver.'

Asheby must soon have known that the treachery was not that of ' the Yrishes ', but of Walsingham. A letter from Edinburgh, by Roger Aston to his brother in England, is written in a very difficult hand, and the original is a half-burned fragment, but this is misdated ' xviii March 1588 '. The true date is November 18th, 1588. Here is Roger's plain tale :

ROGER ASTON TO HIS BROTHER

' EDINB., 18 *Nov*. 1588.

' This day word is come that the great ship that lay in the West Isles is blown in the air by a device of John Smallet's ; most part of the men are slein ; the manner was thus : McLean entertaining great friendship wth them, desired the borrowing of 2 cannons and 100 Hagbuttes to besiege a house of Angus Maculleis, and delivered a foster son of his in pledge for the safe delivery of them again. In the mean time John Smallet, a man that had great trust among the Spaniards, entered the ship and cast in the powder room a piece of Lunt and so departed. Within a short time after the Lunt took fire and burnt ship and men. Whether this be true or not I am not sure, but so his Majesty is informed.'

We next find Asheby writing in this cool fashion to Walsingham on November 26th :

WM ASHEBY TO F. WALSINGHAM

' EDINB., 26 *Nov*. '88.

' There arrived the 24 of this present 24 Spaniards, that were taken out of the ship burnt in the Isle of Mull on the West of Scotland : *the particularities thereof*

83

I thinke yo *hono* *understandes by the partie that laide
the traine, whom we here saie to be comed into England,
the man knowen to yo* *hono* *and called Smallet.'*

'The man knowen to your honour' had done his business and gone to London to report to his employer. As he had incidentally blown up Maclean's foster-son, he could not be too far from that chief.

Perhaps Burleigh was not in the secrets of Walsingham in this matter. At all events, a year later, Asheby writes to Burleigh thus:

WM ASHEBY TO BURLEIGH
'EDINB., 13 *Nov.* '89.

'Here are some 100 Spaniards readie to imbarque at Lythe for Sp: there course intended is to cast about the north of Scotland for feare of interrupcion by the Hollanders; thei appeare to be men of better service than those wch past awaie from hense the last somer being the cheife men culled out of 500 by Maclane, for his service against one of the L^{ds} of the Isles; the remnant perished the last yere together wth there ship at the Isle Mula *by mischance of gunpowder* whiles theise were enterteined by Maclane in service by land, as I remember I then advertised the winter past.'

What Asheby 'advertised' in November 1588 was that Smollett had blown up the ship, and would be with Walsingham in advance of his own letter! The wretched Smollett had ingratiated himself with the Spaniards, on Walsingham's orders, 'had great trust with the Spaniards', and had earned his money. Colonel Foss quotes 'direct family tradition' for this exploit of John Smollett, Esq, of Cameron House, Dumbarton, and cites the author of

Peregrine Pickle himself : ' In one of several bays of safe anchorage which Mull affords, the *Florida*, a ship of the Spanish Armada, was blown up by one of Mr Smollett's ancestors.' It may be asked how Smollett came to be trusted by the Spaniards. It was his trade to provision the western islands, as Irving says in his *History of Dumbartonshire*. In course of business, in victualling the ship, he would have ample opportunity to ' throw in a lunt '.

Having established the facts, we need not linger over the legendary explanations given by Mr J. P. Maclean in his *History of Clan Maclean*. Nor need we prove by Scottish official records, as we can, that Maclean did take into his service one hundred Spanish musketeers, who aided him in his campaign against the Macdonalds of the Isles and of Ardnamurchan.

I quote, however, the news sent to the Lord-Lieutenant of Ireland, in the end of 1588, by Richard Egerton, commanding an English garrison at Knockfergus.

As we see, Egerton had first made inquiries of Scottish merchants, and then pushed researches ' at mine own chardge ', probably in Argyll.

    ' Right honorable my bounden duetie most humblie remembred : takinge occasion heretofore to trouble your Lordship in advertisement touchinge the Kinge of Spaine's shippe that was burnte in M'Lane's countrie, as then I supposed the same to be true upon the reporte of Scottishe merchantes aryving here, so for my owne assuerance therein I have sithence made some further meanes of my owne chardge, that thereby I might manifest an undoubted trueth unto your Lordship, so that your Honor may be assured that that shippe was a gallion of Vennis (Venice) of 1200 tunns, burned by the like accident as I tofore advertised your Honour : in which was the twoe chiefe Captens burned ; V. of M'Lane's pledges, and 700 souldiers and sailors, savinge twoe or three that were blowen on the shoare with the upper decke, so that nothinge was saved that was in her at that instant, and what remained unburned is nowe suncke under water. One captain of smale accompt, with 100 souldiers, was with M'Lane on the shoare, whoe be yet all with him, and take paie of him.'

All returned safely to Edinburgh, as Asheby reported. Twenty-four men on board the vessel also escaped.

In this version the tonnage and number of soldiers are much exaggerated ; only two or three Armada ships were of 1,200 tons, none carried four hundred soldiers, not to speak of seven hundred. The ship is not Tuscan, but Venetian ; by the Pilot-General's account, it is Ragusan—Ragusa being then Venetian. The one hundred musketeers are safe on shore : this was unknown to the men of the *Valencera* who were so long in Scotland, but Maclean may have concealed the fact, as he still needed their services. By ' the twoe chiefe Captens ' of the ship, Egerton probably means Don Diego Tellez Enriquez, and his brother, Don Pedro Enriquez, who was with him, and, as we saw, lost a hand in action.

The incident of the extraordinary escape of two men of the ship, who were blown on shore by the explosion, must have lingered in the tradition of the people of Mull. In a Memorandum written by the ninth Earl of Argyll in 1677 he says : ' two men standing upon the cabin were cast safe on shore '. Maclean, on March 23rd, 1589, received a full pardon for his treatment of the Macdonalds, but not for the burning of the galleon—of which he was innocent.

In 1641, when Charles was trying to propitiate ' gleyed Argyll ', he made him a Marquis, and induced the Duke of Lennox, Great Admiral of Scotland, to hand over to him all the Spanish vessels supposed to be wrecked on the west coast. The ninth Earl, heavily in debt, made various efforts to raise the Tobermory galleon, but only recovered large guns in bronze and iron. In 1677 he had a suit with the Duke of York (James II) for the right to the ship, and won his case. He now made a Memorandum, of which I have only an abridgment in the Argyll papers published by the Hist MSS Commission. He says that the vessel ' is reputed to have been the *Admiral of Florence*, fifty-six guns ' (fifty-two in the *Florencia*, May 1588), ' with thirty million of money on board '. The *Admiral of Florence*. No ship was thus named or was likely to be. Argyll must have misread a crabbed Spanish hand of, say, 1600, which gave ' the *Almiranta* ' (vice-flagship) ' of Flores '—Don Diego Flores. That vice-flagship was the *San Juan Bautista*, wrecked off Ireland (*Scotsman*, September 20th, 1910).

The 30,000,000 ' imagination boggles at '. I find that in several cases flagships of squadrons carried 50,000 ducats : for expenses of the squadron, I presume, but the *San Juan Bautista* was not a flagship.

But now consider the following apparently veracious description of the sunk vessel by Archibald Millar, of Greenock, writing in 1683 (when the ninth Earl was a proscribed rebel) to the Duke of York.

> ' INFORMATION by ARCHIBALD MILLAR anent the Ship Sunck in Tippermorie in ye Sound of Mull. The Ships name is the *Florence* of Spaine.
>
> ' The Ship lyes Sunck off the Shore, about one-finger stone-cast, her Sterne lyes into the Shore Norwest, and

her Head to the Southwest, shee lyes under ye water at ye deepest Nine fatham at a low water, & twelve fatham at a full Sea on High water.

'There is no Deck upon her Except in ye Hinder part, there is one great heap of Timber wch I take to be the Cabbin, I did see one doore there wch I take to be the Steerage doore, and within that doore I did see a number of Dishes both great & small of a White blewish Colour, but whether they are pewter or plate I know not.

'Neer this place I did see one great Gun & her Mussle upright on end, as big or bigger than the Gun I lifted wch would carry a 48 lb. ball, there is a great heap of Cannon shot about Midship, & upon the Shot lyes three Iron Gunns.

'In the fore part of the Ship lyes many great Ballast stones & some shot amongst them, & there wee found *one Silver bell about 4 li weight*, wee got within the Ship at a prety distance the said great Gun wth other two (all Brass Gunns) *the great Gun is eleaven feet length*, & seaven inches & one fourth part of measure in the bore, th' other two were Minions, wee also got two Demy Culverins, two Falcons, two slings all Brass.

'We lifted three Anchors whereof one was eighteen feet of length, th' other was fifteen and the third was ten, I got two brass sheeues weighing Sixty pounds, I lifted also the Rother, & took eight Iron pykes of it, It was twenty eight foot of Length, but there was no peece broken of the same.

'I lifted the Kemp stone of Curious worke, pauled wth a Spring at every inches end, I cannot tell ye bigness, the thing I found would have been two foot in the Diamiter.

' I saw something like a Coat of Armes but I could not reach it being entangled, I saw Guild (gilt) upon severall standing peeces of the Ship.

' *I saw one paper of Lattin Extracted out of the Spanish Records that there was thirty millions of Cash on board the said Ship,* and it tells it lay under ye Sell of the Gunroome.

' *The Lieftenant of the Ship reports the same to the Earle of Argile I mean the Marques's father, & wch paper holds goods of the Lieftenants report.*

' I found something like Mettle betwixt the Ship & shore in soft Osie ground in severall places & thinck they were Gunns.

' The properest time to Dive is to begin about ye Twentieth of May, & continue untill the midst of Augt, *I found a Crowne or Diadem & had hooked the same, but being Chained it fell amongst the Timbers, this Crowne is also in ye Spanish Records.*

' I thinck the Goods of ye Ship may be recovered provided the Timber could be taken away, and I doe not doubt but all may be taken away, provided my pains & expences be allowed and to shew that this is not a Simulated Informacion, though I be an old man I am willing yet to goe alone upon due consideration, for it is a pity that such a great business should be lost where it may be recovered by industry as Witness my hand at Grinock this Twentith day of November 1683.

' I was Mastr of the whole Employmt myself for ye space I dived.

' ARCHIBALD MILLAR.

' Jo. Tailfer, *Witnes.*
' J. Young, *Witnes.*
' Wm. Mathie, *Witnes.*'

(MS found by Mr Purnell in the Bodleian, and published by him in *The Times*, October 22nd, 1910. I take my copy from the original.)

This Crown, hooked by Millar, I know, is remembered in the local traditions about the galleon. More trustworthy evidence is that of the Council of the States of Zealand, writing officially to Queen Elizabeth from Middelburg, the 16th of August. Their fleet, they say, blockaded the Duke of Parma in Dunkirk, prevented him from joining hands with Medina Sidonia, and took three partly-wrecked Spanish galleons; they send the noblemen captured to England. They then mention a report that Philip II was to give to the Duke of Parma (as Viceroy of England) 'the Crown and sceptre of England blessed by the Pope'. The Pope may have blessed the Crown for Philip, but Philip could never extract from him one coin of his promised million of ducats in gold.

Here we have all that I can find about the Crown hooked and lost by Archibald Millar, who seems more interested in the kemp-stone of curious work.

Returning to Archibald Millar, the galleon, with 'a Crown or diadem' aboard, and a silver bell weighing four pounds, seems opulent enough! It is more important that Millar says that he saw a 'lattin' extract from Spanish records mentioning the '30,000,000 cash' and the Crown, and that it is corroborated by the 'report of the Lieutenant of the ship' to the Earl of Argyll of 1588. In that year the Earl was a boy of thirteen, which would permit him to believe in the 30,000,000 of money, but would not account for the Latin extract from the archives of Spain, which also mention the Crown hooked by Archibald Millar!

Now, where and when did Archibald see these astonishing documents? I answer,—at Inveraray Castle, on April

6th, 1680. At that place and time Archibald made his bargain with the Earl for his services in salvaging the property in the sunk galleon. The ninth Earl believed in these documents. He notes that if the famous Crown be recovered, it is to be reserved for Charles II. What can we say to these documents? Did the seventh Earl get them when, as a Catholic convert, he was an exile in Spain? Were they part of a Spanish practical joke?

But there is another conceivable explanation of the ' 30,000,000 cash '. According to Don Alonzo de Luzon, commanding the *Nuestra Señora de la Rosa,* and examined at Drogheda, October 13th, the talk of the Armada ran that the whole of the king's treasure on board the fleet was from 600,000 to 700,000 ducats. Put the ducat at its present nominal value of eleven shillings (and not at the silver ducat of three shillings), and this brings us to a sum (at 700,000 ducats) of over £300,000, which is very like the value of 30,000,000 *rials*, taking the *rials,* loosely, at a hundred to the pound sterling. Moreover, we know from his own despatch to Philip that Medina Sidonia carried jewels of great value. Why, on a distant and dangerous expedition, was the Duke carrying ' precious jewels '? Perhaps Philip, in his unusual confidence, looked forward to blazing with diamonds, emeralds, and rubies, as he sat on the Stone of Destiny in Westminster Abbey to be consecrated King of England.

English accounts from Ireland speak, even the Lord-Lieutenant speaks, of the gold and jewels of the unhappy prisoners. But his Lordship adds that the Irish have got hold of them. Those of Don Diego (not Tellez) Enriquez were seized by Irishmen, whose names are given in the State Papers. The Duke of Medina Sidonia writes that, through Portuguese channels, the English learn that, ' in addition to supplies, there were 500,000 ducats in the Armada, and that His Majesty [Philip II] had arranged for sight-bills in Lisbon for 300,000 ducats to be sent, which money had already been sent thither'. This is rather more probable than the report of the Spanish commander of the forces of Sicily, who gives 16,000,000 ducats as carried by the Armada. He is Don Alonzo de Pimentel, son of the Marquis de Tavara. He commanded the *San Mateo* (850 tons).

It is nowise impossible that Spanish archives did contain records of treasure to the amount, in *rials*, of, say, £300,000. The fleet did carry abundance of wealth. The seventh Earl, in Spain, may have had an extract made to that effect—the *whole* treasure is of, say, £300,000—which the ninth Earl conceived to apply to the treasure on board of his Tobermory galleon.

Nine ships, I remark, are mentioned as having ' great store of money and plate ' by the Portuguese Gregorio de Sotomayor, under examination. The *San Juan Bautista* is not one of these nine, nor is the *Florencia*, if that matters. Among the nine is the captured vessel of Pedro de Valdes, taken on July 31st. The sea captain, Vicente Alvarez, of Valdes' flagship, puts the treasure ' in a chest of the king's ' at 52,000 ducats, with plate and ' great store of precious jewels of the Duke and Don Pedro '. Don Pedro puts it at ' near 20,000 ducats '; Drake at 25,300,—' this I confess to have '. Had nobody else any of the treasure ? Purser Coco states it at 50,000. I fear that Valdes minimised. The *Santa Ana*, a flagship, carried 50,000 ducats.

But the fighting *San Juan Bautista* of Sicily was no flagship or vice-flagship : she did not carry the pay-chest of a squadron—did she ? There is just one outside chance that she carried treasure beyond the money, plate, and jewels of her officers. It is this : On July 31st the gun-powder of Admiral Oquenda's vice-flagship, the *San Salva-dor*, exploded, severely damaging the vessel. It was said that a Spanish officer had beaten a German sailor, who fired the powder which was in open barrels on deck. In any case the Duke of Medina Sidonia tried during the night to tranship the burned and wounded men, but failed. On August 1st he gave orders ' to tranship his Majesty's treasure, and the men ', and to sink the *San Salvador*. The English, in fact, towed away the wreck. On board the *San Salvador* was the Paymaster-General, Juan de Huerta, who appears to have been in charge of a very considerable portion of the whole treasure.

Nobody tells us into what vessel this treasure was tran-shipped. If into one of Oquenda's squadron, that had nine ships, not one of which is the Tobermory galleon. If Diego Enriquez (not Tellez) took the treasure (and *his* squadron had lost its own pay-chest), then the money came into Irish hands. His squadron had nine ships—among them the Tobermory galleon. As the transhipped treasure probably remained in Oquenda's squadron, or followed Diego Enriquez into his squadron, the ships of the two squadrons being eighteen, it is seventeen to one that the treasure was not placed in the *San Juan Bautista* of Sicily, and, consequently that it is not in Tobermory Bay. But if Archibald Millar did actually see and hook ' a crown or diadem ' in the Tobermory wreck, then the crown was probably part of the Paymaster-General's charge, and a sign that the rest of his treasure is also actually on board the *San Juan Bautista de Sicilia*. That is the *spes ultima et exigua* !

Since this paper was in type I have learned, on excellent authority, that old people, natives of Tobermory, used to speak of the vessel from which two or three men were blown to shore with the upper deck as the *Saint John* (*San Juan*). Don Pedro, who ' had his hand shot away ', appears to have been remembered in tradition as ' the one-armed man ', but confusedly, as a Gaelic speaker.

Now, alas, must be told a fact disappointing to hopes of treasure. Sir Walter Scott (Edinburgh, March 1st, 1812) writes to Surtees of Mainsforth, quoting Sacheverille's ' Account of the Isle of Man, &c., including a voyage to I. Columb-Kill in the year 1688 ' (1702):

> ' The fishers showed me [Scott] the place where she [the galleon] lay in the Bay of Tobermory, and said that there had been a good deal of treasure and some brass cannon got out of the wreck. Sacheverel (*sic*) mentions having seen the divers sinking 3 score feet under water, continuing there an hour and returning loaded, whether with plate or money, the spoils of the ocean.'

On the other hand, Colonel Foss kindly shows me a note by a gifted lady who made researches for him, and unhappily died in August 1911. This is a rough note from a document unnamed, but which is clearly authentic, and proves that between 1691 and 1694 the tenth Earl of Argyll, son of the Presbyterian martyr (1685), was dealing with Archibald Campbell, the younger, of Calder, in a fresh endeavour to recover treasure. As the tenth Earl must have known in 1691 all about the results of the operations of 1688, as described by Sacheverel, he must have been of opinion that plenty of plate and money was still left in the wreck. Whether he got it out or not I am unable to say: let us hope that he failed.

Finally, as to John Smollett: in April-May 1589 I find

him ' wanted ' by the Government of James VI in connection with the Catholic and Spanish conspiracy of Huntly and Errol. On August 1st, 1586, the Master of Gray, writing to the deepest of traitors, Archibald Douglas, speaks of Smollett as a person whom he had dealt with successfully for news of such plots, Spanish and Catholic, as Graham of Fintry shared in, to his ruin. It thus appears that Smollett, as an agent of Walsingham, went into the plot of the Catholic earls as a spy, and very probably it was through information given by him that, in spring 1589, Elizabeth's Government obtained the compromising letters of Huntly and Errol to Philip II and the Duke of Parma. In these circumstances Mr Smollett fled, and was protected by the Sempills, who were deep in the plot. He would return to Dumbarton and business when the storm blew over ; and probably, late in 1592, he betrayed ' the Spanish Blanks ', or rather betrayed George Ker, who carried the papers and was lurking in the isle of Cumbrae in the Firth of Clyde,—conveniently adjacent to Mr Smollett's place of residence at Dumbarton. Gentle King Jamie himself was, more or less, art and part in the conspiracy, and nobody was any the worse, except Graham of Fintry. Mr Smollett feathered his nest ; and is apparently the founder of the house whence sprang the author of *Roderick Random*.

[March 1912

5

THE KHAN'S TREASURE

H. de R. Walters

One of the only two roads into India that are suitable for an invading army is the Bolan Pass, and right along-side the Bolan Pass runs the frontier of Khelat; also the ground on which stands our great frontier fortress of Quetta belonged to Khelat, and the Government of India used to pay a rental of 50,000 Rs. yearly to the Khan of that country.

About thirty years ago the Governors of India began seriously to think when it became known that the Khan of Khelat had been having a series of interviews with certain mysterious strangers from the North; the more so because they, the aforesaid Governors, knew that the Khan was a sordid miser, *argenti sacra fames* being his be-setting sin, and quite as likely as not to sell his country and the key to the Western Passes if he could get his price.

This Khan, who bore the somewhat humorous name of Khuda Dad, the Gift of God, was a most unpleasant person, being, among other things, a cruel old tyrant, who ground the faces of his subjects into the dust in extracting from them their uttermost farthing; he was peculiar too, in that, quite contrary to the usual custom of the East, he refused to accept his dues in kind, but insisted on having them paid in silver, and in silver rupees at that.

We had a very able and experienced administrator in the person of Sir James Browne, who, as the guardian of the Western Passes, was keeping a watchful eye on the doings in Khelat, quite determined, when opportunity offered, to have a go at Khuda Dad, and eliminate him from the sphere of practical politics. Sir James had not very long to wait.

Evidently considering that rupees in the hand were better than roubles still in the air, the Khan determined on squeezing yet a little more out of his unfortunate subjects, and summoned his Council to devise the means. The venerable grey-bearded Councillors, all men of considerable standing in the country, duly assembled, and the Khan, explaining that his Treasury was sorely depleted, put it to them that it was their duty to refill it. The Councillors, horrified at the thought of further taxation, protested that the country could not find another anna ; the Khan insisted. The Councillors in all humility demurred. The Khan, quite unaccustomed to any opposition, began to wax wroth, and the more heated he became the more abject was the humility of the Councillors. But they still demurred. Said the Khan, " It is an order." Said the Councillors, not so briefly but to the same effect, " It is impossible." Then the Khan rose in his wrath, and, losing the last rag of his never too genial temper, sent for his executioner, and had the lot decapitated then and there. (This is a euphemism. They suffered a much worse fate, too gross for publication.)

After that things moved with considerable rapidity : a hurried exit from Khelat of the numerous wives of the murdered Councillors, escorted by a large retinue of their infuriated male relatives ; a rush for Quetta ; and a frenzied appeal to the *Lat Sahib* for immediate vengeance on the perpetrator of this dastardly outrage.

They found Sir James quite ready to lend an ear to their complaint, even prepared to redress their grievance : " Should such a miscreant be allowed to reign another moment ? Perish the thought." (Or the border Chief who entertains suspicious strangers from the North ? Not much !)

Next morning we were off, a compact little force of all arms, straight across the hills to Khelat, and a mobile column of cavalry down the Bolan, heading for a certain pass which leads from the hinterland of Khelat into Mekran. We were after one Khuda Dad, not his country, hence the stopping of the bolt-hole. Sure enough, the Gift of God, who, though he had raised the whirlwind, had no mind to ride the storm, fled incontinent straight into the arms of the cavalry at the mouth of the pass.

In the meanwhile the main column ploughed its weary way over stony *tangi* and sandy plain, unscathed save by thirst and dust and unutterable weariness of the flesh, and camped some two miles from the capital city of Khelat. Seen from a distance Khelat looked rather fascinating, ' a walled city of the plain ', the flat-roofed houses, packed tight within the massive outer wall, huddling together under the frowning battlements of the Miri, the fortress-palace of the Khan. The Miri, perched on a little mound within the city walls, commanded the whole town as well as the flat country round it.

Closer acquaintance dispelled all fond illusions. Fascination fled, conquered by the overpowering acrid smell of camel and unwashed humanity amid streets the narrowness of which had to be seen to be believed. A brief rest and then ensued for a few of us most strenuous times, packed with excitement and monotony in unequal parts, the latter predominating, until the final day when excitement grew to fever-heat as we broke through the last obstacle that hid from us the Khan's Treasure. It all began quietly enough. The Political Officer with the force got a message from Quetta to the effect that the Khan was supposed to have left a large amount of money in the Treasury. Would he see to it and put it under guard? This seemed very simple, and the Political Officer rode forth without more ado to find the Treasury and arrange for the safeguarding thereof—but there wasn't any Treasury!

No one knew anything about such a thing as a Treasury. The Khan Sahib took all their money, and what he did with it was no concern of anybody but the Khan Sahib. Off went a message to Quetta to that effect, and as quick as helio could flash it came the answer, ' No doubt of there being much treasure in the Miri ; report says much silver, believed gold and jewels ; take immediate steps find and remove same.'

And then the fun began. The Political Officer took his immediate step by handing the message to Lieutenant-Colonel A, the Officer commanding the Khelat Field Force ; Lieutenant-Colonel A, who in the piping times of peace commanded that same mountain battery which formed the artillery of the force, having assimilated the message, called up his battery officers, and set off with them to prospect.

Having pushed our way through the motley throng of men, camels, sheep, and goats which packed the narrow streets, we found ourselves confronted by some twenty armed scallawags who called on us to halt and showed that they meant it. It may seem undignified to stand rooted to the ground before a crowd of nondescript ruffians whose diversity of costume was balanced by the similarity of the dirt which encrusted one and all from head to foot, but a loaded Snider at twenty paces is an argument that is not to be gainsaid.

Suddenly yet another black-ringleted hook-nosed Khelati dashed out of the Miri, and the whole crowd, bunching together, presented arms! Somewhat overcome by this unexpected politeness, we were hesitating as to our next move when we saw, emerging from the Miri, a tall handsome native, resplendent in broadcloth and gold lace and girt with sword and sabretache. This proved to be no less a personage than the Commander-in-Chief of the Khelati army, one Mir Baz, Durani, an Afghan of the Afghans, cousin to the great Amir Abdur Rahman Khan, now wisely putting himself out of reach of that dread potentate, a servant of the Khan of Khelat. With some ceremony Colonel A introduced his little party and explained the object of their visit, whereupon Mir Baz ushered us in and showed us all over the vast pile except the women's quarters, about which, Khelat being a Mohammedan country, we took care to ask no questions.

Interrogated as to treasure, Mir Baz was quite frank. He knew nothing as to the whereabouts of the Khan's Treasury; that was not his business, but he had often heard that the Khan Sahib had much money hidden away somewhere; in fact, it was said that, many years ago, the Khan Sahib had imported skilled artisans from Hindustan to construct a safe hiding-place; these men had worked long and had been well paid, but, strangely enough (and here Mir Baz, for all his solemnity, had a twinkle in his eyes), as soon as they left the city they were set upon and murdered, and so their secret died with them.

With this somewhat meagre information we had to be content.

The Miri was a huge pile of sun-dried brick, some four storeys in all. Entering by the great gates, one found one-self in a large hall with a guardroom on one side, and a wide archway on the other leading on to an open courtyard which served as a gun-park for the Khan's artillery. At the back of the hall was the staircase which ran straight up to the first floor. Upwards from the first floor the stairs were arranged in a different way, going up one side of the well to a false landing, and then up the opposite side to the floor above. These false landings were built against the outer wall of the Miri, and were indifferently lighted by small windows at some height from the floor.

Of the upper floors it is only necessary to say that they were quite out of keeping with the majestic appearance of the Miri from the outside. But the first floor deserves a fuller description.

As one stepped on to the landing one saw on the right a heavily-curtained doorway which led to the Zenana, while on the left was a similar doorway opening on to a courtyard. On one side of this courtyard were the Khan's private apartments, on the other the Council Chamber, the scene of the late massacre. The Khan's rooms were much more in accordance with the general idea of a palace than the rest of the building, being lofty, well-proportioned, of considerable size, and well lighted by several large windows, but they were very bare. There were three rooms exactly alike, with a stout door in each dividing wall, each room having a broad shelf running round three sides of it, a string bedstead, a strip of carpet, and prac-tically nothing else.

The shelves were laden with a collection of articles,

ranging from the sublime to the ridiculous. Here would be a very dainty gilt travelling clock surrounded by a number of the cheapest alarum atrocities; there a choice bit of china or a beautiful jade vase with, betwixt and between, horrors of the crudest kind; pink and blue vases, gilt-lettered mugs with coloured views, animals of every kind in every conceivable material, and here, there, and everywhere life-size hens in brown china, sitting on green nests!

The beds were the ordinary *charpoy* of the East, but had an interesting distinction. The legs of the first one were of wood, very gaudily painted, the second had legs of solid silver, while those of the third were of gold.

Next day the treasure-hunt began in earnest. Obviously the treasure had been concealed, and the search would have to be very carefully done, so the original party was increased by the addition of two stalwart gunners from the ranks of the mountain battery, genial giants armed with pickaxe and crowbar.

Full of excitement, we started at the top of the Miri and worked our way down, probing here, sounding there, but found no trace of anything resembling treasure, or of any place where treasure could be concealed.

It was unpleasant work. The dozens of little rooms on the upper floors were not only dark, but showed very plainly that even the most elementary laws of sanitation were still unknown in this palace of a king.

Our excitement gradually cooled, and when, on the second day, further search revealed nothing, and a third day's labour bore equal fruit, the thing became frankly monotonous. One more day was given, always probing a bit deeper and sounding a bit harder, even digging here and there, but all to no avail, so we called a halt, and sent a message to Quetta to say that no trace of any treasure could be found. Back flashed the answer, ' No doubt treasure is there ; try again.'

So at it we went again, and for two days we gave that Miri a general battering from roof to basement, but found no signs of treasure.

Another reference to Quetta brought the disconcerting order, ' Search women's quarters ; treasure in Miri somewhere.'

This was really a very tall order. To break into the Zenana of the Chief of a friendly Mohammedan country was simply to ask for trouble, and the Colonel knew it, and, knowing it, flatly refused to do anything of the kind. Having curtly remarked that he would see So-and-so in Hades before he allowed anyone under his command to cross the threshold of the women's quarters, the Colonel proceeded to give orders for a final devastating upheaval of the rest of the Miri, and with that object in view we set forth the next morning. This time, however, we were a much larger party, the two original giants having been reinforced by six others of the same kidney, carrying pick-axes, crowbars, shovels, and two lanterns.

It was pretty obvious that a bulky treasure could not be hidden in the upper storeys, but, taking no chances, we went through those rooms most thoroughly with pick and crowbar, finding nothing, but leaving them considerably better ventilated than ever they had been before.

And so we worked our way downwards with the fixed intention of pulling the Khan's private apartments to the ground, our only regret that we had not the Khan himself to bury in their ruins.

As the Colonel led the way down from the second floor, he stopped on the small landing between the two floors, and stood gazing intently at the outer wall of the staircase well; then, still looking at the wall, he called out, " Run upstairs somebody and see whether any other landing has these funny little arches cut in the wall."

While one departed at speed, the rest of us looked at the wall, and saw three very shallow arches, apparently cut for ornamentation. Now this wall was obviously an outer wall, having windows to light the stairs, and outer walls had hitherto received very scant attention; but when a voice came pealing down from above, " All the other walls quite plain, sir," interest visibly quickened, and the Colonel called to one of the gunners, " Come along, M'Carthy; try a pick on these arches."

Down the stairs swung M'Carthy, reputed to be the biggest man in the army of his day, and set to with a will on the arch next to the side wall. A few minutes of strenuous hacking and he had dug out large chunks of sun-dried brick, and made a considerable hole in the wall.

" Now the middle one."

Up went the pick with a full swing, and ' whung-g-g ', a grunt from M'Carthy heralding a general shout of " wood! "

There was no mistaking *that* sound. After days of the dull thud of pick and crowbar meeting clay, the sound of metal on wood brought our blood up to fever-point again, and another brawny gunner hustling down with a crowbar, the two soon peeled off the thick coating of baked clay—and there stood revealed a door, an indubitable door!

No means of opening it being apparent, pick and crowbar went to work again, and after some very arduous minutes the door was wrenched open, disclosing a very narrow passage, which led into uttermost darkness. Lanterns having been lit, the Colonel took one and went ahead, the rest filing after him in a darkness that could be felt, so blanket-thick it seemed, the feeble little flicker from the lanterns penetrating no distance at all as we emerged into what appeared to be a vast illimitable cavern.

"Now, S, take the other lantern, and go along to the rest with Captain S. Be careful and look where you put your feet."

All groped their way carefully along the walls to right and left for a few paces, when the leaders called out almost simultaneously, " Ends here ; wall at right angles," and turned in the new direction.

Suddenly one of the two young subalterns, whose eyes, being younger, were presumably sharper than those of the rest of his party, plunged forward with a yell of " Look there." All halted and watched a dim figure struggling with some large, quite indistinguishable object : a ripping sound and " Oh, Hell! "

A distinct sniff followed, and then, " How perfectly putrid."

The roar of laughter which greeted this anti-climax was hushed by the quiet voice of the Colonel, " Now then, young man, what's your trouble ? " To which came the reply, " Lot of large jars here, sir, full of some horrible sticky stuff that smells like nothing on earth."

Further investigation disclosed a line of large earthen-ware jars, reminiscent of the Forty Thieves, filled with mustard-oil rancid with age. And that was absolutely all the mysterious cellar contained.

It being very obvious that something more precious than mustard-oil must have been concealed behind that care-fully-camouflaged door, more and better lights were obtained from Mir Baz, and a very minute search made of walls and floor.

A thoroughly vigorous sounding of the walls having produced nothing, the men were beginning to dig up the floor, when Captain S, who was standing in the far corner by the oil-jars, called out, " Give me a pick," and began tapping gently at the wall above his head, very near the ceiling.

Looking closely one could see, high up and almost in the corner, a very slight, almost imperceptible bulge, and it was at this bulge that Captain S was tapping.

After a few moments the distinct tinkle of metal on metal brought us all crowding round, and the excitement grew intense as the persistent pecking peeled off the clay facing of the wall, and disclosed a metal something that shone in the light of the torches.

A few more gentle pecks and there stood revealed a padlock, one of those large cylindrical affairs, common in the East, so formidable in appearance but so completely useless in reality ; but whatever might be its utility there could be no question as to the interest which this wonderful padlock excited, for whoever before had found a padlock embedded in a brick wall seven feet from the ground ?

S handed over his pick and retired into the background, while two lusty mountain gunners, stripped to the waist, set to with a will. A few minutes of earnest endeavour played havoc with the sun-dried brick, and again came the welcome sound of pick-point meeting wood ; but it took some time to clear away all the covering brick-work, and more than one pair of exhausted gunners had to be relieved, overcome by the heat and choked by the dust from the crumbling clods of clay, before the wood was all visible, and again there appeared a door.

And now the why and wherefore of that ridiculous padlock became apparent, for driven into the wood, one at the top of the door and the other into the lintel, were two stout staples, long enough to protrude over the protecting brickwork. What was not quite so apparent was why anyone should have gone to the trouble of padlocking a door which he meant to cover with nine inches of brick.

A crowbar made very short work of the staples, and the same weapon soon prised open the door, when there appeared the head of a very narrow and steep stairway, leading apparently into the very bowels of the earth, so utter was the darkness down below.

Down we went with lanterns and torches, treading on each other's heels in our excitement, until we emerged into another cellar, a smaller one this time, with an opening on the far side, and, on our right, a huge door with three heavy bolts, each secured by a very serviceable padlock.

A wave of the Colonel's hand, and the destroyers stepped forth. No padlock made by human hands being able to withstand those muscles for long, off they flew ; the bolts were drawn back, the door flung open, and there—*at last*!

From roof to floor, a veritable cascade of silver, glittering and twinkling in the rays of the torches, met our enraptured gaze, the resemblance to a waterfall curiously heightened by dark objects, like rocks, protruding from the face of the silver mass, while odd coins in twos and threes slid tinkling down.

It seemed impossible that one man, in the short span of a human life, could have collected all that mass of silver coins, but there they were, six million two hundred thousand no less, all bright shining rupees, a fact which must stamp the Khan as the champion miser of this or any other age.

Closer examination showed that the protruding rocks

were really the ends of boxes, and that the silver was not a solid mass as it had appeared from the door. Some of the boxes had burst open and allowed their contents to escape, but the greater part of the treasure was securely packed, eight thousand rupees to a box, which was fortunate for us, as we had to count them later, and the handling of six million odd individual rupees would have taken some doing!

The narrow opening in the cellar wall, outside the treasure chamber, was found to lead to another stair which ended in a very solid wooden trapdoor: this trap was let into the floor of the Khan's third room and carefully covered by the floorboards, the bed with the golden legs standing guard over it.

The discovery of this trapdoor solved the mystery as to how all that silver could have been stowed away in the cellar without anybody being any the wiser. One can see the old miser pulling up his floorboards in the dead of night, raising the trapdoor, and slinking down the stairs with his bags of rupees to add to his hoard; very possibly the large amount of loose silver was left so intentionally, something to handle and to gloat over, much more solacing than a lot of ugly boxes.

Having solved one problem by finding the treasure, we now had to tackle another—how to get away with it.

Counting the loose silver, checking and sealing the full boxes, and getting them out of the Miri was comparatively easy, but the removal of all that bullion to Quetta was a task of some magnitude.

It took nearly four hundred camels to carry the treasure, and four hundred camels cover quite a lot of ground, offering golden—or should it be silver?—opportunities for a cutting-out party. Luckily we were dealing with

Brahuis and not with Mahsuds. Precious little of that silver would have got out of Waziristan.

And that is the story of the Khan's Treasure. What happened to it is the secret of the Indian Government. All I know is that none of it came *our* way.

[January 1924

6

GOLD FROM SEAWATER

Bennet Copplestone

There is an unforgettable fascination about a gold bar. In his youthful days in the city of London the present writer loved to peer into the courtyard of the Bank of England and watch gold being packed for export by a placidly indifferent workman. The dull yellow ' bars ' lay about naked on the stones, in shape very like Roman bricks, to all appearance unprotected save by their own massive weight. The workman would neatly fit five of them into a wooden case, lap it about with hoop iron, drive in a few nails, and pass on to the next lot. Each bar that he handled weighed four hundred troy ounces (over thirty - three pounds), and was worth some seventeen hundred pounds sterling. Each case of the value of £8,500 had a weight of one hundred and sixty-six pounds. I have watched a man for hours putting up gold bars as indifferently as he would potatoes, and presently assisting an equally indifferent rail-way vanman to hoist those boxes of fabulous treasure into his unguarded van. Maybe hidden somewhere there was an armed guard, or perhaps the prohibitive weight of the gold was its own best protection.

In the strict sense, perhaps, this tale has little in it of distress or of alarm. For that which began in distress, in the sinking of a great ship and a loss of many lives, ended after long years of high endeavour in a triumph of the spirit of man over the powers of the sea. It is a tale far too good to be sacrificed to any pedantic regard for a general title. Indeed, we present this story of Commander Damant's salvage of the *Laurentic's* gold bars off Lough Swilly as a companion picture, in a modern frame, to that other story, now nearly a century old, of Captain Dickinson's recovery of the *Thetis's* dollars at Cape Frio, retold in our 'Dead Men's Tales'. As a study in contrasts and in likenesses, these two stories have many features of interest. Captain Dickinson of the old sailing Navy worked 'on private account' to make what he could for himself and his men out of salvage awards; Commander (now Captain) Damant was working for his country under orders at his professional naval duties. Dickinson had to invent and construct everything for himself as he went along—diving-bells, a vast derrick, and searching gear; Damant had skilled divers from the *Excellent*, and all the salvage plant, explosives, pumps, and mechanical power that the Admiralty could spare for the service. Yet in both cases, though so far apart in details, the enemy fought was the same, and the triumph won was due to the same human qualities. In the twentieth century, as in the early nineteenth, the high spirit of man wrestled with the blind powers of the sea and won through by sheer grit and brains. In these two great jobs of work, separated by three generations, we perceive all through the superb qualities of the British sailor—his cheerful persistence, his indomitable courage, and his unfailing loyalty to his leaders. 'It was the men who did it all,' say Dickinson and Damant; 'it was those wonderful creatures who pulled us through.' Leadership is proved by its fruits. Men do not labour cheerfully, do not prove themselves to be wonderful creatures, unless they are privileged to serve leaders who inspire and sustain them. Whether we read of Dickinson's sailors tipped out of a diving-bell, coming up gasping and half dead, and then eagerly going down again, or whether we read of Damant's divers grubbing with bleeding fingers for gold bars hidden in the debris beneath the *Laurentic's* bottom, we are reading the same story of simple human devotion to the leader who is worthy of it.

In January 1917 the White Star liner *Laurentic* was sunk by enemy mines off Lough Swilly while on a voyage from Liverpool to Halifax, Nova Scotia. She went down in one hundred and twenty feet of water, and three hundred lives were lost. With this big ship of 15,000 tons went forty-five tons of gold bars, valued at over five millions sterling, which were being shipped to Canada at a time of great financial distress. This country was making huge purchases of war material, the United States had not yet ' come in ', and our national credit in America needed the solid buttresses of gold and dollar securities if the war was to be carried on. The sunken gold was wanted badly and at once, so the Lords of the Admiralty ordered Commander G. C. C. Damant, R.N., to go to Lough Swilly and get it. The job at the beginning did not look one of great difficulty for an officer who had made a special study of diving operations and for divers trained in the Admiralty service. The position of the ship was known, and the position of the gold in the ship. Provided that the *Laurentic* would hold together for a few months Damant and his divers should be able to get the gold out of her.

We will deal presently with the difficulties, mechanical and physiological, of diving in deep water and of working when there. For the moment we are concerned with the immediate problem of getting quickly at those 3,200 bars of yellow gold, neatly packed in their wooden boxes, and locked up in the second class baggage-room in the sunken *Laurentic*.

Commander Damant had at his disposal a mooring steamer, the *Volunteer*, five divers from the *Excellent*, and pumping and hoisting gear which, if not in all respects what he would have chosen, could be made adequate to the immediate purpose. He had also a large model of the *Megantic*, a sister ship of the *Laurentic*, and builders' plans, so that he knew exactly where to look for that second class baggage-room of unromantic name and glittering contents. By the end of February he had the *Volunteer*, his plant, and his men at Lough Swilly, with headquarters at Buncrana. After some delay from bad weather the position of the *Laurentic* was fixed in a spot fully exposed to the north and west and not too well sheltered from the south. The *Volunteer* was moored above at all four corners, and the first descent was made. Modern deep-water diving is done from a ship, not from boats, and steam air-compressors are used in place of the old hand-pumps in order to maintain a sufficient supply of air to the divers. The ship was found to be lying on her port bilge at an angle of sixty degrees from the vertical, the entry port on the starboard side leading to the second class baggage-room could be got at, and prospects looked bright. The plan was to blow in the entry port, clear a way to the baggage-room, force the door, and haul out the cases of gold. But the experiences of the first divers to go down suggested that all was not going to be plain sailing.

The trouble—and it was the primary cause of all Damant's woes for seven years—was the motion of the sea in the depths. A short breaking sea affects only the surface, but the long slow Atlantic swell transmits horizontal surges along the sea-floor at the *Laurentic's* depth of a hundred and twenty feet, so that the divers had to cling to the sloping side of the wreck lest they be swept away. All loose tackle lashed like whips about them with the scend of the sea above.

As soon as the exact position of the entry port had been found, the moorings of the *Volunteer* were taken up and relaid, so that the vessel might be placed directly above the men at work, and keep their pipes and lines clear of fouling. Then with a charge of gun-cotton the steel doors were blown in and neatly jammed into the tunnel behind. The next step was to haul these doors out and to clear a way through a mass of casks and cases which littered up the passage beyond. All went well, though the diving vessel was pitching in the swell above, the hoists jerking up and down, and the divers being swung to and fro by the deep water surges. Finally, success seemed to be upon the point of achievement when on 14th March the steel door of the strongroom was reached and opened with a hammer and chisel, and the first box of five gold bars lifted out and sent to the surface. A box of gold is a small object measuring no more than a foot square by six inches deep, but its weight of one hundred and sixty-six pounds makes it clumsy and laborious to carry through narrow ways out of the bowels of a foundered ship. Yet there was on the 14th that one box as an earnest of others to follow, and next day there were three more boxes. It looked, as Damant said, as if a few weeks would see a job done which actually spread itself over seven weary years. All depended on the weather. Damant was to find, as so many have found before, that the sea does not willingly give up its prey.

In his diary under 15th March he wrote : ' Started to blow '. And for many days thereafter the record is one of continuous gales from the north, with the wind blowing ' like the devil '. Down below, the swell, as they were soon to find out, was working on the *Laurentic's* hull in a manner inconceivable to those who have had no experience of deep-water salvage. The water moving irresistibly to and fro seized upon projecting features, such as superstructures and shelter decks, worked them backwards and forwards, and nipped them off as one breaks a bit of tin between one's fingers. Also the pressure of the water squeezed in the compartments that had not been opened to the sea when the vessel sank, and decks became piled upon decks. All this havoc was discovered as soon as the weather moderated and the *Volunteer* could get back to her moorings, and it was a havoc which postponed indefinitely all hope of getting at the gold bars in bulk. For now with the collapse of the decks—the whole ship was found to have been shut up like a concertina—the heavy gold had made its way down to the lowest depths near the sea floor. The lamentable consequences of that series of gales and the collapse of the *Laurentic's* hull were realised when, after great toil and amid constant perils, the divers had again blown their way into the crushed strongroom and found it empty. The room itself was forty feet lower down than at the earlier entry. The gold had all escaped, fallen away to port, become mixed up and overlaid with deck-frames and plates, and must now be searched for bit by bit as Dickinson had to search for the dollars of the *Thetis* when she had, in similar fashion, been broken up by the seas. From a rapid operation the work of salvage had become one of immense toil and of indefinite duration.

The one bright spot was the disappearance of immediate

urgency by the entry in April of the United States into the war. The buried gold which had so sorely been needed to finance our American purchases was no longer of vital necessity, and Damant, in the long years that lay ahead, could have for his operations all the time that he required. One may, however, doubt whether the prospect of unlimited days of nibbling at that clotted mass of jagged steel looked sweet in contemplation.

The problem was no longer one of removing gold boxes from the strongroom of a ship, for the once proud *Laurentic* had ceased to be a ship. She was just a litter of crushed and split and tangled metal splayed about on the sea floor, and the gold bars escaping from their splintered wooden boxes were no longer in one closed sealed room, but in three thousand pockets wherever they had fallen or crept. At every gale the Atlantic swell churned and broke the tangled mass of steel more and more, and redistributed the gold hidden within it and beneath it. And seeing that he could no longer remove the gold in bulk from the wreck, Damant had to contemplate the removal of the wreck from the gold, by cutting right down through it, by clearing a way to the bottom of it, and then picking up the gold bar by bar. As time went on those bars which were not early discovered would bury themselves more and more deeply until it might become necessary to follow them into the sea floor itself under where the wreck had been. That was the tremendous task, carried out primarily by manpower at a depth of one hundred and twenty feet, with the watchful care and slow deliberation necessitated by deep-water diving—if his gallant men were not to break up and die on their leader's hands,—Damant had not only to contemplate, but to plan and to carry out. And that is, in brief, exactly what he did. Since he could not remove the gold from the wreck, he removed the wreck from the gold.

As himself a skilled diver and master of divers, Commander Damant had outstanding qualifications for the conduct of undersea work. Twelve years before he had been sent to Lough Swilly to fetch up the *Laurentic's* gold, Lieutenant Damant, as he was then, had, as a naval specialist, been lent to the Admiralty Committee on Deep-Water Diving for 'experimental work'. This meant that not only would Damant carry out experiments, but that he would submit his ' vile body ' to the experiments of others so that the dangers to life and health of deep-water operations might in his person be discovered and eliminated. And so he did, submitting with Mr Catto, Chief Instructor in diving at Whale Island (*Excellent*), to experiments at depths up to thirty-five fathoms, or two hundred and ten feet, and enabling the Committee to arrive at their invaluable conclusions. It is in accordance with the rules of this Admiralty Committee of 1905, of which Dr J. B. S. Haldane was the medical inspirer, that deep-water diving is carried out today. The two physiological dangers incurred by divers are carbonic acid gas poisoning due to insufficient volume of pumped-down air, and nitrogen bubbles in the blood caused by prolonged exposure to high air-pressure. The first is prevented by increasing the supply of air in proportion to the depth by means of steam air-compressors of sufficient capacity. Nitrogen bubbles are more difficult to deal with, and unless eliminated will cause paralysis and death. The worst of the evil effects are got rid of by bringing a diver up in stages, with intervals for rest. At the depth of the *Laurentic* the men worked in thirty-minute shifts, and took thirty-three minutes to ascend, the longest rest of a quarter of an hour being at ten feet from the surface. Even then the divers frequently suffered from what are called 'bends', severe pains in the joints, and were then put into a decompression chamber in the diving vessel, and gradually made accustomed to normal air-pressure. During the work on the *Laurentic* Damant often went down himself, knew exactly what his men had to do and how they suffered in doing it, and so completely won their affection and confidence that recovering divers would insist on coming out of the decompression chamber, and enduring the return of those horrible 'bends', to make room for him rather than that their skipper should linger in pain outside.

So the long work of cutting down through the wreck began. The tangled structure had to be removed beam by beam and plate by plate by men whose vision under water did not extend beyond three or four yards, and whose every movement had to be communicated by telephone to those above. The masses of metal were cut by explosives, and when detached were hoisted to the surface for ultimate dumping at a distance. Cutting metal beams by explosives is an art in itself, and Damant explains how it was done. A charge on one side only bends a beam; two charges directly opposite one another produce no effect; but if two opposing charges are stepped a little so as to give a shearing stress upon explosion, the beam is neatly severed every time. Day after day through April and May this picking to pieces of the wreck went on until a crater had been driven nearly to the bottom, and then on 22nd May the divers came upon a pocket of gold bars separated from their cases. They secured twenty-two that day, worth about £37,000, more than enough to pay the whole working costs of the salvage party for a season! This was most encouraging; it showed that the searchers were on the right road. On many days in June gold was found in smaller quantities, and then on 20th June came a bumper day, which Damant permits himself in his diary to underline heavily and describe as ' splendid '. The divers struck a rich lode, and four of them in successive shifts found and sent up no less than 224 bars (value £380,000). One man to his own bucket scored 109, while another man raised no more than three. This shows how much luck there was about the game. By a very wise regulation the men engaged on the underwater work, and those above in the diving vessel, shared in the bonuses on gold recovered on a fixed scale unaffected by individual scores in gold bars. The whole job was team work and not personal pot-hunting.

The work on the wreck during that first season was not continuous. Frequently it was interrupted by weather, and for many days Damant with his *Volunteer* and divers was called off for other salvage jobs. Altogether ninety days were spent grubbing in the *Laurentic's* bowels, and on thirty-one days gold was found. The total haul of the season up to 31st August was four boxes (five bars each) and 522 bars—542 bars valued at about £920,000. Towards the end of it all, on 28th August, we find this delightfully human entry in Damant's diary : ' Found two wires ashore. Frightened ! Bad—worse—dead ? No—a daughter, 3 A.M. All well.'

The effect of explosives under water was curious and rather erratic. The area to the North of Ireland in which the *Volunteer* was working was one favoured by German mine-layers. Now and then our sweepers would explode a mine. Once this happened at two miles distance from the *Laurentic*, and a diver at work received a most violent and dangerous shock. After that work was suspended when minesweeping was in progress within five miles. While the divers were blasting their way into the wreck the decks would be covered with dead fish and attract the eager attention of shoals of dogfish. Charges would be exploded in the midst of these dogfish, yet they never seemed to be hurt. 'On the contrary,' says Damant, 'they could be seen rising to the surface almost in the foam of an explosion, and tearing at the bodies of the freshly killed teleosteans.' He came to the general conclusion that fish do not seem to be killed outside a radius of two or three hundred yards, and he noted that those without swim-bladders did not seem to be affected at all.

The year 1918 was blank insofar as gold hunting had claims upon the Admiralty's attention. There were other and more urgent things to do, so that eighteen months elapsed before Damant was ordered back to Lough Swilly to dig once more into the carcass of the *Laurentic*. It was now 1919, and he was able to secure the assistance of the fully equipped salvage steamer *Racer*, a type of vessel which, like the famous *Ranger* of the Liverpool Salvage Association, is a self-contained travelling workshop. There were for the future to be no more troubles with defective air-compressors—that in the *Volunteer* was constantly going wrong,—and the decompression accommodation for divers suffering from 'bends' approached the luxurious. A diver could lie inside a great steel cylinder undergoing compression and have tea passed in to him through an airlock.

In general appearance there had been few changes at the wreck, though for eighteen months the Atlantic swells had had their will upon her. The job of burrowing into the vessel and clearing the old crater was resumed, at first with fairly gratifying results. But then the pockets petered out, and it became clear that the greater quantity of the bars had been widely distributed. The rich lode of 1917 was soon exhausted in 1919 (it yielded 315 further bars, about £535,000), and the hunt had to begin again on a wider and more laborious scale. Hitherto Damant had been intent upon driving a shaft down through the wreck ; now he had to remove the wreck itself piecemeal. It was not until gold ceased to come up from the initial boring that he was compelled to face the larger, and for a long time less fruitful, operation.

The winter gales of 1919-20 helped by breaking up the remaining superstructures and depositing plates and decks upon Damant's crater. These were peeled off, and taken to the surface, and then it was found that a new and formidable obstacle had obtruded itself. From above and around broken fragments of chairs, planking, baths, tiles, and so on had been swept into the crater, and from below sand and stones had pushed upwards from the sea bottom and become caked into a solid mass reinforced with cot frames and spring mattresses.

The years 1920 and 1921 were almost blank as regards gold, though they were chockfull of toil and disappointment. As plates and solid lumps of metal were blasted away the sand would well up, inexhaustible and resistless, and fill the space again. Large centrifugal pumps and dredging grabs were tried, but failed for lack of space within which to work, and Damant was driven back upon slow and terribly painful hand work. In fine weather the divers gained ; in bad weather the sand. 'Very fortunately,' he writes, 'a few odd bars of gold turned up and kept hope alive when failure seemed to be threatening.' The fruit of 1920 was seven bars, and of 1921 forty-three bars—fifty bars, or £85,000 in two toilsome years. Not the least of Damant's anxieties at the end of those two unfruitful years was to convince My Lords at the Admiralty that the gold was there in the wreck to be found, and that it could be found and salved by removing enough of the wreck. Fortunately even in his two bad years he had recovered more than enough to repay the costs of the salvage work, which were some £20,000 for a season.

By the end of 1921 so much of the wreck's structure had been blown away and brought to the surface that the port side of the shaft tunnel and the tank tops could be seen among the mass of debris. This showed that the salvers had burrowed right through the ship from top to bottom as she lay and reduced the steel scrap-heap to some semblance of order. The two seasons of patient labour were duly rewarded in the spring of 1922, when operations were resumed. The first diver to go down actually saw a number of bars sticking up out of the sand in a spot where the sea had kindly washed them clear. Nineteen bars were seized the first day. As the men expressed it : " They came up like lambs." Damant was now right down on the skin of the ship, and set to work to clear as large an area as he could. This season was the turning-point, for it not only proved rich in gold, but revealed the true method of dealing with accumulated and accumulating debris. The contrivances of modern engineering, centrifugal pumps and grabs, had failed ; they got out less than a hundredth part of rubbish dug. Hand power must, after all, do the job if it were to be done. The divers were assisted by hosepipes from the *Racer*, which projected water at seventy pounds pressure. With the nozzle in one hand driving away sand and stones, a man would grope with the other hand for the instantaneously recognisable 'feel' of soft yellow gold. Many bars had lost their shape, they had been moulded like putty, they had pebbles and bits of steel driven into them, yet the magic touch of them revealed their identity instantly to the sensitive divers. After a spell of work for many days together, the nails of the men would be worn away to a quarter-inch strip, their finger-ends would be palpitating pulps of raw flesh, yet they went on. Leather gloves were offered and refused. Gloves, the divers declared, spoilt their sense of touch; they could not react to the odd thrill of soft gold, as distinct from hard metal or stones, unless their hands were bare. So they went on, though their nails were worn down far below the quick, and their wounds were tortured by day and night with the salt of the sea water. The bars usually lay eighteen inches or two feet deep in the sand, and the divers could just reach them with their tender finger-tips.

Where mechanical means of clearing a way to the treasure had failed man-power succeeded. ' The corner was turned,' writes Damant describing his struggle with encroaching sand, ' as I am convinced by the simple device of weighing and recording the amount of sand dug out by each diver in his spell below. Here was a new competition, and one with no luck in it. For ten or twenty working days the weights of sand per man steadily increased as brains came to the aid of muscle, as new dodges for saving twenty seconds here and getting an extra three or four pounds there with the aid of some queer-shaped scoop made by the blacksmiths came into action. . . . A standard, and a high one, had been set up which no diver's pride would allow him to fall below; and till the excavations reached a depth point ten feet below the level of the surrounding seabed the sand trouble was overcome.'

At the end of the season of 1922 Damant was able to report that 895 bars (about 1½ millions sterling) had been recovered in seventy-seven diving days out of a season of one hundred and ninety-eight days, and that there had again been no accidents to life or limb. Indeed, the freedom from serious accidents from first to last in the many perils of the work shows the degree of care which was exercised throughout. Once in the early days a diver became imprisoned beneath a large plate owing to the breaking of a wire hoisting cable. He called for air and more air, for he felt that his spine was being broken, and he got some relief as the extra pressure swelled out his diving dress. But though the diver might call for more air, Damant had to balance the risks. Too much air would certainly burst the dress and drown the diver. So the supply was actually throttled and the man's spine risked, while a rescuing diver rigged a new wire to the imprisoning plate. In nine minutes the first diver was released ' unruffled and none the worse '. This instance of shrewd quick judgment makes one understand the unlimited faith of the divers in their commander.

The long years of labour culminated in the season of 1923 with the recovery of 1,255 bars of gold of a value of over two millions sterling. This brought up the total number of bars salved and stowed in the Bank to the credit of the Treasury to 3,057 out of the original consignment in the *Laurentic* of 3,211 bars. Over ninety-five per cent had been recovered ; less than five per cent remained. Something like three-quarters of the huge vessel had been picked to pieces and removed, and, except for the intrusive sand, her bottom plates were almost clear. It was a great work, and one is glad for Damant's sake, and for the sake of his dauntless divers who had fought the good fight with him—fifteen of them—that the job was not left uncompleted. As now tried and proved artists in salvage, they craved permission to put in those final touches which make immortal a perfected picture.

So with light hearts they set forth in the spring of 1924 for the last lap or varnishing day, or whatever one may elect to call it. The great carpet of plate upon which and under which they were now to search for those last 154 bars was not continuous. There were rents and portholes in it, and under the action of the sea it crept so that gold which had fallen through apertures might be hidden beneath unpierced plating. The weather proved excellent. The sea knew that it was beaten, as it always does when man stands up to it and fights it to the uttermost. There is a strain of bully in the soul of the sea. The last layer of the wreck was cut away and hoisted off, and then some 2,000 square feet of the sea floor itself was uncovered and searched. Divers working with the water-hoses and bleeding fingers could not now be denied, and they were rewarded by tracking down one hundred and twenty-nine more bars, leaving just twenty-five unaccounted for. That was in September 1924, when the operations were concluded, and one feels that there was a touch of the higher artistry in leaving that little something in the clutches of poor Father Neptune. He had been badly beaten, and knew it. It was as if Damant flung him a consolatory *pourboire* of £42,500 after dragging £5,416,000 out of his grip.

" And how," I asked of Damant, " did you store all these lumps and masses of treasure as the work went on, and how transfer them safely to the Bank of England ? " He replied that in the early days the bars used to be stowed under the Master's bunk in the *Volunteer*, probably the safest place in such a ship. When things got bad in Ireland the Admiralty provided the salvers with a destroyer as escort, and any gold would be transferred and locked up in her magazines after each day's work. " When a quarter of a million or so had accumulated," he went on in the airy style of a wholesale collector of bullion, "arrangements would be made for the destroyer to run over to a convenient port (e.g., Stranraer), where a 'representative of the Bank of England'—total stranger, bowler hat, plausible manner —would appear with lorries and take it off to the train." It all sounds delightfully casual, yet the total stranger in the bowler hat and the plausible manner always was what he represented himself to be, the lawful guardian of the Bank of England's gold. Had this tale been fiction he would, for once at least, have been a superlative crook out of a cinema film.

The total cost of the salvage work spread over seven seasons was less than two and a half per cent of the amount recovered, and was conducted all through by Commander Damant to the account of the Admiralty. The salvage party, in addition to their naval pay, received at the end a bonus of one-eighth per cent on the gold salved. Contrast this modern method of doing things with Captain Dickinson's salvage of the treasure in the *Thetis* on private account, and his subsequent legal fights with his own admiral and with underwriters at Lloyd's. Ours is a more dignified and at the same time a more economical way. Had this operation been carried out on a salvage contract 'no cure no pay', it would have cost the taxpayer at least ten times as much as it did.

And of the men, the true heroes of this little epic, listen to Captain Damant, their leader. In March of this year, when kindly supplying me with all the notes and papers upon which I have freely drawn in this tale, he wrote:

'I have often wondered why my divers all behaved like angels all the time. Most men do when there is a life to be saved, something that appeals to all mankind educated or not. Possibly ditto with the real red gold. Every deed could be evaluated. No one was enriched by anyone else's labour. A common religion, absolute unity in aim, reality, danger and boldness, to give pleasure. The only sad days were the ones when we could not get out to the wreck and had to mope in harbour.

'No question of award apart from actual service pay ever arose. I mean not one of the divers ever suggested that any bonus, or more bonus and pay, should be given them, and, of course, I never raised or commented on the question with the authorities. They did, voluntarily and spontaneously, award something just under £7000 which was divided among about seventy officers and men, who were all very well satisfied and grateful.'

In my rendering of this tale I have tried to hint, not obscurely, why Damant's divers all behaved like angels all the time.

[September 1926

7

ELDORADO UNLIMITED

L. A. Bethell

It may come as a shock to most of us to remember that before Vasco da Gama rounded the Cape in 1498 and opened the sea route, the only road into the vast Peninsula of India lay through one mountain pass : a gut so narrow that, till we English built a road through it, parts of it would not take two laden camels abreast. In those days Bombay, Calcutta, and Madras were not, and the existence of Ceylon was hearsay ; but through the Khyber Pass, and on across Afghanistan to Balkh, lay a single-file camel track which joined India to the immemorial Silk Route of the East, where Chinese silks and porcelains jostled the jewels, carpets, and spices of India as the two tides merged in a westward flow to the markets of Byzantium and the Mediterranean ports : a thin stream of great price, whose last feeble flicker is even now seen in the camel caravans which, twice a week and cheek-by-jowl with the new railway, thread slowly down the Pass to Peshawar, halt for a day, and as slowly drift back again, the last fizzle-out of a romance which may well be three thousand years old.

No bulk came that way, but only things of great intrinsic value, whose sale would profitably cover the immense overhead charges of transport and much middlemanship over a camel journey which often lasted six months, and which was beset throughout its length by every conceivable risk in an age when insurance was not.

Now, as we know, in any sound system goods pay for goods ; but there was nothing which the West could send in exchange for the treasures of the East but things of bulk—things which were an uneconomic load for camels. The West, therefore, paid in cash, and the packets of treasure flowing eastward crossed more and more caravans flowing westward—caravan loads which created a mighty thirst for beautiful things, for silks and fine raiment, in Imperial Rome, and which brought about the sumptuary laws of Tiberius. More and ever more of them passed west and north, till Byzantium outshone Rome, till Venice and Genoa arose as the carriers, and on the inland seas grew up a breed of corsairs whose direct descendants overflowed into the nineteenth century.

The East sent things of price, and the price travelled back in the gold of Rome, of Byzantium ; later, of Venice and Genoa and the coins of Central Italy. Many of these have been discovered in the recent excavations on India's North-West Frontier.

That portion of the coin which reached China and paid for her silks and porcelains was legitimate stuff applied to a legitimate end. China was, as she still is, a land of honest and energetic traders with a high standard of commercial morality. She had, and still has, a sound banking system with good credit and good trust ; and the coin which she received she put straightway into circulation to finance the trade, mainly by inland waterways of great antiquity, which went up and down a land extensive enough to make, within its own borders, an exchange between the goods of a cold to temperate north and the subtropical products of the south. In a lesser degree the junks of the coasting trade helped.

China never hoarded wealth. The genuine riches of the Chinese arose from a solid trade in marketable commodities, and from a banking system which still operates successfully alongside the western variety within their own borders, in spite of the seasonal dog-fights which today scar the land and which, in any land less based on the ages, would paralyse the system.

India, however, was, and till our arrival remained, in far different case. With neither roads nor waterways, with no movement of goods up and down the peninsula save by the small and toilsome convoys of the ox-driving *brin-járas*, with no coastwise trade by a race which would not venture on the waters, with no banking system, and with inveterate mistrust between man and man, the coin which she got from the West did not go into circulation. It produced nothing. It drifted into the pockets of those Hindus in high places, in Northern India and down the rich Ganges Valley, who financed the westward trade and whose influence and power protected the Route. They never put it into circulation, and since, from the highest to the lowest, every man mistrusted his neighbour, the money was hoarded.

History does not tell us in what remote age this state of affairs commenced, since, in Northern India, proofs of civilisations, each more ancient than the last, are still being excavated. But we know from our own records when the change took place which should have modified the whole situation, and which in the end only accentuated it. In 1498 Vasco da Gama, at the bidding of Prince Henry the Navigator, rounded the Cape and found the sea route to the East. The trade of Europe with India and China multiplied in direct proportion to the widening of the avenues of access. By a coincidence this expanding trade synchronised with a stronger purchasing power in Europe, and a widening tendency for even the common people to use spices for the preservation of their winter meat instead of the rough and unpalatable salt. The ships, at first infrequent, later organised into highly financed fleets, filled their holds to overflowing, and sailed home. India, Malacca, China sent trade vast beyond all comparison with the old and toilsome camel loads. By all reason the Silk Route should have starved; but it took far more than what were, after all, only the nibblings at the edges of these vast territories to divert into new channels a trade which had flowed in one set course from time beyond memory. The factors of the trading companies drew great store from the coastwise districts, leaving the inner areas untouched, and what returned into the East in exchange was mostly cash. We hear of hardware, cottons, and broadcloth being sent to Calicut and Canton; but these were trivial in bulk and poor in value, being mainly regarded as peculiarities and bought in the East as one might buy an unwanted gilded teapot at a fair. ' *Marchandises de nouveauté*,' as one of the French factors described them.

Broadcloth. To India! One cannot think that the buyers were in earnest. No. The ships going eastward went largely in ballast; and somewhere in the lazaretto under the captain's cabin lay the bars of bullion which paid for what was taken.

As time passed and we English became masters of India, we opened up the land by road and rail. Then, and then only, did the Silk Route wane, though even today it is anything but dead. John Company, ousting his competitors, sent the products of Ind in ever-increasing bulk overseas to England; while India, slow to learn the need of England's goods in exchange, took ever more and more gold and silver.

Today India takes our cotton goods, machinery, medicines, motor-cars in a measure comparable with the increase of her needs for the trappings of civilisation—a pace as slow as that of a tortoise. Pushed and pulled, combed and harried by the energetic English at her principal ports, she exports more and more goods, till, on this day and month of 1928, the level of her surplus of exports over the goods she takes in exchange has reached 29 millions sterling annually.

A number of us there are who, travelling eastward on an Australia-bound boat, have transhipped at Aden for Bombay. We have leant over the side and have watched a lighter alongside the ship; a ship's white officer standing in the bows of the lighter, counting into her hold, bar by bar, the ingots of greasy-looking grey silver destined for India. Ingots weighing 1,200 ounces; each worth £120. For half an hour the stream of solid treasure flows: a pause: then follows a string of small but stubborn-looking boxes. "What are those?" "Oh, those are the gold bars. Too soft to handle loosely." And in they go, on top of the rest—one of the periodic consignments of bullion for India; part of the 29 millions annually, from the gold and silver brokers in London to the consignees up and down the land of Hindustan.

As with the Bight of Benin, 'there's little comes out, for all that goes in'. Practically, nothing at all. Financiers in high places will tell you how, normally, their clan can say where, at any stated moment, lies the trade of the world, where its credit, and where its cash. The movements of gold, and the effects of gold at the time of speaking, are known to them. But the one imponderable factor which always upsets their calculations is India. The present world output of gold, annually, is 80 millions sterling, of which the British Empire produces 70 per cent ; and of this annual total how much will be absorbed by India and never seen again depends entirely on what India's surplus exports are—this, again, depending on a monsoon good, moderate, or wholly lacking. Meteorology, therefore, as a further complication to an already complicated science, strikes them as unfair ; and their references to this particular subject leave nothing to be added to, in their crispness.

Revert, then, to what we have seen. From times immemorial down to A.D. 1928, India has steadily absorbed treasure, in whole or in part, in return for her exports, and has swallowed it up with a finality as definite as her refusal to put it into circulation in the veins of that commerce which, in the last recourse, depends on trust between man and man. To what the total amounts, nobody can guess ; pre-history has no figures for us ; but from the time when the sea route opened, down to today, we happen to know that the figures have reached a total of 553 millions sterling in gold, and 4,556 millions in silver—proportions to the whole world's treasure, throughout that period of comparatively slow output, of 14 and 34 per cent respectively.

Compare the case with that of China, with a much larger and infinitely more industrious population, where, for the past thirty-five years—the only period for which the figures are available—only 16 per cent of payment has been taken in treasure ; a proportion barely sufficient to finance her internal trade and to keep her banking system going.

The figures, were they not authoritative, would be incredible. What in the name of heaven, it may be asked, can have happened to it all ? The country must be simply running over with wealth. What do they do with it ?

A sullen silence pervades the whole question. Nobody knows. But one may quote the words of a highly-placed servant of the Indian Government, lately retired, who said that if in 1920, India had been combed thoroughly, she could have paid the bill for the whole costs of the war, on both sides and on all fronts, and not have felt the loss.

Who has it all ? And where ?

Who can tell ? It is in the nature of every Hindu, of no matter what class, to hoard ; and hoarders never tell. Little can be gathered in a land where a professional money-lender, who may be a millionaire, goes about in a suit of cotton worth ten and sixpence, and lives in what we should call a slum. We know even less of the East nowadays than did our grandfathers ; but in John Company's days, when his white servants in India were in closer touch with the native than we are today, some strange things must have passed in the written reports to the Honourable Directors. A single instance came to public notice when Warren Hastings was arraigned. Here we find a minor potentate of Oudh dying and leaving buried in the vaults of his zenana a treasure of twenty million rupees. Of a moiety of this Warren Hastings rightly mulcted the surviving Begums ; for which act Sheridan exposed him to five hours of the most impassioned hot air that has ever disgraced long-suffering Westminster. He would have it that the poor Begums were impoverished. They scarcely felt it.

The money passes into India and vanishes. It goes underground ; it goes behind the purdah ; much of it goes into the temples ; much more goes to buy the glittering gems which increasingly swell the treasuries whose beginnings lie in dim antiquity, and whose full extent will never be guessed. They are incredible.

Incredible or not, the fact has been common knowledge throughout the ages. Of the great waves of predatory invasion, two only took the easy route to Europe. Attila, whose Mongol cupidity had been aroused by the treasure caravans passing eastward through his country, pictured the West as a land overflowing with riches. He invaded it. The only treasure he got was the blackmail paid by Rome and Byzantium to keep him from raiding them. Thanks to the Roman banking system, the wealth of Europe lay in commerce, in goods, in credit, everywhere fluid and nowhere tangible; a land where commodities flowed freely and hoarding was not. From him might his lineal descendants, whose fingers itch round the idea of the capital levy, have learnt that the wealth which they would loot does not lie about in attractive chunks in banks, or in the homes of the idle rich; but it floats on the sea, runs on rails, or, in the last resort, lies on the back of a sheep grazing in the backblocks of Australia; and that nothing but that trust between man and man, which they would destroy, makes it available to the human race.

Attila made just about as much out of it as would keep him in wine and women; and, after his death, his following dispersed to Asia as poor as when they came.

Genghis Khan's empire, again, swamped Russia; sat there for two hundred and thirty years—and got nothing, where nothing was to be got.

But with the exception of these two, history, since history has been, is full of the invaders of India. Not for them the easy open plains which led westward. Each and all fought their way toilsomely through the tangle of mountains which bar the way to the narrow gut which leads into India. For a thousand years ? Two thousand years ? Setting aside the countless raids of the Early and Middle Ages, two thousand two hundred years ago Alexander of Macedon heaved his solid phalanx half-way across Asia, to conquer Persia and descend on India ; the traditional goal, even in his day, of the strong man singing to himself in an undertone a tune about ' they may take who have the power, and they may keep who can '.

India, the quest and quarry of all who dreamt of quick and easy riches, of those whose conscience was salved by the lip-service of a modicum offered to the gods. India, silent and secretive, whose obstinacy defeated each treasure-hunter in succession, sending him empty away.

The pelf has some aspects peculiar to itself, which may be worth examining ; one presumes that few of us have a soul above these things.

Why should gold be not only a thing of price, but also the mainspring of much that has made the history of individuals and of nations ? It is a useless thing in itself, come to think of it. With the exception of a tiny quantity used by the dentists, it has no uses whatever in a practical world. It cannot even be turned into a decent garden spade.

It depends for its value solely and entirely on a desire, deep-rooted in us all, for personal adornment. Its value, as the basic factor of human prosperity, is therefore quite fictitious ; and should some epidemic ever smite the human race with, as its *sequela*, say, a horror of yellow as a colour, gold would straightway become valueless. As it is, it keeps its value, and the difficulty of finding it prevents it from becoming too common. Its rate of production, 80 millions a year nowadays, just about keeps pace with the increasing prosperity of the world at large ; and it supplies, for those countries fortunate enough to have it, the means of backing their paper on which an equivalent amount is persuasively written in ornamental script.

Silver, in a minor degree, is ornamental, and consequently valued. But it suffers from violent fluctuations in production, and therefore fails as a standard of value. The places where it is most prized are those lands which learnt to set store by it in the dimly remote ages when its rate of production gave it a fixed valuation based on its rarity—the unchanging East. India and China use this jumpy metal as a standard of human welfare, because their remotest great-grandfathers valued it. Elsewhere, its jumpiness has reduced it to more or less of a token, when coined, depending for its importance on arbitrary laws made by its owners in consultation, whereby it has a standardised relation to its elder brother, gold.

Coins are therefore minted in both metals ; and lest the rarer metal become unmanageable if minted too small, silver coins big enough not to get mislaid (*pace* our universal enemy, the threepenny bit) represent its subdivisions. Both metals are so malleable that they are in danger of losing their worth by wear and tear if minted pure ; in civilised countries they are therefore alloyed. 24-carat gold is chemically pure. 22-carat is what we find in our sovereign. But the first king to mint sovereigns was our late liege Henry VII ; that miserly king who, dying in 1509, was undoubtedly the richest prince in contemporary Christendom and whose idiosyncracies we meet no less in Kipling than in the ' day-book ' of the realm's expenditure, which all may see at the Record Office (these eyes have seen it), with his great sprawly royal initials in ink against every tiny item. He, as a consequence, was able to bequeath to his son Hal a million and a half of personal wealth, representing a modern equivalent of ten millions. He, viewing a sovereign as a thing to be cosseted and petted, minted it soft, at ' 995 fine ' or within five-thous-andths of chemically absolute purity ; a noble coin, weighing 240 grains as against our present piece which assays at only '916 fine', and is just half the weight of its forebear. Admirable king; admirable. And for that very reason, quite unlovable.

Gold, pure, is softer than silver, and nearly as soft as lead. Both gold and silver are exported to India in as chemically pure a condition as the refineries of the West can make them. India, trusting nobody, takes no alloy in her metals ; India, where commercial mistrust is universal. It ranges from a chemical analysis of her imported bullion, down to the man who buys a farthing box of matches at a bazaar stall and rattles it against his ear to be sure that it is not empty, forgetting that if it were really full it would not rattle.

The purity of the gold and silver she gets is therefore absolute. The 1,200 ounce bricks we have seen, lowered into the lighter ; the sturdy boxes, therewith, contain short truncheons of the yellow metal about as long and as thick as a desk ruler—just such a handleable size as will allow bits to be snicked off it with a heavy knife, in the bazaar or the counting-house, the ceremony being performed after dark behind barred shutters and by the light of a cheap kerosene lamp, the ministrants squatting in a tight circle on the white floorcloth and gazing fixedly at the ritual.

To revert. Why should not India, after all, hoard the precious metals ? It is nobody's business but her own ?

Your pardon. It is.

An adequate annual supply of gold—and, with it, we

include its satellite, silver—is necessary to the world at large. It gives a fundamental value to those paper securities which are the written expressions of the trust between man and man which alone makes trade possible. Any shortening of this supply means a stringency of money, a growing distrust in the written promise, falling prices, and a consequent general depression of the world's economic life. In addition, it must be remembered that wealth is not static; it is continuously wasting, in the struggle against Nature and against other men, and is as continuously being recreated by private enterprise and by brains and labour. And, as the pace of the struggle increases, so, *pari passu*, does the consequent wastage. Axiomatically, the need arises for more and more of the sinews of this struggle, gold; and if the struggle is to result in progress instead of retrogression—if wealth is not, in the end, to run like water into the earth and disappear—there must be no lessening of the basis of fundamental values.

At present, the 80 millions of fresh gold produced annually keeps pace with the world's economic progress, and any milking of it lessens *pro rata* our advance to that hoped-for point where everybody is comfortably well-off as well as being fully employed in congenial and heartening labour.

' Progress ', that overworked word, is, by the way, not an absolute term. We are inclined, for instance, to speak of the increasing speed of movement about the earth's surface as progress. Progress is a comparative, not an absolute, term. A may be said to progress for just such a time as he is going five miles an hour faster than B ; but if A and B are both of them going sixty miles an hour, they are just as well or as badly off as when they were each going four miles an hour ; stalemate, in fact. So with all other factors of movement, existence or possessions which we see about us. Whittling off all the trimmings and complications with which we, nowadays, obscure clear issues, the only clear standard by which to measure progression or retrogression is whether all men have a sufficiency of acceptable and strenuous work and, therewith, sufficient monetary return to give them a decent and quiet life free from anxiety or ill-health, moral or physical.

Freedom, in fact, from FEAR.

By whatever the world falls short of this, it may be said to be retrograde; by however much it approaches the ideal, it may be said to progress. All other references to progress are the most damnable misnomers.

Is India, *ergo*, an enemy to the human race ? Should we be so much nearer to our longed-for goal if this hoarding could be stopped ? Unfortunately, this is the most complex subject which ever wore the appearance of complete simplicity ; and though we shall, *en passant*, touch on bits of it its full consideration would demand a chapter to itself ; for which there is no space. The wealth-chasing brain of man has, in its strenuous striving through the ages, produced involutions in the conditions of wealth and commerce which defy simple corollaries ; and he would be a brave man who would cut the knot with a statement such as this. Cure there is, as will be seen ; but the cure can be only as slow and painful as has been the growth of the distemper.

We are told, also, that there are other hoarders in the world. We are told that the United States has, since the war, become the world's gold-drainer ; that all available gold now flows to America.

Not so.

Every nation is entitled to as much gold as will give

reasonable backing to its commercial paper-commitments. In the case of the United States, the amount of gold in the country represents only 7·7 per cent of her floating securities and bank deposits, a proportion slightly in excess of England's 6·5 per cent. The national wealth of the United States now stands at the colossal total of 50,969 million dollars ; and if her prosperity goes on increasing at its present pace she will need all this gold, and more, to back up her securities. Pin that fallacy to the board.

Anyhow, what happens to the stuff in the lighter ?

The firms, mainly British or Parsee, at the principal ports of India which accumulate from up-country centres the produce shipped overseas, take, in exchange, goods from England or the surplus balance in gold and silver. This gold and silver is obtained either by credit notes against bills of lading with white banks at the ports which order the bullion from London, or by direct order on firms of bullion brokers like Samuel Montagu of Old Broad Street, or Mocatta & Goldsmid of Throgmorton Avenue. The former specialise in silver. There are about four firms of bullion brokers who can, at any moment, lay their hands on any quantity of the two metals, standardised to the requisite fineness, and made up into the bars or ingots which experience has found that the Indian bazaars demand.

The bars, consigned to the P & O mail route, travel to Bombay, whence they are distributed up-country by the importers to the shroffs, or hereditary produce-dealing money-lending class, whose trade it is to accumulate exportable goods from the cultivator. At this point the stuff enters the catacombs of *lenideni*—the Indian ' give and take ' which represents personal manipulation of money,

—and all trace of it is lost.

To understand what happens in this subterranean traffic, it is worth while exploring a matter which throws light on many side-issues which have puzzled the West for centuries. Anciently—that is to say, verifiably three figures B.C., and conjecturally four—the Indian social order was divided into four watertight compartments. These, in order of seniority, were: kings or warriors; priests (Brahmans); traders; cultivators and artisans. The caste system is nothing new, nor is it peculiar to the East; it is as old as the social order. We see it in the squabbles between patricians and the plebs, in Rome, where matters of *connubium* and *commensalitas* were burning inter-class questions. We see its apotheosis in Upper Tooting today. This simple quadrisection persisted in India till 600 A.D., by which time the Brahmans had succeeded in ousting state-protected Buddhism and in making their own religion supreme. Simultaneously they fought for top place in the social scale, with eventual and lamentable success. No sooner did they find themselves unassailable at the top of the tree than the social order, to serve the Brahman purpose, began to suffer that comminution which we see in the caste-system today; in which every class, trade, or occupation is shut up within itself by barriers of priestly making; which has therefore a pseudo-religious sanction; and in which the power of the priests, as arbiters of every tiny daily action performed or abstained from by 216 million Hindus, is as fixed and as immovable as the stolid and unchanging acquiescence of the dupes.

With a social order crystallised into immovable compartments into or out of which no man might move, heredity of aptitude for the particular job became an irresistible feature and, through the centuries, acquired a force which

142

we in the West shall never be able to understand. As an instance, a man born to, brought up in, and meticulously trained to a profession of money-lending which ran centuries old in his veins, inherited a proficiency in the subject which needed neither the sleepy assent of his victims nor the blessing of priestly approval to make absolute.

Into the hands of such a hereditary expert the cultivator fell like a ripe apple. The system debarred him from being his own merchant and from marketing his own goods. To do so he would have had to step outside the rigid bounds of his place at the bottom of the social scale, and to join the one above it—a move which the self-interest of the merchant class, no less than the trammels of the system, made absolutely out of the question. A preying middle-manship was therefore superimposed on him, an incubus from which nothing could ever free him ; and since, in spite of all its tyranny, it saved him the pains and troubles of thought and prevision—his two pet enemies—he ended by almost blessing it.

The merchant caste took his produce and marketed it. They paid him for it ; more often they lent him the means of producing it, and held a mortgage on the ungrown crop. The interest on the loan—also a fixture since records have existed—has been, and ever will be, 5 per cent charged monthly, or 60 per cent per annum. Throughout India, it may fairly be said, every single son of the soil is in the fixed and irremovable toils of the nearest shroff, who takes everything that the peasant does not himself consume, and, in return, just keeps him going with enough small cash and involved credit to keep him alive and exploitable. The spider in the web has learnt to stall his fly.

Before the English came, the shroff was protected against an *émeute* of his creditors by the overlord who, in his turn, profited not a little by his complaisance. When we came, and our laws were used to enforce mortgages and to protect the life and safety of the mortgagee, the land was gradually passing by foreclosure into the hands of these moneylenders; till, to remedy an age-long abuse, we passed the Land Alienation Act which practically put a stop to any further foreclosures. This, you might think, would have stamped out the money-lending. It raised a squeal against us, almost feminine in its shrillness. But the money-lending went on with scarcely a check; the cultivator, accustomed through the ages to look to the shroff for a market for his produce and a small supply of ready money, entered into an alliance with him against our protective measures; driven to it, indeed, by the fact that unless the shroff were pacified there would be neither trade nor pocket-money, nor anything for the hoard; for, impossible though it may seem, the needy Indian peasant yet find means of imitating his betters by putting by a hoard, however exiguous.

Again, the shroff tentacles are such as absolutely to debar the *ryot* from having any wish to buy agricultural machinery, even a decent iron plough, wherewith to get better value from his land. Were the annual 29 millions to be expended in modern farm-tools, imagine for a moment what would be the agricultural wealth of India!

The shroff, then, commands the situation. He and his unholy caste are universal throughout India. He it is that collects the produce and marks up its value against the ever-mounting debt. He it is who sends it down-country for shipment, and who orders either piece-goods in exchange which he, again, sells to the cultivator at a fabulous profit, or bespeaks the grey and the yellow stuff which vanishes into the unknown the moment it reaches him—29 millions sterling a year.

Between the uncountable profits of usury and the clever manipulation of export and import, he grows fabulously rich ; and though something of what goes to him reaches its proper destination, and is there again subdivided into the fluid and the hoard, the vast body of it stagnates. In the old days, whole chunks of it went up the social ladder, and a moiety dribbled downwards ; nowadays, when unbribable law takes the place of the immemorial protection, the upward flow no longer exists.

Now, in the human body, the blood-flow, pumped unceasingly from the heart, reaches the capillaries in the tips of the fingers and toes and thence returns steadily to the heart, reviving and energising the whole body in its passage. Should any drop of it stop and stagnate anywhere, dire trouble results. So with money, the life-giver of trade. What leaves London, the commercial heart of the world, should, by every law, return thereto ; to be sent journeying again. India clogs the flow. This, by all analogy, should bring about painful symptoms and the most dangerous consequences. You would think that an inevitable Nemesis would supervene. But just as the East, through long custom, is proof against enteric and the outward evidences of more unpleasant troubles endemic in the race, so does it seem to be proof against that moral septicæmia which, in races of a newer and cleaner standard, would bring with it the instant and inevitable retribution of Providence. The East, therefore (let us get our definitions clear), flourishes where the West would rot.

Let us consider for a moment in what this hoarding consists ; and, in doing so, note the fact that throughout these figures the requirements of the Indian Government for minting purposes are definitely excluded.

145

Taking the year of discovery of the sea route as our starting point (since no figures were recorded before it for the immense sums absorbed, the extent of which will never be known), India's total absorption throughout the 430 years to date has been 553 millions sterling in gold and 4,556 millions sterling worth of silver, the annual ratio throughout the period being something over one million gold to eight and a half millions silver. This has progressively altered to the present annual ratio of 18 millions gold to 11 millions silver—a figure based on the returns of the last ten years. It shows a steadily increasing tendency in India to hoard gold instead of silver, despite the absolute embargo on the former metal throughout the war.* Indeed, in 1924 alone, as though to make up for the stinting which preceded it, the absorption of gold rose to 52 millions, or 65 per cent of the year's output for the whole world; a mouthful which did something to stay her hunger since, in the year following, she took only 27 millions, or $33\frac{3}{4}$ per cent of the world production. Touching this matter of world production, if we take a slightly more extended view covering the last thirty years, we find that in that period the world produced 2,248 millions sterling of gold, of which India took 355, or an annual average of nearly twelve as against China and Egypt whose combined annual average was barely two.

Again, narrowing the field, we find that though in the few years preceding the war India absorbed an annual

* India, hungry for gold during a war in which every other form of value seemed to be tottering, must have been tantalised beyond measure by the barely concealed fact that our home Government lodged at Bombay the whole of each annual gold output of South Africa destined for the Bank of England, sooner than expose it to submarine perils on the homeward voyage. It accumulated to an immense sum.

average of only 10 to 20 per cent of the world's production, yet, of the last three years, the annual average has touched fifty.

This increasing tendency to absorb gold instead of silver is one of the most disquieting symptoms of the whole situation. It would seem as if the very vastness of the sums now being swallowed had grown unmanageable in its bulk, and had to be condensed into something more portable. Again, it is necessary to remind ourselves of the direct interest of civilisation in having at command a fluid supply of gold wherewith to give value to its written promises. Also, here or hereabouts, we may take notice of the existence of a large and clamant group of Indian politicians who, in season and out of season, shrill to the skies the cry that we English are exploiting India for our own selfish ends, and are impoverishing it.

Now, are we to panic ? Are we to foresee a day when India will own all the gold in the world—a broody hen sitting on the whole egg supply of the farmyard, though hatching nothing, while England stands outside the coop with a stick, to keep off intruders ? Not so. Of the localisation of gold we know more now than we did before the war, since it is chiefly held by central banks and is not in circulation. We therefore know that, at the moment of writing, the world's surface, less India, owns 4,923 million sterling of the metal, of which 2,137 million is in coin. So that even though India may steadily be eating into the annual 80 million increase, it will take her a long time to eat as far into the margin as to bring the danger-point into imminent view. When, of course, that happens, we shall have to look round for something short, sharp, and rather heavy, and apply it to her ; but till then we may sleep in our beds.

How, now, is this all hoarded ?   Whither does it all go ?

The traditional hole in the ground may exist, in the case of the under-dog cultivator, taking the place of the stocking in the chimney in a land which possesses neither ; but the idea of holes, with the grades above him, may be scouted. Possibly the medieval ghettos of Europe, to whose conditions the modern Indian bazaar closely approximates, could have given us a few hints on the subject.   One thing, however, is certain.   Little, if any, of the wealth goes into banks or into the keeping of white man's commerce.   The hoarder trusts nobody ; though an elaborate network of inter-shroff credit exists.   Each knows the other, his caste brother, personally or by name.   It is possible to get a letter of credit on any other shroff, however distant.   The writer, travelling once from Assam to embark for home at Bombay, and being unwilling to carry a large sum on so long a journey, applied to an inconsiderable local merchant for a *húndi* in exchange for his rupees.   He got what looked like a Coptic love-letter written on rose-coloured tissue paper in a script designedly cryptic, the bulk of which probably conveyed a lot of mixed local commercial information and held in its body some such offhand remark as ' give this dog five hundred rupees '.   Two shroffs in Bombay saw it before it was handed to its addressee ; both offered to cash it on sight.

Does this argue against an absence of trust ?   Within the strict limits of the shroff fraternity, yes ; but, in their case, one remembers the old Indian dictum that ' dog doesn't eat dog '.

The corollary may have occurred to him whose patience has carried him thus far that, with all this carpet of wealth under its feet, the Government of India must be fabulously rich ? Surely it takes its share ?

The income of India's Government is mainly derived from a multiplication of tiny sums obtained as land-tax from the cultivators, who form four-fifths of the population. Income tax is collected from the incomes of white men, of Government servants, of white trading concerns. But income tax is difficult to levy in a land where the native refuses to put his money into discoverable circulation ; where, in fact, he may be said to have possessions but no income. You cannot tax him on his visible possessions, since he keeps these down to a minimum. Attempt a tax on his house ; he will prove to you, by bell and by book, that it belongs to his wife's second cousin. Examine his books—of which he is credibly reported to keep two sets, one for use and one for inspection—and the inevitable conclusion at which you will arrive is that he is running his business, year in, year out, at a loss ; even though his profits on his last twelvemonth of trading, alone, may have made him worth his worthless weight in straight shining coin.* If there be gold and silver in the shape of ornaments, or in jewels, these are hidden behind the purdah where no man may venture, or are so mixed up in inter-family ownership that the tangle is inextricable and

* To those who like skylarking with figures, it may be of interest to know that a well-grown man of 11 stone weighs 5,989 rupees and four annas. A millionaire in rupees (and there are many such, up and down the land) will thereupon weigh 167 men, or, say, five full platoons of infantry. Should Dives, however, prefer himself in terms of gold sovereigns, he will reduce his fighting strength to 108 men and a bit. He may object to this translation, being by nature non-combatant ; whereupon we may comfort him with the assurance that he is worth the weight of three regimental brass bands plus one bass drum, four pairs of cymbals, and an E-flat clarinet.

the possessor unidentifiable. Bateman has yet to draw for us the picture of a Hindu filling in a return for income tax, and Heath Robinson a machine for extracting it.

Other means of touching the deadweight of stuff are barred by modern civilisation. The most effective means disappeared with the dentistry appliances of King John, and cannot now be revived. At any rate, by a civilised Government. Though there *are* Governments which. . . . H'm.

Well, now ; granted that all this is, apart from a definitely sordid aspect, a drawback to human prosperity, is there no remedy ? Cannot India be made to disgorge ?

The Lord forfend. That would be catastrophe indeed. If the floodgates were, by any conceivable means, opened and the tide let loose, the resulting stream would so cheapen both metals as to make them all but valueless in a world which depends on their value. It would, indeed, result in the wiping off of all international debts, but only because the nations would thenceforth be in danger of having no coin of any value whatever to offer, each to each. An immense sum in gold could probably be absorbed by the United States wherewith to enlarge the backing of her ever-increasing commercial prosperity and the paper which covers it. But the silver ; goodness knows to what extent the silver would cheapen ; the imagination boggles. For one thing, the Government of India, which, after the Indian people, is the largest holder of silver in the world, would be very hard hit.

The real remedy would seem to lie not in disgorging, but in the prevention of future engorging. It is difficult to see how this can be brought about, since it presupposes that India will, in future, take goods instead of bullion, will invest her money in straightforward commerce and in banks, and will trust her fellow-man with her money. Counsels, alas, of perfection. How far she is from these three conditions precedent, let those say who know India.

In many lands rich or over-rich, one of the first evidences of the glut is seen in the development of the æsthetic. It is as though Nature were taking her own line in a corrective reaction from the surfeit. The arts of Byzantium, of Florence, Genoa, Venice, bring us by traceable cause and effect to our most precious possessions, which are even today finding a new home across the Atlantic. By all logic, therefore, we might expect Hinduism to show such artistic perception, such an expression of the beautiful as would, commensurably with its overflowing riches, surpass all other art.

Yet we find, throughout India, that art, from architecture down to illuminated manuscripts, is the sphere of the Moslem to the definite exclusion of the Hindu ; and that even in his religious representations, where you would expect any art to come to the surface, the Brahman's gods and godlings have a claim to popular respect that is purely, and for the most part lamentably, physical.

Such Hindu æsthetic feeling as there is has stopped short at that elementary expression of the artistic which we find in the most primitive races, and which is based on the desire for ornament. In this, the cult of precious stones is engrained in human beings as the simplest aspect of the æsthetic. The wealth-hoards of India have, for thousands of years, largely been expended on gems ; and these, as they now are, not only form an integral part of the accumulated riches of the country, but by their shape, grouping, and setting often give a rough clue to the date at which the accumulations began. This, to all appearances, was in the remotest ages; the types of setting are often distinctly anterior to those synchronous with the old Norse and Celtic jewellery, and the blunt-looking practical ornaments of the Merovingians. The gamut of types ranges from very distant times down to today, and is characterised throughout by a flashiness far removed from what we Westerners would accept as good taste. This jewellery has always been the apanage of the ruling classes, if only because rich and striking personal adornment was a political necessity in the presence of subjects whose very soul lay in money and its outward evidences; a race so miserly in nature that, to this day, it has no verbal equivalent for our two simple expressions of spiritual generosity—" I'm sorry " (for fault admitted), and " Thank you ". To this race the ruler who forbore ostentation had already joined the ranks of the under-dog who had something worth looting, and concealed it under a humble exterior, thereby travelling half the road to abdication.

But this Eastern æstheticism, expressed in outward display, is still very elementary. India which, since the opening up of the new worlds, has ceased to be the source of precious stones, still absorbs them largely; but, as is well known, the stones she takes are in a large proportion those flawed, ill-cut, or defective in colour which are debarred from the markets of the West. Let them but glitter, let them be of a piece with the glass chandeliers, coloured glass balls, gilt mirrors and other gimcrack adjuncts of what are often noble palaces and a stately pageantry of demeanour, and their buying is assured.

Stones ill-cut, stones hardly cut at all, lest a portion of their bulk be lost; stones looking like oysters set in soft gold, depending for their value on their deadweight of substance; these you may find in myriads in the heaped treasuries, the accumulation of uncounted years. For it is a fact that from the beginnings of written history down to the discovery of the new worlds in the sixteenth century every gem of which we have any conspicuous record has come from India. Setting aside that well-known activity in the world of precious stones which has always accompanied the uprising of any famous beauty in history, from Cleopatra down to her namesake de la Mérode, there has been a steady westward stream of historical gems each of which has a place in the chronicles and each of which, being indestructible, will continue to be the centre of events till the end of time. The diamonds of Golconda, the rubies and sapphires of Burma, the pearls from Ceylon and from Bahrein, any and every precious gaud with the single exception of the emerald, all came to us from the East tucked into the waistbelt of the traveller along the camel route.

Of some of the names we hardly need reminding. Of the diamond, that stone which Pliny describes as ' the most valuable of gems, known only to kings ', we know the Koh-i-Noor, the Orloff, the Pitt, the Great Mogul, the Darya-i-Noor, the Nizam, the Taj-i-Mah, the Baroda, Tavernier's blue diamond, the ill-omened Hope, and a dozen others. The procession becomes tedious. They are of all weights from 787 carats * down to 40 ; from the size of a moderate paper-weight to that of a pear-drop, from clearest sparkling white to a full rich green. Some are in the treasuries of kings, some have suddenly vanished ;

* He who, in common with the large number of us, is unaccustomed to visualise bulk in terms of carats, may be reminded that if he walks down Bond Street and sees displayed in a jeweller's window a single magnificent diamond set as a solitaire in a ring, and priced at £350, the weight of that stone will be—as near as makes no matter—three carats.

some belonged to kings who will never be kings again. Some are mild in nature, starting from warrantable trove and passing by fair purchase from hand to hand; some seem to gather to themselves blood and violence at every step; so ill-omened are some that the owner, however legitimately he may have come by his possession, is dogged to the very last by crushing misfortune.

Of the rubies, sapphires, pearls, and minor treasures of the East, there is no end. A list of historical names would be wearisome. But one shines out among them all, both for its size and for its history: the great balas ruby given to the Black Prince by King Pedro the Cruel, irregular in shape, rounded *en cabochon*, of an angry blood-red, and flaming as the centre of Queen Victoria's crown.

Each and every stone of the galaxy is indestructible. Each, already infinitely old, will still be accumulating history and the strenuous passions of men ten thousand years hence. Things of wonder they may be, but, in all humility let us say it, thank God you and I do not possess a single one of them.

But there are those of other mind, those to whom ostentation is not only a personal joy but a necessity of their position. Endowed, by the accumulations through the centuries behind them, with the power of gratifying it to an unbelievable extent, there are occasions when the kings, kinglets, and other inheritors of riches unlock the treasure chambers and bring to light the things of which the brown masses speak with bated breath.

The writer's most vivid recollection is that of a scene at a historic Durbar, that of Lord Curzon in early 1903. This, an even more gorgeous display than that for our King in 1911, was packed with every notable throughout the land whose position or possessions could add to the éclat of what was a twentieth-century Field of the Cloth of Gold. The festivities culminated in a levée held in the Dewan-i-Am of Delhi Fort, a Moslem hall apparently less the work of stone-masons than of jewellers, and to this day a place of pilgrimage for the traveller.

Into this marbled fairyland were packed civil and military officers, rajahs, maharajahs, nawabs, princelings, Rai Bahadurs, Rai Sahibs—the skimmings of the cream-bowl of the great Indian Empire. Literally packed, for the great hall could barely hold the press, since a tiny circle was with difficulty kept free about the steps of the dais where Viceroyalty sat enthroned. Kitchener, in mid-sea, projected head and shoulders, even as he stooped to courteous conversation with two Japanese officers in their undecorated blue full-dress. Knights were there from England, the jewelled Garter hardly discernible where legs stood as thickly as larch-poles. Dotted here and there and in clumps shone the blue and gold of civil uniforms, the blaze of gold-laced politicals, the broad splashes of unrelieved scarlet where stood the soldiers. All these were foreign to the land and incidents only in such a wealth of pink and blue and mauve, of filmy white and dull purple, in colours shot and striped and, be it almost said, ring-straked, as the dreams of the Maker of the Rainbow could hardly have conceived. Through the air, heavy with jasmine scent, glittered and twinkled every dart of light which could emanate from jewellery.

The Indian part of the concourse ranged from stately nobles of immemorial ancestry down to the *bunniah* who had appeared in the latest birthday honours, for the *nouveaux arrivés* are no more unknown in India than they are with us ; and it was noticeable that personal ostentation varied in inverse ratio with breeding and lineage, for the ennobled shopkeeper class seemed to be the one which carried the greater number of king's ransoms strung about it.

Ropes of pearls there were; not the ropes as we know them, where a moderate fortune may hang in one, or at most three, curves round the neck of elderly femininity. But here were literally festoons of the precious things, ranging in size from a pea to the frankly incredible, varying in ill-assorted colour from the purest white to a sickly pink, strung all ways, worn anyhow, as long as the wearer might display them; not, indeed, from necks tall and gracious which they might well and fittingly have adorned, the necks of personable women, but hung and hung and hung again from jowly male throats, round moist dewlaps; close-packed, down and down in row after row till they echeloned out on to the waist-line.

Jewels of every shape, size, and colour stuck about wherever they could stick. Sewn on, patched on, tied and threaded, they glittered everywhere, while nodding aigrettes gave a finish to the *coup de théâtre*.

Through it all the eternal slipshodness of the East leapt to the eye. For the whole glittering pageant was obviously and childishly insecure; not, indeed, in danger from snatching or burglary, but insecure with the slovenliness of a race to whom a serviceable knot, a safe clasp, or even a sound carpenter's hinge are things of neither use nor understanding. Fear of theft, indeed, there must have been; for next to us in the crush stood a queer pair; the owner of the spoil, unreservedly parvenu, who was manifestly the real thing; and, pressing close on him, one who had obviously been chosen for his close likeness to his master; dressed in exactly similar raiment, he wore such a travesty of gimcrack imitation jewellery as would hardly have deceived a child. Every stone, every pearl, closely imitating that of his master, might well have emerged from a cracker. A soapstone sword-hilt hung askew from the top of a patently empty scabbard, aping the purest jade of the Rai Sahib's original. But, balancing it on the right-hand side, a weighty short-barrelled service revolver dragged into untidy folds the muslin trousers' pocket which failed to conceal it. Here was the buffer between the master and sudden misfortune; here the stalking horse. Here was the one to be mistaken for the original, and his shoddy snatched at while the real thing dodged; and imagination boggled at the thought of what would have happened had that very serviceable revolver been drawn and fired, in a moment of panic, through that packed Golconda.

The insecurity of pearls threaded on silk never renewed and rotting in the Indian heat was, a moment afterwards, apparent. Two yards away, suddenly and without any warning, one of the milky festoons burst asunder, and the precious things pattered and hailed on the marble floor. Ah, then indeed was Bedlam; sixteen stone of panic sank to the floor, squeaking short yelps of dismay while it grabbed and patted and scrambled for every elusive sphere; legs parted, as far as legs might in that crush; curious eyes searched and tried to help; but not a soul stooped to pick up a gaud, lest the owner should think him to have given back one where two had been collected. Sobbing and distraught, the owner rose at last, and thrust a fistful of trove deep into a baggy pocket which, in the sequence of native probabilities, inevitably had an un-darned hole in it.

Later in the evening it was our privilege to see a young magnifico courting disaster. Hospitality stood open-handed at a long buffet near the door, where liquids popped and gurgled, and all might drink who wished or who could elbow a way to reach a glass. This youth had evidently been a winner, nor could he possibly have realised the potency of what he had won; for just as long as the crush buttressed him, the roseate delusion upheld him; and as he, backing outwards, reached comparative freedom, his luck held good; it gave him a wall against which to prop himself. Leaning against this in his last conscious moments, he slid and pawed his way along to the outer air. Fortunately for him all steps had been eliminated, and a smooth gentle slope led down to the exit. With muslins and jewellery pulled into converging lumps, and a diamond aigrette sagging from a turban half-adrift, this tottering Crœsus felt his way to what he must have seen as a multiple doorway. Here stood two magnificent Sikhs of the Bodyguard; sentries. We saw one of them prop his pennoned lance against the fretted lintel and, with a good-humoured grin, catch up the wanderer under the armpits, lifting him clear of the floor. Without a moment's afterthought, he carried him bodily to the entrance of the main courtyard, and " *hai-ee-e, gharrywán!* " he shouted. An ordinary bazaar tumtum drove up from the outer darkness. Into it the Sikh bundled his burden and slammed the door, laughing up at the barefoot urchin on the box.

" Where to ? "

" *I* dunno. Better take him down to the bazaar and ask! "

Did the wanderer arrive bereft of half his jewellery? Or with none? One doubts it. Rather does the vision arise of the driver carting his unconscious burden from pillar to post through the night for hours on end, till someone, anyone, took delivery; and then of the age-long haggle with the consignee for twice the proper fare—in annas. Honesty ? Not a bit. Rather the *idée fixe* of one whose mind runs for ever on the tiny fruits of extortion, missing, in its stride, lifelong wealth sprawling on the cushions.

Is the picture overdrawn ? On the faith of a scribe, every word and syllable of it is true ; and the recollection of much besides must retreat into the background, lest it crowd the canvas.

" Well—of course India is rich. We all know that. So why make such a song about a unique occasion ? " And yet one must remember the countless minor wealth-hoarders who were not bidden to the feast ; they whose aggregate possessions far overtopped even the hereditary treasuries of the upper classes. One must remember that for all the deadweight of barbaric riches hung and plastered about the gathering, no single member of it but left at home ten times what he could carry on him. Hardly one of them but could say, " Take me and put me on the scales. Add my sons, and my sons' many mothers. Heap up the balance till it will hold no more. Then pour my treasury on to the other side—and watch the weighbeam! "

The prosperity brought by the white man, say you ? The wealth which has grown up under a secure Raj ? When our forefathers were trotting about these woods, clothed in blue tattooing and little else, India went stately, in silks and fine raiment.

India, tired and sleepy with the weight of wealthy ages behind her. India, the shrinking prey of every invader, till the English came and, with fearless honesty and fairness, secured to each in the land the snug possession of all that he had and of all that he might acquire.

To Asia at large, and to those most particularly and hereditarily Asiatic, the Soviet, we English are the only barrier between them and the unlimited power which would come with taking this boundless wealth.

The Soviet have learnt in China the lesson which Attila learnt in Europe—the inconvertibility of fluid and legitimate wealth. The rebound towards India's static and lootable hoards is as inevitable as the human sequence of established history. The old tradition is as deeply engrained in the East as is hunger, or thirst, or the love of women. India; the treasure-house of the world.

Something there, beyond the Passes !

Hsh, comrade ; something there !

Will you come with me, and look ?

[November 1928

8

KUH-I-SIM, THE TREASURE OF TURKESTAN

P. S. Nazaroff

Many years ago, when still a student, I was engaged on a geological expedition in the Kirghiz Steppe, far from any dwelling or *aul* of the nomads. One late autumn day a snowstorm overtook me. The wind blew in gusts of great violence, and obliterated the path; the tired horses could hardly move their legs. Faced with the disagreeable prospect of passing the night in the steppe, and even, perhaps, of freezing to death, I asked my guide, a Kirghiz, " Which is the way now ? Where can we find shelter ? "

" If we push on, *Khudai khalasa*—that is, if God wills —towards evening we may reach Hazret, and there we shall find a comfortable shelter and a good reception. He has a big stone house; there is not another like it in the steppe, and Hazret is a very learned holy man. It will be nice for you to meet him," replied the man.

With great difficulty late at night we succeeded in reaching Hazret's home. His medium-sized stone house stood on the banks of a stream in a small copse, a great rarity in the treeless steppe.

I had already heard of this Hazret, a learned mulla who enjoyed an immense influence among the Kirghiz,

161

who related many tales of his wisdom, learning, and sanctity, and so was very glad of an opportunity of meeting him.

I was still more glad when I went into a bright, clean, warm, nice room, the best in the house, which was placed at my disposal. In it there was no furniture at all; it was entirely hung with and spread with splendid Bukhara carpets, and the walls bulged with satin rugs and cushions. How good it was to stretch oneself after ten hours in the saddle, and after the cold of the blizzard to drink boiling hot tea and satisfy one's hunger with a splendid *pilau*, prepared as only they know how who have lived in Bukhara the Noble, 'Bukhará-i-Sherif'.

Hazret received me very kindly. "Live with me as long as you like," he said, "and as soon as the fine weather comes, then I will give you guides and fresh horses, and you can ride straight through to Djaman Kalá."

He was indeed an interesting man. A Kirghiz, son of a rich father, with a thirst for knowledge, he had gone as a young man to Bukhara, the seat of Mohammedan learning. There he had lived as a student in the *medress* or university for eighteen years, and then performed the *haji* to Mecca, travelling on horseback through Afghanistan and Persia. He was now living quietly among his own people, reaping the fruits of his wisdom. He produced on me the impression of a medieval scholiast, crystallised in his opinions. It was curious to hear his account, for instance, of Bukhara, which he quite sincerely considered the most learned and enlightened city in the world.

"Everywhere light comes down from above, but in Bukhara it arises from the ground," he said, repeating the boastful assertion of the mullas of the city.

"In Holy Bukhara you may learn all knowledge, all sciences which are available for mankind," he said.

" And what did you learn in the *medress* at Bukhara ? "
I asked him.

" Moslem law, historical books, the philosophy of Aflatun,
the works of Abu ibn Sina, geography, and the Arabic
language in which all these things are set forth."

This was the scope of Moslem teaching, and I recognised
in unfamiliar guise the names of Plato and of Avicenna,
the famous geographer who lived in Khiva in the eleventh
century and became an authority in medieval Europe.

" Yes," he continued, " I will show you some of my
books," and he brought and laid open on the carpet some
old tomes in ancient leather bindings.

" These," he explained, " are all very old and expensive
books. For this one alone I paid one hundred golden
till; it is nearly a thousand years old, and by it I learnt
geography."

I smiled to myself that he should pay such reverence,
and such a price, about £30, for this treatise on geography,
which, of course, did not include one hundredth part of
the world as we know it. I took the book, and at once
my glance fell on a large map showing the universe in the
form of a flat circle surrounded by a broad belt of ocean.
Northern Europe, the eastern half of Asia, and the greater
part of Africa did not exist. The outlines of all continents
and countries were distorted, and in the place of Great
Britain were shown the Isles of the Djinns.

I could hardly repress my smiles at the sight of such a
strange chart of the universe.

" Are Moscow and St Petersburg marked here ? " I
asked.

Hazret looked at the map and said, " No, these towns
are not shown."

" Well," I could not help answering, " what is the use

of a geography which does not show such important cities?"

"Here you will find shown rather Mohammedan countries," answered Hazret. "See, here is Bukhara and there is Samarkand."

"But where is Tashkend?" I asked.

"Tashkend is not there."

Then I could not help smiling.

"Well," I said, "what is the use of a treatise on geography like this? You cannot learn anything about the world from it; it is not worth anything," I exclaimed with a smile.

Hazret thought for a moment. It seemed to me as though a shadow of doubt in his own learning began to dawn in his crystallised Moslem brain.

"Well, you see," he began, after a little consideration, "I do not treasure so much what exists in the world today that is new. I value and am interested only in what existed in the days of old, at the time of the Prophet, whose name be blessed!"

"An answer worthy of a sincere orthodox fanatic," I thought to myself. In those days I was young and proud of my own knowledge won at the university. Many years later I understood my error and failure to appreciate the lore of this learned mulla and his love of the past.

Noticing some big town marked near Samarkand, I asked Hazret what it was.

"Oh, that is a large and very wealthy city, Tunkent, the capital of the Principality of Ilak; there is a great deal about it in this book," he said, brightening up.

"What does it say about Tunkent?" I asked, never having suspected the existence of such a town in Turkestan.

"See, here among these mountains," and he pointed

with his finger to a spot on the map, "is the most famous and richest silver mine in the world; here they quarried pure silver like so much rock. This mine belonged to the principality of Ilak, and in Tunkent they minted money and made various precious objects and works of art which circulated through the entire world in exchange for different kinds of merchandise, which came into Tunkent from all lands. The town abounded in luxury, palaces, mosques, and for a long distance round was encircled by wonderful gardens."

"That must be what in old days they used to call Samarkand," I suggested.

"No, Tunkent was a totally different city and richer than Samarkand; in Samarkand there was only an Emir, who governed all Khorassan," replied Hazret.

"Look," he continued, "there is an immense and terrible cavern, to the end of which no one has yet penetrated. There is an underground river, and across the river a bridge, and on the far side there is a terrible dragon which guards the uncountable treasure of gold and precious stones. It kills everyone who ventures to go by."

"But that is only an old fable of ignorant folk in ancient days. You, as a learned man, you know yourself that nothing of the sort really exists," I tried to persuade him.

"No; this is truth," he answered. "I myself read in Mecca on the walls of the chief mosque an inscription about this same cavern, and pilgrims from Kokand told me that not long ago three Kirghiz who had returned from Mecca went into the cave to seek the treasure and never returned. Then their relatives collected, no less than forty men, all well armed, and went in to seek them, but they too never came back. After this the folk of the neighbourhood shut it up with stones, and covered the main entrance with earth. The learned Moslem Abu ibn Sina, who lived nine hundred years ago, describes this cave in detail in his book; it is called Khan-i-Gut—that is, the Mine of Destruction,—and he gives all instructions for prayers to read and for charms against the dragon should anyone want to go in and get the treasure."

I was no longer listening. Fatigued with my adventures, I was dozing into a slumber, and do not know what more Hazret went on to say about the cave and the treasures of Turkestan.

Many years after I was sorry that I had paid so little heed to those rare old books which Hazret showed me, that wise old connoisseur of the Arabic language and ancient Arabic literature. Fate willed that I should spend the best years of my life in Turkestan, seeking out its mineral wealth. I was the pioneer of the mining industry that was just beginning to bud.

The fame of Turkestan as a land rich in gold and other valuable and useful minerals was dissipated like smoke after the Russian occupation. The first prospecting expeditions by miners of the Urals and Siberia soon showed that the country was very poor. This opinion, too, was confirmed by the geological investigations of Professors Mushketoff and Romanovsky, and Turkestan for a long time ceased to attract attention in this respect.

My first researches into its geology, however, showed these opinions to be false. The more I investigated, the more and more convinced I became that Turkestan is no poorer than the Urals themselves in useful minerals, but, of course, the deposits do not occur near big towns or main highways of communication. Gold, silver, quicksilver, copper, lead and zinc, vanadium ores and wolfram, oil, coal and abundance of excellent iron ore, asbestos, and recently the discovery of radioactive ores and deposits of tin found by me would have enriched the country had circumstances been more favourable. Nature has given it, too, precious gem stones, abundance of marble, and lithographic stone.

Apart from the richness and variety of this mineral wealth, I was struck by the remains of ancient workings, with tools of bronze and stone, that I met at every step. There are also workings of the recent past by the khans of Kokand, but the greater part of the old mines, in places with immense workings, belong undoubtedly to a very remote historical period, the golden age of prosperity and culture of Turkestan.

In one remote spot in the mountains were great hills of slag, covered with grass and scrub, the remains of extensive buildings, old shafts and underground galleries, and immense excavations in the rock, all converted by the lapse of time and action of earthquakes into natural caverns, the walls of which were already covered with a coating of calcareous matter, and here and there from the roof there hung big stalactites. It required a very experienced eye and careful investigation to recognise the work of men's hands, and to see what ores had been worked and from which spots. It was remarkable, too, that in many such mines the chief seams and entrances of the adits and shafts had been artificially sealed, cemented over, and very carefully masked. To the eye of the layman they were simply caverns and natural grottoes. To this concealment nature had added screes, falls of rock, bushes, and trees.

A rich and highly developed mining industry had flourished in this place; the spot had once teemed with life, and been such a hive of industry as can be seen today in England and parts of Belgium. Then suddenly all life ceased; something happened and converted the flourishing industrial district into a desert.

Whatever it was it had happened not abruptly nor unexpectedly, and the miners had had time to make their preparations and conceal their wealth from other and hostile eyes until happier days should return, such as, for this unhappy country, never arrived.

The cavern called Khan-i-Gut, about which Hazret had talked so much, turned out to be well known and had been often explored. In the days of the khans they had sent condemned prisoners, promising them life and pardon if they made their way through to the end and returned to report what they had found in the recesses of the cavern, but not one had ever come back.

The Russians, too, had made several attempts to explore it, but each time some difficulty had stopped them.

That entrance which now opens into the cave leads into a huge open cavity, at the edge of underground abysses, into immense halls and chambers and deep wells, and finally to an underground river. The air in the cave is very pure, it is excellently ventilated, and there are no traces of dead bodies. Inside there is a spring of splendid pure water, remains of old wooden bridges and timbering of wood that has not rotted, of the juniper known locally as 'argi' (*Juniperus pseudosabina*). But strong nerves are wanted to wander about the narrow and slippery paths over dark and sombre precipices, glittering evilly in the flickering light of a magnesium flare, or white glare of an acetylene lamp.

It was easy enough to see in the endless chambers and passages, to go through all of which would take days, an old mine. A part of these great cavities was made by nature and part by the long-continued work of men's hands through centuries. The regular methodical workings were there, the timbering, the deep shafts, with appliances for going down and coming up, though only a monkey could use them one would think ; in places, over steep or vertical descents down marble cliffs, were artificially cut rings for the attachment of ropes.

The path is covered with the dust of ages ; when this dust is removed a bright marble floor is revealed, polished by hundreds of bare feet that had walked over it in the course of centuries, smooth as the marble of ancient statues. There are astonishing, long, pipe-like holes, drilled in some unaccountable manner through the hard rock by the hand of man.

In the cavern there is a very rich silver-lead ore, galena, and gold ore. There is zinc ore, but if that was worked it was only for medicine.

After exploring the recesses of the cavern for two days I came to the conclusion, from various signs, that the air inside was rich in radioactive emanations. A scientific expedition which explored the cave before the Great War confirmed my opinion, and proved that the air inside is strongly radioactive. At the northern foothill of the mountains where Khan-i-Gut is situated, in a lovely spot where there is the tomb of a holy man, the Hodja-i-Tahraut, is a spring of beautiful water forming a green oasis among the barren mountains. This place is considered by the natives to be miracle-working, and they come in thousands to the tomb of the holy man to drink the wonder-working water, which showed upon investigation to be highly charged with radium emanation.

In the big mountain Kara Tau, above the tomb, there has been found pitchblende.

Another strange mine interested me very much. I came across it by chance in a wild and remote part of the Turkestan mountains, in an isolated, shut in, desert valley. What struck me in this valley was the fact that, in spite of its inaccessibility, everything in it gave the impression of a remote life long since passed, and activity of man, who left his traces everywhere on every side, but traces already planed over and masked by time and nature.

It was possible to go through the valley only on horse-back, and that with difficulty, yet in it, from below to the top of a lofty mountain, there went in zigzags a broad carriage road, admirably laid out. Now it is all grown over with herbage and trees. This road leads to the ancient workings, which are very numerous and extensive : a part has collapsed, another is covered with falls of rock due to earthquakes. In the main workings, which look like an immense cathedral, the floor was covered with a thick layer of blue guano and covered with huge boulders that had fallen from the roof. But the galleries were entire, astonishing, broad, admirably cut out of the hard marble, and blind—that is, they led nowhere. All pointed to extensive workings through the course of centuries, all on an 'industrial capitalistic' scale.

After attentive examination of the falls, slag, and work-ings, I clearly saw that here silver had been worked and some other metals. But the veins themselves, the actual ore, and the ends of the galleries had been carefully sealed and artificially masked.

A layman would find it difficult to discover the spot where the main ore body occurs and where work might be resumed. For specialists I will say that this mine belongs to the so-called 'contact-metamorphic' type, such as occurs also in the Banat of the Danube plains.

On examining this ancient mine, the question kept arising in my mind, Who worked these ores ? To what historical period do they belong ? What kind of people were they ? And when was this extensive mining industry developed in this now forgotten and almost inaccessible valley, an industry that is now extinct, and whither did the output go ?

Of course, it could not be the work of the present inhabitants of the country, the Sarts, with their very low level of technical knowledge and their indolence. And, too, their character and devotion to agriculture and stock-breeding are quite opposed to the idea of an intensive mining activity.

They remember former workings, but the winning of iron and copper in the days of the khans was of a very primitive character, and the natives discriminate these quite clearly from the ancient mines on a grand scale such as I have described. These, they invariably say, were worked by the Chinese, which is out of the question.

About the time of my tale there was found in Samarkand an ancient astronomical observatory, once the property of Ulug Beg, grandson of Tamerlane, a famous learned man of the Middle Ages. A Table of the Stars drawn up by him has significance even today for astronomers. He is the author of that very true sentence often repeated in his writings : ' The study of nature unites mankind, but philosophy and religion disunite.' How truly the history of the twentieth century confirms his words of wisdom !

When looking at this observatory I met a Russian archaeologist who had paid great attention to the history of Turkestan. He asked me if I had ever come across, in my geological expeditions in the mountains, any ancient silver mines.

" Why do you ask ? " I asked in turn.

171

"You see," he explained, "we are naturally not interested in the actual mines, but in their position on the map, as according to ancient Arabian guidebooks we might be able through these mines to determine the position of seven ancient cities of Turkestan which have now disappeared, and, above all, the situation of the town of Tunkent, capital of the principality of Ilak. We hope to find there a good deal of very interesting antiquarian remains of the pre-Mohammedan period of Turkestan and of the first centuries of the rule of the Arabs."

"This mine," he went on to say, "was called Kuh-i-Sim, which in Persian means the Mountain of Silver, or the Silver Peak. In its day it supplied the whole Moslem world with silver, and also Russia. In the Hermitage in St Petersburg there are quite a number of coins dug out of old stores in central and even northern Russia, with inscriptions that they were struck from silver from Kuh-i-Sim in the city of Tunkent."

I then remembered Hazret, and told him about this learned Kirghiz and his old books.

"Yes, indeed," said my friend, "those were certainly very rare books; a pity that you did not pay more attention to them and did not note the titles and names of the authors."

"Yes," he went on, "in Bukhara there are still a fair number of rare old books and manuscripts, but the local mullas value them very highly and conceal them from Europeans."

All this interested me so much that I resolved to take up the study of the history of Turkestan. In the Imperial Public Library of St Petersburg there was a splendid edition of De Gué, *Bibliotheca Geographica Arabicorum*, but its Arabic text was a closed book to me. Luckily, such Arab writers and geographers as Idrissi, Istakhri, Ibn Khaukal, Ibn Khoroat Bek, and Abulfeda are available partly or entirely in translation into some European language. These writers opened my eyes about Turkestan, which I, like many others, thought was a ' new country ', only recently discovered and opened up to culture and civilisation ; that it had hitherto been only a sombre, strange, wild, Asiatic barbarism. It entered my head that the soil of Turkestan contained traces of a high civilisation when the nations of Europe were savages, and in the forests of Russia, in the expression of the old chronicler, men lived ' in the manner of beasts '.

Already in the seventh century, before the arrival of the Arab conquerors in Turkestan, the country was far ahead of the states of Europe in civilisation. The Arabs found the town of Samarkand rich, and in the highest degree prosperous. It had, for instance, a water supply, which through lead pipes gave the citizens a splendid drinking water from springs in the mountains ; the beautiful and luxurious gardens and the streets of Samarkand were watered and irrigated by a special system of canals. I will remark in passing that neither Samarkand nor Tashkent, capital of Turkestan, has any water supply today, and the inhabitants are obliged to drink water from filthy wells or stinking gutters.

In the time of the summer heat the poor inhabitants of ancient Samarkand were supplied with ice free of payment, a luxury which is unknown today even in Europe !

The open places in the city were ornamented with huge bronze statues of horses, bulls, camels, dogs, etc. The chief religion at that time was the teaching of Zoroaster, Mazdeism, which inspired love and respect to animals, especially domestic, among which the dog held the first place, as the chief companion of man given him by Ahura Mazda for the protection of his family, home, and flocks, as is set forth in the hymn of the Zend Avesta composed in honour of the dog. Confirmation of the truth of these assertions is afforded by the bronze foot of a camel found in a water-channel at Dirhan, near Samarkand, and now preserved in the Tashkent Museum, unless it has been stolen by Bolshevik commissaries, as is their wont.

The town of Samarkand was full of temples, not only of the Zoroastrians but also of Buddhists, Manichaeans, and Nestorian Christians, for at that time in Turkestan there was full religious liberty. The Arab conquerors of Turkestan were not destroyers; Islam was introduced gradually and its acceptance accompanied by sundry privileges, such as the giving of money payments for going to the mosques.

For this reason in the ninth, tenth, and eleventh centuries the country reached a very high degree of prosperity and wealth, which it has never since been able to attain. This was the time when the dynasty of the Samanids, founded by Said Nazar, governed Turkestan. The Samanids were distinguished by their love of culture and education, and very properly soon became Emirs, quite independent of the caliphs of Baghdad. Their rule extended not only over the present area of Turkestan, but also over the northern portion of Persia and Afghanistan. All this district then bore the name of Khorassan. Commerce and industry flourished in the land.

In Samarkand excellent paper was made from the bark of the mulberry tree, and the glass made there was famed throughout the world. The Chinese emperor sent a special embassy to Samarkand to request the Emir to send skilled craftsmen to China to make glass.

It was famous, too, for its silks. According to tradition a Chinese princess who married an Emir of Samarkand secretly hid in her hair and brought with her some silk-worm eggs to Samarkand, and thus started the silk industry in the country. The Chinese jealously guarded the secret of their silks, and the exportation of the eggs was an offence punished with death.

In the mountains life hummed. The smoke of the smelting furnaces mounted to the heavens ; iron was poured forth, and copper and lead and silver ; gold was won and quicksilver ; there have been found remains of stone apparatus for the amalgamation of gold and silver ; gems and precious stones were won.

Coalmining began in this country four centuries earlier than in Europe.

All these descriptions of the old Arab geographers strike the reader by their circumstantial accuracy ; they are useful even today as guides, for those who know how to read them. They say, for instance, writing about a certain colliery, that the ash from the coal was useful for bleaching tissues. This seems strange, but an analysis which I made of the ash showed that it contains zinc, so that evidently the ancients made zinc white out of it. The Arabs also praise the tin of Turkestan for its purity, although this metal was totally unknown in the country until I came across an easily smelting tin-ore. When I was being hunted by the ' rule of workmen and peasants ', and hid myself in the mountains, I stumbled on a deposit of topaz, sapphires and rubies.

The commercial relations of Turkestan in those days were very wide. Its iron, famed for its purity, and its *bulat*, or steel, was sent as far as Damascus, and formed the blades that gave that ancient city its fame. Turkestan was always, and still is, famous for its melons. These, packed in ice in boxes of lead, were sent by courier express to the table of the caliphs of Baghdad, surely the first recorded instance of the export of perishable fruit in cold storage.

The Arab writers paid special attention to the silver mine mentioned above, Kuh-i-Sim, and to the town of Tunkent.

If we collate all data arising from Arabic sources, I am convinced that the remarkable silver mine discovered by me is the famous Kuh-i-Sim. Down to the smallest detail everything points to it. Even the statement that not far from the mouth of the river of the silver mine there is an observatory corresponds to facts. I used often to visit this mine, and every time was more and more convinced of its identity and its remarkable richness. I always postponed a detailed investigation and survey till a more suitable occasion, which, alas, has never arisen.

This highly developed civilisation, this vigorous industrial, and commercial life, these flourishing cities, and smiling gardens, all were swept away by a wave of barbarians, nomads who came out of the east, the wild hordes of Genghis Khan. The infusion of Mongolian blood and the material ruin of the country led to the intellectual decay of the population. Only for a short time under Tamerlane and his immediate descendants did Turkestan attain any degree of civilisation again, but this also swiftly passed away.

Islam, once it became the dominant religion, turned a spiritual culture into savage fanaticism and hatred of unbelievers. This state of affairs lasted till the occupation of the country by Russia. It was on the very eve of this conquest that the two English travellers, Stoddard and

Connolly, died a martyr's death in Bukhara by the orders of the Emir Muzaffar Eddin.

The rapidity of the spiritual decadence of the population is illustrated by the following incident. In Samarkand was found the original surveying instrument used for making plans by the old surveyors. Its design is so convenient and practical that it was seriously proposed to put it on the market as a modern pattern. It bore an inscription which is admirably preserved, to the effect that it was made in Samarkand by such and such a craftsman. But neither in Samarkand nor in Bukhara today can be found a single native, even among the learned mullas, who could explain the significance and use of this instrument.

I was also lucky enough to find the site of the ancient capital of the principality of Ilak, the city of Tunkent.

It was a wintry blizzard on the Kirghiz Steppe that drove me by sheer chance to make the acquaintance of Hazret, from whom I first heard of Tunkent. By an odd chance it was also through a snowstorm on the steppes of Turkestan that I fell upon the spot where once upon a time stood the proud and prosperous city.

It happened in the following manner :

After a very successful day's boar shooting I sent my man home with the half a dozen pig that I had killed, and proceeded to spend the night on the steppe in an *aul* of Kirghiz. Next morning before sunrise I was off again, calculating that a couple of hours' ride would bring me to a small caravanserai on the road where I could rest and break my fast. It was a cold morning and misty, a drizzle began which soon turned into a thick dry snow, and a strong cold wind sprang up from the north-east.

Riding against the wind was very difficult. The snow

covered the ground, and the wind hardened it. The snow hurt my face, covered my eyes. My hands were numbed, but still my good horse pluckily struggled on, as it seemed to me, along the road.

Two hours passed thus; then three, four. But the familiar caravanserai did not appear in sight. The storm obscured vision, and I realised that I had strayed from the path and was riding in the wrong direction.

I peered round in the hope of finding some sort of shelter where I could stop and rest, get protection from the weather, and wait till the storm passed. I could not see more than ten or fifteen paces ahead. Everything was covered with a thick mantle of hard snow.

At length, unexpectedly there gradually appeared on the right the outline of something protuberant. I rode up to it, and found a piece of an old ruined wall forming an angle. This made a good shelter from the wind, and I made myself snug there with my horse, which was as glad as I to get into the lee from the blinding hurricane. Hooking the reins over my arm, I tucked myself right into the corner, rolled myself as tightly as possible in my coat, and fell asleep.

When I awoke, the storm had died down, and soon stopped altogether. The sky cleared, and I crept out of my shelter and climbed on to the wall to have a look round to try to pick up my direction.

What I saw caused me the greatest astonishment. For a long distance all round, as far as the eye could reach, there lay stretched out before me the plan of a great city of natural size, picked out in black lines against the white background. Whole streets were clearly marked: the sites of houses, buildings, irrigation canals, cisterns, towers, walls, and the city walls. The dry snow driven by the wind had filled in all depressions in the soil, throwing out into relief the protuberances, and thus marking out the town, which had at some remote time been razed to the ground.

In the summer, when the steppe is covered with grass, and in winter when it is all hidden beneath a monotonous greyish yellow uniform, these small depressions and elevations are not apparent; but now, when a mantle of snow, a rare occurrence in this part of Turkestan, covered the ground and the wind had planed it off, the plan of the ancient city, long since destroyed, lost and forgotten, appeared once more, like a photographic negative. It was an interesting, rare, and instructive sight.

The next morning the sun would melt the snow, and the wonderful plan again disappear. How sorry I was not to have a camera with me, or that I had not with me the means of making a sketch plan of it on a plane table, which would have been better still.

A long time I spent riding round the streets and parks of this ephemeral Pompeii, trying to imagine what it all signified, the meaning of this or that right angle or curve. It was strange how the city gates were shown. It looked just as though the foundations for a new town had been laid out.

Towards night I came to a large river, where I bivouacked in a hamlet. Home again, I carefully measured out on the map the distances and directions I had ridden, and looked up my notes from the old Arab writers. I came to the undoubted conclusion that this was the spot where once upon a time stood the mysterious city of Tunkent, whose momentary plan sketched in snow I had thus strangely gazed upon.

It may be asked, what was done with these discoveries of mine, of Kuh-i-Sim and of Tunkent?

My notes, plans, and manuscripts were taken by the Bolsheviks with all the rest of my property, and burnt by these 'agents of scientific Socialism'. During the hard winter of 1918-19, when I was hiding in the native *auls*, the Bolsheviks for some days fired their stoves with my papers and documents containing the results of my life's work, geological surveys, and prospects in Turkestan.

Kuh-i-Sim, hidden from the savage Mongol hordes, is hidden too from the barbarians of the north, who have wiped out the mining industry which was just beginning to bud in Turkestan. A heavy earthquake, some time before the war, has covered up and completely hidden the approaches to the mine; now there is to be seen only a mass of tumbled rock and stone.

[August 1929

9

THE LOST CITY OF MY QUEST

P. H. Fawcett

When Colonel Fawcett set out in 1925 on the expedition into the unexplored interior of Brazil from which he failed to return, he hoped to find a large ruined city of the remote past. In this article, written not long before his departure, he describes the original discovery of that city.

It is certain that amazing ruins of ancient cities—ruins incomparably older than those in Egypt—exist in the far interior of Matto Grosso, the vast and still largely unexplored inland state of Brazil. And here, for the first time in print, so far as I am aware, is the arresting story of the discovery in the year 1753 of one, presumably the greatest, of these. It was a chance discovery, made by a Portuguese expedition whose real business was treasure-seeking.

A century and a half and more previously, exceptionally rich gold, silver and diamond mines had been found in the interior of Brazil by Melchior Dias Moreya, a half-Portuguese, half-Indian soldier of fortune, who figures in the history of early colonisation under the name of Moribeca.

Enriched by his discoveries, Moribeca, about 1610, offered his silver mines to Don Pedro II in exchange for the title of Marques das Minas, stating that they would yield more silver than there was iron at Bilboa. But he was made the victim of petty deceit by the authorities, and becoming aware of this, he declined to give any information. They imprisoned him for two years without result, when on payment of nine thousand crowns he was released. He died in 1622 with his secret undisclosed. Blood and treasure were freely spent to discover the lost mines of Moribeca, until, as the historian says, a century and a half-failure dispelled the illusion of the existence of a new Potosi in Brazil.

In the year 1743 a native of Minas Geraes, whose name has not been preserved with his record, was fired by the ambition to discover these mines. It was no small matter to penetrate the wilderness. It is not today. His party consisted of himself, five Portuguese from Minas Geraes, some dozen Negro slaves, and a following of twenty to thirty Indians, small enough considering the risks and in comparison with the expeditions known as the Bandeirantes, which rarely numbered less than three hundred well-armed men. Animals were difficult to take or preserve through trackless country, and to feed upon the forest for perhaps years was a precarious matter demanding the endurance of real men. There were hostile Indians to face, and the exigencies of a climate which varied from cold to extreme heat and from drought to a deluge. But the blood of the Portuguese navigators ran in their veins, and neither wild beasts, venomous reptiles, disease, nor a paradise of the insect kingdom could deter these adventurers, bitten by the lure of the precious metals. Exactly where they went is conjectural, albeit it is known to two or three; roughly, it was to the north.

Their absence grew into months, the months into years.

In 1754 the remnant reappeared in the coastal region of the State of Bahia. This is their story:

Reduced by ten years of wandering in the wilderness, often completely lost but always enthusiastic in the search for gold, they were in 1753 feeling their way eastward towards the Atlantic coast. They had not discovered the silver mines of Moribeca. Such a quest in those days would be like looking for a needle in a haystack. For there were no maps or any knowledge of the interior, nor was there in the party anyone skilled in the art of navigation on land. They had lived as other forest pioneers lived, and must still live, upon fish, flesh and fowl secured mainly by the skill of an Indian following; sometimes upon maize and bananas from the plantations of the indigenes.

They had emerged from thick, dry and dense forest known as *catinga* on to grass pampas covered rather freely by short bush and with picturesque islands of palms and low trees, which gathered around the sources of a few streams. In front of them towered a lofty ridge whose jagged summit cut the sky in extravagant shapes. They were not ordinary mountains. In common with so much of the volcanic area of Brazil, they were extraordinarily rich in crystals and in that slightly opaque and glassy quartz which is so abundantly enriched by crystals of malachite, tourmaline and aquamarine.

It was after rain, and the glow of the setting sun in the west lit up the wet surface of the rocks into sheets of flame. Stars of red and yellow shot from the face of a thousand large crystals. The rocks seemed ablaze. Streams leaped from rock to rock, and over the exquisite scene the low arch of a brilliant rainbow seemed to indicate within the treasure-house of an empire. Small wonder that the report smacks of extravagant description. ' Could there be a better omen that we have found the lost mines of the great Moribeca ? *Vamos barracar.*' The party camped in extraordinary excitement.

In the morning the jagged rocks and abrupt cliffs, a black and grey mass obscuring the rising sun, somewhat damped their enthusiasm. With no little dismay the adventurers found everywhere abrupt unscalable precipices. All day they followed the foot of the cliffs, struggling over boulders and examining crevices, stepping warily, however, for the rattlers were numerous, and there was no remedy for the poison of the Brazilian species. The afternoon was well advanced when their leader called a halt. " For," said he, " we have marched three leagues to no consequence. It would be better to return to our old camp and seek a way northwards. What say you ? " The party agreed to camp and retrace their steps on the following day, casting glances of disappointment at the white rocks with their streaks of colour and glow of crystal. " *Logo !* away with you, José and Manuel, and *busca lenha*—wood for the fire —*pronto, amigos.*"

Manuel, half a mile away, gathering dry wood amongst the scrub, had almost secured an armful, when he espied the standing trunk of a small dead tree, the best of all for fires. He made his way towards it, and emerging from behind some bushes put to flight a stag, which disappeared round the corner of a cliff, its white tuft of a tail high in the air. " A white deer," he ejaculated, " *que sorte !* " He dropped his firewood, and running for his gun was soon upon the trail of the animal. It had vanished, but in front of him was a cleft in the precipice, a path by which the summit could undoubtedly be reached. He forgot both deer and wood. " *Patrao ! Patrao ! ó camino ! ó camino !* " The almost breathless Manuel dashed into camp and broke the news. There was no further talk of return. Hump packs and up the mountain ! " *Adiánte, Manuel !* "

The crevice in the mountain widened somewhat inside. It was not a steep ascent and, marvel of marvels, it was surely artificial ! True, the going was rough, but there were short stretches of what seemed like paving, and the loose stones which littered the ascent appeared to be worn smooth on one side. Even the sides of the crevice or gorge were suggestively artificial in places. The Indians were clearly frightened. Lumps of perfectly clear rock crystal, long hexagons of malachite and frothy masses of semi-transparent quartz, in which here and there were embedded green and blue crystals of aquamarine, delighted and amazed the rest of the party.

The roughness of the path made the ascent none too easy, and it was after three hours that, leaving the gorge, the trail of stones wound up to the summit of the ridge. But from there what an amazing view to repay the effort ! To the north and north-east an unbroken forest extended almost to the horizon, losing itself in the faint bluish haze of distant hills. From north-west to south-east the mountains stretched as far as the eye could reach, the white quartz caps of the jagged peaks appearing like snow. In the immediate foreground lay extensive plains brilliantly green, with patches here and there of silver water, changing to yellowish brown and dull greens as they drew near the foothills.

On this was a sight that made the adventurers gasp and hastily draw back behind the crest-line. For, at a distance of some three or four miles, and so clear that buildings could be distinctly made out, was a huge city.

From far below, where the rocky trail crossed the ridge and dipped down out of the range of vision, could be observed the narrow ribbon of loose stones winding over the plain and losing itself in the brown environment of the walls. Nothing could have been more unexpected than this extraordinary sight. Was it some colony of the Portuguese? Was it the hated Spaniard? Was it some unknown wonder of the mysterious Orizes Procázes, remnant of the Tapuyas, who had shown such indisputable signs of some civilised origin and had vanished into the west under the stern lash of the white invasion? If not, what was it? One by one they crawled over the skyline and regathered on the trail against a background of rock and scrub. From here, when they had gazed their fill, they descended cautiously to the plain, and leaving the trail, decided to camp in opportune bush near a tiny stream of clear water. Fires were avoided, and the party talked in whispers. The sun was well up, for it was scarcely past midday, and it was decided that two Portuguese and two Negroes, all well armed, should reconnoitre as near the city as possible and discover what sort of people dwelt in this mysterious place.

Impatient with curiosity and fanciful with apprehension, the main party waited for their return under constant false alarms. For the forest in these solitudes is always full of voices, soft whisperings and cries of animals easily mistaken for cock-crowing or evidence of humanity by nervous folk. The scouts returned. They had not ventured too near the city, but from a distant point of vantage had observed neither inhabitants nor smoke. To the Indians it was just as mysterious as to their more civilised companions. They had vague traditions and very definite superstitions regarding this part of the country which had kept it taboo, and they were fearful of they knew not what. One man was found, however, who volunteered to go alone and discover what there was. He started early next morning and returned about noon, obviously frightened, but asserting that there existed not a trace of living man.

On the following morning the whole party set off cautiously along the trail, an advance guard of four scouts preceding them by about half a mile. Drawing near the city the scouts rejoined the main body, corroborating the Indian's account that there was no sign of human life. The whole party thereupon came into the open, and, disposed in strategic order, approached the walls.

The trail led directly to an entrance through three lofty arches built of gigantic stones, the middle arch towering above the others. The stupendous masonry was black with age, and the grandeur of the architecture tied every man's tongue. No one could speak above a whisper, and orders were issued in a strangely unnatural voice. The overwhelming dignity of the design, the awesome silence and mystery of an old abandoned city possessed them, rough men as they were. High above the crown of the central arch, and deeply engraved into the weathered stone, were characters of some sort. They knew enough to realise that this was no familiar script. The arches were in a good state of preservation, but a few huge blocks had fallen from the summit, and portions had slipped somewhat out of plumb. Passing through the archway they found themselves in a wide street, littered with fallen masonry and broken pillars. They gazed in amazement. There was not a sign of human occupation. It was all incredibly old, and yet in its age amazingly perfect. Here were two-storied houses on either side, all built up of carefully squared blocks carved in elaborate time-worn designs. In many cases roofs had fallen in, in others great stone slabs still covered the dark interiors, and he who had the temerity to enter the windowless chambers through the narrow doorways and to raise his voice, fled at the echoes hurled at him by the vaulted ceilings and solid walls. Fallen stones and an accumulation of bat droppings covered any vestiges of human occupation, had there been such. Dumb with amazement, the party, huddled together like a flock of scared sheep, passed down the street into a vast square or plaza. Here they must have ' looked at each other with a wild surmise ', for in the centre of the plaza, dominating its surroundings in sublime majesty, was a gigantic black stone column set upon a plinth of the same rock, and upon it the statue of a man, one hand on his hip, the other arm extended with the index finger pointing towards the north—magnificent in design, perfect in preservation. In each corner of the plaza had been great obelisks of black stone covered with carvings. Three of them had been broken off short, the upper parts lying on the ground prominent amidst the litter of stone. The whole of the right-hand side of the plaza was occupied by a building so magnificent in its design as to have been obviously a palace, its square columns intact, but walls and roof partly demolished. A vast entrance hall was approached by a broad flight of steps, much of which was displaced. The interior of this hall was rich in exquisite carving, and still showed signs of a brilliance of colouring comparable with some of the finest relics of Egypt. The interior exit from this hall was blocked by fallen masonry. The deep droppings of the bats during hundreds or perhaps thousands of years made the atmosphere acrid and unpleasant to breathe, and multitudes of tiny white parasites, known as *guanacos*, attacked the intruder and poisoned any exposed flesh. The bats fluttered in countless hordes around their disturbers, beating their faces with wings and creating such a deafening noise with their shrill notes as to make the explorers only too glad to get back to daylight. At the junction of the street with the plaza, above what appeared to be the principal entrance, was carved in semi-relief the figure of a youth in excellent preservation. The figure was naked from the waist up, had shield in hand and a band across the shoulder. The face was clean-shaven and the head crowned with a wreath of laurel. Of the worn characters below the figure it was possible to make out the following:

K ʊ 𝒫 ɪ ʔ-

In the plaza opposite the palace was the ruin of another huge edifice, evidently a temple by its magnificent façade and general appearance. It was entirely unroofed, but on the weather-worn walls were still to be traced figures and designs of animals and birds. Over the entrance were the characters:

Beyond the street and plaza the city seemed to be entirely in ruin, and much of it was buried. Gaping chasms in the ground, into whose fathomless depths a stone dropped without sound, left no doubt as to the agency of destruction. Around these dreadful gulfs great blocks of stone elaborately carved, slabs of rock, portions of stone and broken columns were piled in an awful confusion. The explorers could imagine something of the ghastly tragedy of this unknown cataclysm, whose resistless force had displaced and thrown down monolithic stones of fifty tons and upwards and destroyed in less perhaps than one fearful minute the civilisation of a thousand years.

On the far side of the plaza the city was open to a river some thirty yards or so in width, flowing with easy current from the hills to the north-west and disappearing south-eastward in a vista of soft green banks and a few occasional trees. Evidently there had been a highly decorative terrace to this river, but most of it had been swallowed up or lay beneath the waters. On the far side of the river were what must have once been fields of cultivation, covered now with coarse grass and a wealth of flowers. Here and there were shallow swamps where rice had continued to plant itself, and whose waters and environment were alive with waterfowl, so unfamiliar with man as to show no fear whatever. About a quarter of a mile outside the city and standing by itself was a palatial building with a front of two hundred and fifty paces, approached by a broad flight of steps of many-coloured stones. It was heavily columned all round, and the noble portico opened upon a vast hall, whose mural decorations and gorgeous colouring still remained more or less intact. From this hall opened fifteen smaller chambers, in each of which was the carved head of a serpent from whose open jaws poured a small stream of water, which, so far as the debris everywhere would permit it to be traced, led to a central basin in the outer hall, from whence it probably escaped by some covered channel to the plain outside.

In front of the portico stood a huge squared monolith,

on whose surface were deeply engraved the characters below :

It was long before they could tear themselves away from these awesome ruins, for whose existence they could imagine no explanation. The grandeur and opulence of the place astounded them, but this feeling soon gave place to an intense lust for treasure, inevitable amongst ignorant men. If they could have filled their pockets with gold, they would willingly have destroyed every stone of this priceless relic of a lost civilisation. Their report reeks of this impulse. It is the buried wealth which attracts them, not the mystery.

One Portuguese of the party, Joao Antonio, had picked up amidst the litter in a chamber a small gold coin, spherical in shape, and showing on one side the figure of a youth on his knees, and on the other a bow, a crown and a musical instrument of some sort. There must, they argued, be any amount of these to be found, for the population could not possibly have removed money or jewels in so dreadful a catastrophe. No doubt they did find signs of more. The document suggests this, but it is guarded over details.

The leader of the expedition was anxious to return better equipped for this purpose. Moreover, the bats had daunted him. The many vampires made sleep dangerous from continual loss of blood, nor had ten years of wandering left them any too strong. There were circumstances to balance the abundance of food. If the plains across the river abounded with duck easy to knock on the head with a stick, they also swarmed with snakes attracted by

191

the same abundance. They lurked by the riverside, and even penetrated the buildings after the bats. In the swamps, anaconda, big enough to attack a man, invested duck hunting with considerable risk. There were not only waterfowl but innumerable kangaroo rats, or jerboa, which, he says, 'hopped like fleas', and seemed to have no desire to run away. The Brazilian wild dog, almost as big as a wolf and not very common elsewhere, found the place a veritable paradise.

Not a man would sleep near the ruins at night. They had found a suitable place about half a mile away, from which they could at sunset watch the millions of bats issuing in endless columns from their sanctuaries and spreading into the sky with a whirring of wings that simulated the approach of a terrific squall. By day the air was thick with swallows, as greedy for the prolific insect life as the wolves and serpents were for the wild-fowl and rats.

Having no notion where he was, but with every confidence that those Indians who remained with him would remember the country, the leader decided to follow the river down on the chance of striking some civilised settlement. Three days down, however, say twenty to thirty miles, the river precipitated itself over a cliff in a fall of considerable size. Beyond the fall the river, in place of being deep and narrow, broadened out tremendously, spreading itself into swamps and backwaters in the manner common to these tributaries of the mighty Amazon. Seeing that there was plenty of game, he decided to camp a while here and send on an advance party to reconnoitre the lower river. Several of his men were down with fever and the Indians were uneasy. Soon after the departure of this party he found to the east of the fall unmistakable signs of mining. Shafts whose depths he had no means of plumbing excited his curiosity. On the surface of the ground were specimens of silver ore of great richness, presumably brought up from these shafts, encouraging him to believe that he had really discovered the lost mines of Moribeca. Further investigation revealed other features of interest. There were caverns hewn out of the solid rock, one of them sealed with a great slab of stone on which were engraved the following characters:

$$+ = \mathcal{V}^{P} \zeta \mathcal{U} o \varsigma$$

No effort, however, could move the slab. Others were similarly closed, the stone showing the characters:

$$+ \overline{m} , \overline{m} , \overline{m} , \overline{3} , \overline{\frown}$$

and many more. Possibly they were the tombs of the priests and kings of the city. The party pictured themselves as rich men. They agreed that, excepting to the Viceroy, to whom their leader owed a debt of gratitude, they would say nothing, but return reconstituted, unearth the treasures and work the mines. Gold, too, was easily panned from the banks of the river.

In the meantime the scouting section, after following the lower river for nine days without result, caught sight in a backwater of a canoe paddled by two white people with long black hair and dressed in clothing of some sort. But on firing a shot to attract attention, the canoe spurted ahead and disappeared. People of this appearance were reported again and again by Portuguese explorers up to about half a century ago, and no explanation has ever been vouchsafed. Afraid of running up against strong Indian tribes with so small a party, and weary of the fatiguing business of making wide detours around swamps and lagoons, they retraced their steps. Unwilling to risk a collision with Indians unknown to his own following, and aware that his own Indian contingent would be liable in such case to melt away, the leader then decided to march eastwards through the forest and leave it to chance what part of the Atlantic coast settlements he eventually struck. Where he ultimately came out he does not say, but after some months he was on the banks of the River Paraguassu (Paraoaçu), for the report from which these details are quoted was despatched from that river.

He tells in his report no more than is actually necessary, but he recommends the Viceroy to retain the services of the Indian messenger as a guide, and to leave the penurious circumstances of Bahia and make use of the abundant wealth that is to be had for the trouble of visiting the old city. Whether his Indians deserted him from fear of the taboo and he lost himself, as so many did in these vast solitudes, or whether the insatiable greed of these early explorers ended in quarrels and tragedy, is unknown. Neither he nor a single member of his party was heard of again, which is not surprising when one recalls the fact that an expedition of 1,400 souls left Sao Paolo for the forests in the seventeenth century, of which not a single man returned to civilisation.

Meanwhile the Viceroy pigeon-holed the report, which never saw light again for upwards of half a century. The Government made some half-hearted attempts to find the place about the middle of the nineteenth century, but they failed to discover anything, and, truth to tell, the search was not conducted very intelligently. It must be borne in mind that it was not easy for a people steeped in the narrow doctrines of the time to imagine such a thing as an old civilisation in the new world. Archaeology was in its infancy, the Egyptian hieroglyphs were still a mystery, and there is little doubt that the ecclesiastics discouraged anything likely to upset the simple story of the Old Testament.

But the story must not be lightly dismissed. It is too circumstantial for that, and the details are beyond the imagination of more or less illiterate people. Moreover, this old city is not alone of its kind. There are others. There is one, relatively close to civilisation, around which the forest has grown like that in Doré's illustration to 'Atala'. The late British Consul-General at Rio de Janeiro visited it alone with a caboclo in 1913, but the goodwill of the Indians is needed to reach it. There are, or were, at least three men who know of the other places, so far as the general location and surrounding topography are concerned. One was a Frenchman, whose last attempt to get there cost him an eye, and it is probable he will make no more; the second is an Englishman who before he left the country was suffering from an advanced stage of cancer, and is probably no longer alive; the third is the writer. The Jesuits of the seventeenth century seem to have known of their existence. Not only, however, are information and forest experience imperative for a successful attempt to get there, but it is improbable otherwise that any but the forest city will be found by chance until the interior is properly colonised and the wild Indian has vanished or been tamed. The explorer of the present day is soft in comparison with the hardy Portuguese pioneers, and is dependent upon too many luxuries. Nor will pottering about the rivers ever discover anything new.

Even the Indians to be met there are shockingly degenerate.

Is the investigation worth while from a scientific point of view? Assuredly, yes. It must be doubtful if there is any archaeological and ethnological research more important today than the study of these ruins and the relics contained therein. Look at the characters! Are they not suggestive? What is the significance of the hundreds of inscriptions scattered throughout the forests in characters resembling some of those contained amongst the oldest scripts known to us elsewhere, themselves as yet a mystery? May there not be somewhere another Rosetta stone? Who can estimate the value of such a discovery of ruins compared with which those in Egypt are modern?

[January 1933

10

THE TREASURE OF BEGRAM

Sir Kerr Fraser-Tytler

Some day, no doubt, the story of the Treasure of Begram will be told by experts, who will be able to appraise the value of this remarkable find at its true worth and place it in its correct historical perspective. But it will be some years before this can be done, and in the meantime the story of the actual discovery and of the people who made it is liable to be forgotten. The principal actors are dead, and so is their devoted henchman, Karl. Meunier may perhaps be alive, rotting in a German prison camp, or he, too, may have been swept away in the great cataclysm of 1940. There is no one else to tell the tale unless I do it myself—I, who only came into it as an interested spectator and played no active part until the last act when the story was all but told. But I should like to tell it, piecing together the fragments such as I know them, because it is a fine story of the crowning achievement in the lives of two people who, having gained their object, turned aside to sacrifice everything they had in the cause of freedom.

The story goes back a long way, back to the days, three hundred years before Christ, when Alexander of Macedon, leading his victorious army to the farthest limits of the

Persian Empire on the great River Jaxartes (Siri Darya), passed up through what is now southern Afghanistan, till he came to the valley of the Kabul River. It was winter when he reached Kabul, and the piercing cold of those snowy uplands drove him to seek shelter for his army in the beautiful valley of the Koh-i-Daman to the north. Here on the banks of the Panjshir River, some forty miles from modern Kabul, he wintered his weary troops and awaited the return of summer which would clear the snow from the passes of the Hindu Kush and enable him to pursue his way across the mountains to the broad Oxus valley beyond. Here, too, at a spot where the Panjshir and Ghorband Rivers join, he founded a city and gave it his name. The site he chose was worthy of the city and of its founder. Standing on the high southern bank of the river, the city looked northwards across a wide valley which sloped upwards to the foothills of the Hindu Kush. Beyond these the great ridge of the main range rose, tier upon tier of massive peaks, covered for nine months of the year with a dazzling mantle of snow. To the west and south the broad, gently sloping valley was filled with countless orchards and vineyards, watered by the streams flowing from innumerable ravines. The site was both fertile and important. It covered three of the main routes from the north—the Ghorband, the Salang, and the Khawak—and it stood on the main highway between India and Central Asia.

There is little record of the fortunes of the city of Alexandria-under-the-Caucasus, as it was called by later historians, after its founder entrusted it to the charge of a Greek satrap, Nicanor, when he set out on his march to India in 328 B.C. After his death it flourished for a while under the Greek colonists, but soon passed under the dominion of Chandragupta, first of the Mauryan Emperors, whose kingdom included all Afghanistan south of the Hindu Kush. On the break-up of the Mauryan Empire, this part of the country and much of northern India passed again into the hands of the Græco-Bactrian rulers, whose successors, the Kushans, ruled a vast Empire stretching from Benares in the south to the Pamirs in the north and east. The greatest of these, Kanishka, who reigned during the first century of the Christian era, held his court at what is now Peshawar in the North-West Frontier Province of India, while retaining Alexandria as his summer residence. After his death the Kushan Empire was gradually reduced by the invasions of Ardeshir, first of the great Sasanian dynasty of Persia. But while Ardeshir carried his conquests eastward as far as the Indian Province of the Punjab, he does not appear to have penetrated far into central Afghanistan, where Kushan principalities continued to flourish under the shelter of the mountain ranges till possibly the middle of the fifth century A.D. At about this time there occurred one of those early nomad invasions, precursors to the great Mongol invasions of a later date, when the Ephthalites or White Huns, crossing the ranges from the north, poured down upon the pleasant valleys and peaceful inhabitants of the little Kushan states still maintaining themselves amid the ruins of their once great Empire. We know nothing of what befell these states. Some day, perhaps, archaeologists, patiently delving among their ruined cities, may unfold the history of their downfall. But it seems probable, if we compare this invasion with those greater ones which followed it some eight hundred years later, that the ruthless nomads from the north, caring nothing for the civilisation and culture of a settled people, destroyed and laid waste the flourishing cities and fertile valleys, till nothing was left save a great silence amid a greater desolation.

The city of Alexandria disappeared from the records of history. Armies passed that way; Ghenghis, Tamerlane, and Baber led their forces across the mountains within a few miles of its site. Travellers came and went; peasants of a different race gradually filled the valley, planted vineyards, tilled the fields, and established crude mud villages amid the ruins of a forgotten people. But the site of Alexander's city, known among the local inhabitants as Begram, remained untouched. For fifteen hundred years no hand was laid on it, save the hand of some poor peasant scratching its surface with a wooden plough. The ramparts crumbled into shapeless mounds, the water channels dried up and disappeared, while the strong dry winds from the Hindu Kush swept across its surface till the land turned arid and parched, and the dust of centuries filled every depression and obliterated the traces of the city's contours. The fact of its foundation remained, of course, in history, and men like the remarkable traveller Charles Masson, who visited Begram in the early part of the nineteenth century, found there vast quantities of coins of the Græco-Bactrian and later periods. But the record of what the city was like, and what manner of men dwelt in it, what was their culture and their way of life, vanished utterly.

In 1922 King Amanullah of Afghanistan, among other foolish acts, gave a monopoly of archaeological excavation in his country over a period of years to the French. The folly of this act lay in the fact that France, impoverished by four years of struggle against Germany, had neither the will nor the resources to maintain in Afghanistan an archaeological mission adequate to the work which lay before it. For all Afghanistan is a cemetery of vanished Empires.

From the vast ruins of ancient Balkh, the Mother of Cities, in the north not far from the Oxus, to the deserts of Seistan in the south, where the ancient Sasanian cities lie buried in the sand ; along the old Silk Route through Badakshan ; down through the gorges and across the passes of the Hindu Kush where the great statues of Bamian testify to a faith which has long since vanished from Central Asia ; by Ghazni and around Kabul, still remain traces of ancient civilisations which grew and flourished and decayed while the forebears of the present rulers of the country were as yet unknown. Such a field for exploration might well have occupied the attention of half a dozen fully equipped expeditions. But the French Government maintained only one mission, and that one was undermanned and often poorly equipped. In 1924, however, they appointed as its chief M Hackin of the Musée Guimet in Paris, who in the years that followed proved his worth in the magnificent work he carried out in Bamian, in his excavations of the Buddhist sites near Kabul, and in the expeditions he undertook in the Oxus valley and in the difficult desert country north of Seistan.

But always, so he once told me, his thoughts turned back to Begram, and to the possibility that among its mounds might be found something which would throw light on the ancient capital of Kanishka, and on the manners and customs of the little-known Kushan Empire. Two or three times shafts were sunk into the layers of sand and rubble covering its ruins, only to reveal the remains of what had once been the bazaar, or poorer quarter of the city. It was not till 1937 that M Hackin, with his devoted wife, was able to turn his full attention to the task of excavating a site some hundreds of yards farther east, which held out hopes of richer reward.

While engaged on work at the site of Begram the Hackins established themselves in a ruined and deserted mud village nearby. With all the genius of the French for disregarding uncomfortable surroundings, M and Madame Hackin and M Karl, with their Afghan assistant, settled down to three months' work, until in July the hot wind off the sand, and the dust and the flies, would drive them into their Kabul headquarters some forty miles away. And here one Sunday in May 1937 I came to lunch with them, driving out from Kabul down the valley and across some twelve miles of rough country road. It was a privilege to lunch with the Hackins; to arrive hot and dusty and be met with a cool drink and a warm welcome; to walk out a few hundred yards to the excavations and watch the labourers patiently working away, removing the sand, and digging into the ruins of some ancient house while Mme Hackin and the Afghan assistant superintended the work; to lunch in the little room off chicken *pilau*, washed down with French wine, while much good talk went round the table, and M Karl propounded some new and startling theory on how to catch the local fish, a pastime of which he was inordinately fond; to return finally to Kabul in the evening refreshed from a day spent with kindly people, who were masters of their job, and most delightful hosts.

On the Sunday in question there was no sign that the day was in any way different from other days, save that M Hackin, instead of taking me directly to the diggings, walked out on to a rampart of the old city overlooking the river, and there stood looking across to the foothills and to the curious escarpment of the Singing Sands (Reg-i-Ruwan) beyond the river. He stood there awhile, talking of the old Kushans and their Empire, and of the wonderful site for a city chosen for them by Alexander, and then led the way back. When we reached the little courtyard where they lived, he paused.

" I've something I want to show you," he said, and led the way into one of the rooms. And there on the floor, tenderly cushioned in boxes lined with cotton-wool, lay the first-fruits of the Treasure of Begram.

Madame Hackin had come on it the day before. Patiently working away with a pick and small shovel in the packed mud which filled a chamber of what had been a part of the old palace of the Kings, some nine feet below the ground, she had unearthed pieces of painted glass of exquisite workmanship, ivory plaques, and ancient vases of strange design, which had no counterpart in the surrounding villages, and had, in fact, never before been seen in Afghanistan within the memory of man.

How they came to be there, what was their history, and why for fifteen hundred years they had escaped the attention of the surrounding neighbourhood, is a matter for the experts. M Hackin was reticent on the subject, unwilling to commit himself until much further evidence, possibly in the shape of coins, should provide some reliable data on which to base an opinion. But from the little he was ever willing to say, it is permissible to hazard a guess that Alexandria-under-the-Caucasus fell to some sudden onslaught of the savage Ephthalites from across the mountains at the beginning of the fifth century A.D. One might perhaps try to imagine the scene when news reached the city that the barbarians had crossed the ridges and were even now descending the long valleys of the Panjshir and Ghorband Rivers and converging on the capital. One might picture the hasty flight of the weaker inhabitants with the women and children, carrying with them their gold and silver treasure and ornaments—for, with the exception of two small gold elephant heads, none of these were found among what was left behind—while the warriors manned the ramparts in a vain attempt to stem the on-coming tide. It would appear also that, before they left, the inmates of the palace collected what they could of the beautiful specimens of Greek and Indian and Chinese art which adorned its precincts, and piled them into two stone-built chambers within its walls, and there left them, little thinking that one and a half thousand years would pass before they again saw the light of day. For if this story bears any resemblance to the truth, it would appear that for some strange reason the invaders never penetrated into these chambers, or, if they did, that the exquisite ivories and other treasures held no attractions for the savages of a nomad race whose possessions were limited to little be-yond the bare necessities of a life of endless movement across the great pasturelands of Central Asia. But all this is mere speculation, liable at any time to be falsified as a result of further excavation and research, which well may give the key to the mystery of the origin and history of the treasure.

For two long summers the work of emptying the cham-bers of their contents went on. On occasions in June and July 1939 I went out to the site and was privileged to sit with Madame Hackin in one of the chambers and watch her at work, while the hot winds of the summer swept across the valley and tore at the slender canvas canopy overhead. And delicate work it was. Seated on a stool on the floor of the chamber, facing the great pile of earth that filled it, Madame Hackin would gently scrape the packed earth with a dentist's pick, and remove the particles with a camel's-hair brush. Gradually as she worked there would appear out of the mud where it had lain so long the design of yet another strip of beautifully carved ivory, or the contour of some exquisite vase or piece of painted glass. Very gently the glass or pottery, or perhaps some little bronze image of Greek workmanship, would be prised from its setting and removed, while the ivories, too fragile to stand the strain of being lifted as they were found, were treated with hot glycerine by M Karl, always ready in the background with his spirit-lamp and blow-pipe.

Thus the work went on, through 1937 and then again, after the return of the Hackins from France, throughout the summer of 1939, while the war clouds gathered over Europe and the shadow of a far vaster cataclysm than that which destroyed the last remnants of the Kushan Empire brooded over the modern world. By the end of 1939 the two chambers were empty, and their contents, delicately repaired and carefully photographed by Karl, were packed and transported to Kabul, there to be most scrupulously divided by M Hackin between the Kabul museum and the Musée Guimet of Paris. It is impossible for a layman to describe the treasure, either accurately or in detail. But I remember that there were many beautiful ivory strips of South Indian workmanship, but no longer found in India, elaborately carved with figures of men and women, of animals and birds, and of a curious mythical creature called a hippo-griff, all most vivid and lifelike, and that they showed traces of once having been held together by copper fastenings so as to form a framework, possibly of a throne or couch. There were plaques of pure Greek workmanship, exquisite painted glass with the colour as fresh as when it was designed; a beautiful little bronze statuette of a charioteer and other images; many delicate vases of alabaster and porcelain; lacquer work from China which crumbled to dust as soon as it was brought to the light and air; and several large drinking-vessels of strange design and unknown origin. It was, in fact, apparent that in this city of the Kushans had been gathered together works of art from all Asia, brought by the caravans westwards from China by the great Silk Route, or northwards across the hills and plains of India, and perhaps eastwards from Macedonia, to adorn the once-flourishing capital of their Kings.

Nothing resembling these specimens of ancient culture and art had ever been discovered within many hundred miles of Alexander's city. It was a find to reward a lifetime spent in patient archaeological study and research.

In 1940 the work was resumed on an adjoining site; but little progress had been made when in June the world was shaken by the great disaster that had befallen France. When news of the surrender of France was broadcast on the radio M Hackin was at Begram, while Madame, convalescing from an attack of dysentery, was staying in my house. Within forty-eight hours M Hackin had packed his camp and was in my study, with a telegram in his hand to General de Gaulle in London, unreservedly offering his services in the cause of freedom. The offer was accepted, and a month later M and Madame Hackin with M Karl left Kabul *en route* for England. It is easy, looking at the past now from the angle of 1944, to say that he did the only thing a Frenchman and a man of honour could do, but it was not so easy in June 1940 in Afghanistan to come to such a decision. He was no longer a young man, and his life's work was not complete. He was asked by the Vichy Government to remain at his post and was offered a handsome salary to take over their interests at Kabul. It would have been so easy and natural to do so, particularly when in June 1940 no one outside the British Legation, however friendly disposed he might be, dared to think, or to say if he did think, that the British Empire would endure for another three months. But M and Madame Hackin never hesitated, and never for a moment counted the cost. They and their devoted assistant, M Karl, dined with me the night before they left Kabul, and after dinner we sat out in the soft moonlight of an August evening while Karl played his ukulele. M Hackin's last action was to hand over to me the final case of precious ivories with strict injunctions that in no circumstances were they to fall into the hands of Vichy.

The rest is soon told. The little party arrived in London in September 1940 in the middle of the blitz, and were soon hard at work. I heard once from M Hackin, a cheerful letter describing life in London during those grim months, delighted with his reception at the Foreign Office and with an honorary membership of the Athenaeum which was offered him. But he had no illusions about the struggle that lay ahead, only believing that his sturdy common-sense, knowledge of men, and real affection for the British people might be of service to his country and his cause. But this was not to be. He accepted an appointment in the East to strive to counteract the spirit of defeatism then spreading over the French dominions. He set out with his wife, and one dark winter's night in the Channel the ship in which they were travelling was torpedoed and sank, only one man being saved. M Karl did not long survive the only two people on earth for whom life held any meaning to him.

[June 1944

11

CRADLE OF GOLD

Alan Stewart

A year ago, if I had given the matter any thought, I should probably have associated Ophir and Sheba with the Hanging Gardens of Babylon and lazily assumed that, with one as with the other, a name from ancient history had been transmuted by a rhapsodist to legend. And if I had been asked the whereabouts of the fabled Mines of Solomon there would have been vague visions of darkest Africa, of ivory and gold and beauteous queens, and, undoubtedly, I should have referred the questioner to the works of Rider Haggard. That was before I became resident on a gold-mine in the Hejaz.

It was in the London office of the American-managed mine that my curiosity was stirred and conjecture first began.

" The mine is about two hundred and eighty miles east of north from Jedda and it lies at the back of beyond," I heard. " It has ancient surface-workings and, although there's no record of its having been worked in modern times until we took it over, it has always been known as Mahad Dhahab, which, we're told, means Cradle of Gold. The Hejazis insist that the ancient cuts supplied Solomon with a good deal of his glory ; but," as I smiled my unbelief, " perhaps you'll be able to prove or disprove that when you've lived there for a while."

An air passage was then arranged for me to Jedda and, a little later, there was the luxurious boredom of the Hermes flight to Cairo. There, a leg-stretching halt took up much too short an hour until an elderly Dakota, which discarded luxury at least, took me on board and made leisurely use of the Red Sea as a navigation guide to Jedda airport where a garish, roistering dawn proclaimed the warmth of welcome the Hejaz had to offer.

I had had a passing acquaintance with Jedda long before it was an airport, and my recollections were of an ancient, mud-walled town with narrow tortuous lanes that gave cramped passage only to a rider and his mount. Houses, then, heeled awry across the lanes, peered into each other's shuttered, latticed windows, and threw a welcome shade for passers-by; while, in the open spaces ringing the bazaars, couched camels, with the sands of distant lands in their matted coats, groaned and uttered heartbroken calls of anguish regardless of whether their burdens were being eased or newly placed upon them.

Now Jedda's wall has gone and a wide, hardpacked, coral-based and dusty road encircles and bisects the town, making a racetrack for modern forms of transport. Speed is limited only by engine-power, and the arbitrary road-rules are dictated by the forcefulness and personality of the individual driver. At road intersections a khaki-clad policeman stands on a crushed-coral pedestal with a wooden shade overhead, and directs converging traffic not so much by commanding as by invocating gesture.

The town itself is a medley of old, crumbling, mud-built dwellings, of sturdy, fortress-like stone houses dating from the Turkish overlordship, and of the shells of pretentious, gimcrack-looking modern buildings—ungainly shapes of things to come. The bazaars are little changed. Judged by the standard of comparable Middle-Eastern towns they are poor in structure and in the goods they have to sell. A lack of local industry and of native crafts-manship is apparent in the utility sections, which are stocked with cheap imports from India and Japan; the restricted luxury trade is confined almost entirely to cars, watches, fountain-pens and cameras from the West. A sad reflection on the economic position of Western luxury-exporters is that local prices for these goods are usually much lower than in their country of origin.

A section of the town that intrigued me was a reclaimed stretch of wasteland covered with rows of rough, white-washed, single empty rooms. These, I was told, house at a price the privileged among the hordes of visitors who arrive each year for the pilgrimage to Mecca. The houses have no furniture, no light or water supply and, as far as I could see, no provision for sanitation; but their rental value adds considerably to annual tolls exacted from the uncomplaining devout.

Devotion in the Hejaz is a grim affair. Any expression of happiness or joy appears to be a deadly sin. Teashops, which in other Eastern lands would be noisy with blaring radios or gramophones, here are silent, and the few that are in evidence apparently exist on invisible patronage. The people are unsmiling, and there is a general air of extreme austerity and poverty. Both undoubtedly are there; but, in Jedda, an unseen wealth keeps European bank branches very much alive, and the austerity, unlike charity, may not necessarily begin in the seclusion of the Hejaz home.

The days I spent in Jedda were uncomfortably hot and

humid, and an evening swim in the Red Sea shallows made only the difference that I was wet all over at one time instead of being cooled on land by the irregular coursing of rivulets of sweat that spontaneously erupted with the slightest movement. Between bathes I walked the coastal edge of the sandy, parched plain, the Tihameh, that stretches to the hills twenty miles away, and found the only break in the level of desolation was given by occasional beach-hills of sandstone invariably fronted with large masses of embedded shells and coral. In the sea itself there were glimpses, from time to time, of the reddish tinge which, my reading tells me, derives from the presence of zoophites, red coral or red seaweed, which gives the sea its name. Much later in my stay I mentioned this theory to a learned Arab friend and was overwhelmed by the vehemence of his protests to the contrary.

" Read your Bible," I was told ; and he quoted extensively what he said were appropriate passages from the Old Testament. The Israelites, he adduced, called any sea *yam*, and when they qualified it to define the sea of the Exodus it was described merely as *yam suph*—*suph* being a woolly, grey-green seaweed that is thrown up abundantly on the shores.

" No," he said, " the sea did not derive its name from the colour of its waters, but from Himyer the Red who succeeded the Joktanites and Cushites, and who headed the chief family and then dominant tribe of Arabia Felix."

According to my friend, Himyer's name is derived from the Arabic *ahmar*, meaning ' red ', and his people, the Himyerites, gave their name to the waters that lapped their shores : ' The Sea of the Red Men '. If one accepts his view it becomes possible to treat the Greek and Roman stories that the sea received its name from ' a great King,

Erythras, who reigned in an adjacent country', as distortions of the Himyerite tradition.

Whatever the derivation of its name, I derived no pleasure from the Red Sea's sultry atmosphere and I left Jedda for the mountain country with uncomplimentary alacrity. It took about an hour to cross the desert plain by car and then a steady climb began on a track bulldozed by the mine's engineers through the massif that runs from Aqaba to the Yemen. The foothills leading to the forbidding mountain range were mainly of fossiliferous limestone, arid and featureless, without even a bush of camel-thorn to relieve their utter desolation; but, shortly after they joined the main, granitic range, water storage, fed by the mountain-sides and tapped by a series of wells, gave life to the tiny village of Esfand and its cultivated area of some fifty fertile acres. A few miles beyond the village an ancient, deserted, Turkish fort was perched atop a solitary hill a hundred feet in height. It stood back from the mountain pass it guarded and its solid, well-built granite blocks still seemed capable of withstanding assault by anything less than a heavy artillery bombardment. With all its strength it had its Achilles heel; for the hill on which it stood had neither well nor water-catchment, and the neighbouring hills offered excellent cover for besiegers.

The climb from Esfand was steady and unspectacular. We followed narrow wadis or dried-up watercourses where the closeness of the walls of rock and the twisting nature and easy gradient of our route denied any impression of gaining height. The wadis, in fact, resembled flights of shallow steps which climbed at irregular intervals to ascending landings of small plains varying from a mile to perhaps five miles in breadth. The lower plains were dotted with camel-thorn; and, occasionally, what appeared in the distance to be heat-haze, or a ground mirage, resolved itself into sparse, blue-grey, waving, wiry grass about three inches high, with each blade standing fastidiously aloof from its fellow. It was while crossing such a plain that my driver suddenly stopped and, jumping from the car with the starting-handle as weapon, gave chase to a moving object that at first sight appeared to be a slowly running hare. When he returned with his quarry he proudly displayed an enormous lizard. If a lizard has withers, then its withers were twelve inches from the ground; and from the nose to the base of its scaly tail it measured about three feet in length. The driver assured me that its flesh was more succulent and tender than the fattest chicken, but its repellent appearance left me no desire to dine with him.

As we gained height we left aridity behind and entered wilderness entire that stretched (my surroundings made me quote) ' from Dan to Beersheba '. The peaks that encircled us wherever we made open ground were of black, shining, volcanic rock with broken terraces of lava-flow on every side to suggest a possible origin of the old conception of flaming hell as the destiny of the damned. Basalt, porphyry, and granite alternated along our track, the only exceptions being two dome-shaped hills, narrowly divided, that stood at the entrance to the largest plain we yet had crossed. Their unusual appearance made me stop to examine their formation, and I found one to be of black and the other of white marble. My driver had a rude phrase to describe this local version of the Paps of Jura. The plateau that spread beyond them carried our track like a white, gravel ribbon spanning a seemingly limitless level field of dark-brown earth turned up by a master ploughman. But the furrows, I found, were basalt shards spread evenly over the vast expanse with not a single piece bigger than a man's clenched fist. My desire to find a cause or origin for everything I see assured me that the plain, in the distant past, had been thinly carpeted with lava-flow, and that weathering through the ages had reduced the carpet to the knots that had bound it as a piece.

Our journey's highest point, 3,400 feet, was reached at Wadi Hama, which was also the half-way mark. Here the mine's road engineer had built himself a lonely house of local stone, and, for company and commissariat, had gathered round him turkeys, hens and goats, gazelles and a chattering young monkey. I appreciated most the cool water from his deep-sunk well to replace the contents of our thermos-pail, which had become tepid and undrinkable in the blazing sun and searing wind that fought against us all the way from Jedda. Beyond Wadi Hama we crossed the ancient, pilgrim trail from Medina to holy Mecca; for it had swung from its direct line to make contact with a mountainside reservoir of stagnant water. The reservoir was a square-shaped pit lined with dark, granitic blocks, carefully faced and smoothed and skilfully bonded together. Each side was thirty feet in length, but its depth was doubtful; for lack of care had allowed silt, which resisted probing, to form beneath its two-foot depth of water, At one corner a kneeling camel dripped water from its slavering mouth back to the pool below, while its owner alternately bathed and, after brushing the surface-scum aside, scooped up by hand the muddy water to refresh his inner self. This Bedu, answering my inquiry, told me that the reservoir was fed by an unseen spring and that it had been built, countless years ago, by Suleiman. Although I had placed it as contemporary with the Turkish fort farther south, I pricked up my ears and asked, " Which Suleiman was that ? "

" The Suleiman who took gold from The Cradle, six days' march away," was his reply.

For the remainder of our journey we kept to the high-level plateau we had gained at Wadi Hama, winding and twisting our way round the desolate peaks that thrust everywhere from the level of the plain and climbed perhaps five hundred feet above our heads. At dusk there was evidence that we were nearing our destination. A corrugated-iron shed stood off from the track, covering the ' boosting-pump ' for a water pipeline that emerged from a narrow valley to the west and ran in the darkening before us to the mine. We followed the pipe and, an hour later, turned west from the darkness of the plain into a narrow valley that, by contrast, was garish in its dazzling illumination. On the left, a forbidding mountain peak threw grim, mysterious shadows in the light of powerful floodlamps that picked out the entrance to the mine and its surrounding buildings. On our right, tiny scintillating beams emerged from windows and doors of a scattered group of houses and coalesced to form a terraced haze of light rising from the valley floor to the top of the hill on which the houses stood.

In daylight there were no such romantic illusions. The mine site stood bare and cheerless in the wilderness of its setting—a world of barren, volcanic peaks thrust at random to the skies. Our containing valley was about a quarter of a mile in breadth and a mile in length, hemmed in on the north by a detached ridge of stony, sandy soil which housed administration offices and staff quarters. On the south a mountain face of rock rose almost sheer from base to summit. Veins of quartz criss-crossed the face, and deep-cut, surface scars made manifest the ancient quest for gold. Where the rock-face fell to plateau level on the east the modern quest was evidenced by a shining, ruthlessly efficient powerhouse, a mill capable of crushing daily five hundred tons of the rock on which it stood, and a mine-shaft that sank six hundred feet to produce gold in quantities beyond the dreams of Solomon's most ambitious treasurer. But these production aids would have been useless without an adequate supply of water; and in this arid land it was a stroke of providence, aided by no mean engineering ingenuity and craft, to find an underground lake some twenty miles away, sink wells a hundred and fifty feet in depth, and pump more than a million gallons each week to meet the mine's requirements. A wooden post erected near the mill, with arms pointing east and west, proclaimed that it stood exactly on the cartographer's Tropic of Cancer line.

The ancient workings intrigued me and, in the course of my stay, I tried to find out who the workers were and when they had left their mark. From the start it was obvious that authentic records would not be found; for in this eremitic land untrammelled archaeological research has always been unwelcome, if not denied. The cuts in the mountain face were undoubtedly of great age, and technical experts of the mine estimated the age at roughly fifteen hundred years. When I remarked that Solomon reigned about a thousand years before our Lord one man shifted his cud of gum and said, " I guess I could be out that much. If I'd known what you were after I'd have estimated three thousand years."

It seemed impossible, from examination of some of the cuts, that grown men could have worked in their narrow confines. They varied in surface length from ten to a hundred yards and in depth from ten to fifty feet; but in almost every instance the breadth was not more than a foot. In fact, they were the narrowest of slit-trenches carved from solid rock. I edged my way through the cuts where the necessarily sideways motion of my progress, the fact that I could not bend my knees and that my arms could move only in a lateral direction, established that the digging was not done by swinging blows from hammer or pick tools. Earlier finds of charring in the bottoms suggested that fire had been applied to the walls, and that when the rock temperature had been sufficiently raised, the dashing of cold water against the face resulted in fractures which permitted the leverage of thick slate-like sections from the laminar main body. The broken rock was then carried to the valley floor, where it was crushed between circular, hand-operated, basalt stones, roughly two feet in diameter and varying in thickness from four to six inches. (These stones, black, coarse, abrasive as a file and pitted to a sponge-like appearance, still lie in their hundreds on the plain, and are in common use as stepping-stones or scrapers wherever they are needed in the modern camp.) Washing and smelting completed the extraction process, but the extravagant crudeness of the mode of working left the valley covered from side to side with artificial hillocks of ancient tailings which are now being garnered by a power-shovel and, under modern methods of extraction, have been known to show a higher gold-content than the deep-mined, hitherto untouched ore.

My amateur research had a negative value only; for if there was no evidence that the mine dated to the days of Solomon, equally there was no positive proof of working having started at a later date. The erudite Arab scholar who advised me had no doubt that gold had been taken from Mahad Dhahab long before King Solomon reigned and, if nothing else, he made me add considerably to my acquaintance with Old Testament writings in seeking proof of his contentions.

"Before being conquered by the Himyerites," he said, "southern Arabia was peopled by the Joktanites, and in the tenth chapter of Genesis you may read that their kingdom stretched 'from Mesha, as thou goest unto Sephar a mount of the east'. Mesha," he went on, "lay adjacent to and to the east of Canaan, while Sephar was situated in the south-eastern corner of Arabia on what is now known as the Indian Ocean. In other words, the whole of central and southern Arabia was then a Joktanite country."

According to Genesis, Joktan was a great-great-grandson of Shem, son of Noah, and of Joktan's many sons (Genesis x. 28, 29; 1 Chronicles i. 22, 23) Sheba and Ophir gave their names to their spheres of jurisdiction. At that time the chief countries mentioned as producing gold were Sheba and Ophir. Their gold was proverbial for its fineness and, in fact, the word Ophir itself was used to denote fine gold.

"Some scholars," Abd-ur-Rahman continued, "would limit these countries to what has been called Arabia Felix, or the Yemen; but their limits are unknown, and if the present Hejaz was not included in their rule it was, at least, their next-door neighbour. Undoubtedly it was from these countries, the only lands his puny ships could reach, that Solomon obtained his gold; and other scholars who tell us that the gold came from the Moluccas, from Peru, Africa or India, forget that the ships of those days, venturesome though they were, were hardly built to cross the oceans."

He quoted Herodotus as his authority for saying that, after the pre-historical Phoenicians, Sesostris (Rameses II)

was the first to navigate the local waters; and three centuries later Solomon's fleet was built (1 Kings ix. 26) ' in
Ezion-geber, which is beside Eloth, on the shore of the
Yam Suph, in the land of Edom'. Jehoshaphat, too, 'made
ships of Tharsish to go to Ophir for gold but they went
not, for the ships were broken at Ezion-geber '.

It is small wonder that the ships were broken; for Red
Sea craft of the time, described by Pliny, were ' built of
papyrus, like the boats of the Nile '; and, at a very much
later date, El Makreezee, the Arab historian, writing in the
first half of the fifteenth century, spoke of ships that sailed
from Eydhab, on the Egyptian coast, to Jedda: ' The
jelebehs which carry the pilgrims on the coast have not a
nail in them but their planks are sewed together with fibre
taken from the coconut tree. They caulk them with fibre
from the wood of the date-palm and they " pay " them
with butter or the oil of the palma-Christi '.

Eloth's situation on the Yam Suph, in Edom, has been
identified with the Gulf of Akaba (that is, ' of the mountain
road ') which is the termination of the long valley of the
Ghor, or 'Arabah, that runs northward to the Dead Sea—
a convenient overland route to Solomon's kingdom, and
probably the route taken by the Queen of Sheba when,
with her great train (1 Kings x. 1-13), she paid diplomatic
homage to the ruler of her limitrophe lands. Abd-ur-
Rahman's comment on this incident had a touch of humour:
" She was probably a minor wife of the then ruling king
of Sheba who had heard of Solomon's successes with the
ladies and who, in paying tribute, was glad to see her go."

The sum of our deliberations was that the Joktanite
sphere of influence extended from central Arabia to the
Red Sea and the Indian Ocean, and that the sections
governed by Ophir and Sheba lay on the western and

southern seaboards. The Arabian capital towns that bore these names cannot now be traced; but this is not surprising, for they probably moved with the changing circumstances of their lords; and the fact that towns that bore the name of Ophir have been recorded in more distant lands is most likely due to the use of the word Ophir as a synonym for fine gold.

We concluded, too, that the Cradle of Gold was originally worked by Joktanite tribesmen who man-handled its precious produce to distant Jedda or to Yenbo, an ancient, little-known port situated north of Jedda on the Red Sea coast. There it was bartered to treasure-seeking fleets and transported to the kings and wealthy buyers of Mediterranean lands. Solomon's collectors, we decided, would return to Eloth, and from there a baggage-train would carry the coveted gold along the 'Arabah, through friendly Edom, to his adjoining homeland. Having come to this decision, I could not avoid comparison of the old-time with modern transport methods; for today I scrape my muddy boots on an ancient, rough-hewn, circular basalt stone before entering an air-conditioned room to learn from wireless-news if the ton of gold that went off yesterday has yet been safely air-delivered at its European destination.

There are, however, other old-time customs that are little changed. The traditional tribute of the conquered and the partisans and the lordly munificence of the ruling power are still maintained. When His Royal Highness, Prince Saud, eldest son and Heir Apparent of King Abdul Aziz ibn Saud, recently came to see our mine, he was lauded by welcoming Sharifian descendants—and fêted by men of the West. The Prince was pleased with his reception; among other marks of royal appreciation and favour he nonchalantly detached a superb American limousine from his mile-long baggage-train and presented it, almost carelessly, to the manager of the mine. Gold, in the shape of watches, each bearing a graven image of the Prince, was for the lesser fry.

And when, on the eve of Christmas, the Westerners paid homage to Our Lord of Nazareth, the loudest voice among the carol-singers was of an Arab Christian who, ordinarily, was a meek and self-effacing sort of man. His faith was probably stronger than our own and his reverence sincere ; but when the exhortation ' Come to Bethlehem ' was sung, there was a poignant, fiery passion in his voice that, I am sure, did not derive wholly from religious fervour.

[May 1953

12

DIAMONDS

Lawrence C. Green

I am back in my birthplace, and if you can approach
great wealth without envy, I will show you diamonds worth
millions.

Kimberley can never hide its past. Here is the 'Big
Hole' again. My head for heights has not improved since
I was a child; indeed, I am so acutely uncomfortable on
the edge of this steep, gaping scar that I have to remind
myself that Nelson was always seasick and that Napoleon
dreaded cats. I have flown over this same place without
the slightest feeling of nausea; but then the aircraft had
become my world, there was nothing connecting me with
the earth, and the impression conveyed to the brain was
space, not height.

My fear of heights must have had its origin in that
gigantic 'Big Hole', for there were no other heights in
Kimberley as far as I was concerned. Once there was no
hole at all. In the early seventies of last century, when
the first diggers were working their claims, this was just a
pock-marked area. No one imagined that Cecil Rhodes
would secure enough diamonds from it to pay for the
occupation of Rhodesia.

I stood there once with a man who had known it as a

shallow pit in the midst of a town of canvas and tin. " Sometimes there would be a burst of cheering from the diggers," he told me. " That usually meant a find. There was no jealousy, for one digger's luck encouraged hundreds of others. Few women came to the diamond fields in those days, so every hat came off and the loudest cheers of all were heard when a white woman appeared on the rim of the crater."

As the series of pits went deeper they became the Kimberley Mine. Diamondiferous ' blue ground ' was hauled to the surface in buckets. Thousands of ropes were used, and in the moonlight the huge crater resembled a monstrous spider's web. Landslides and rockfalls hampered the work, but in course of time the area of the ' Big Hole ' at the surface was thirty-eight acres. Before the mine closed down in 1909, it had yielded diamonds worth £100 million. A shaft had then reached a working level of 3,601 feet, which made it the deepest diamond mine in the world.

From the observation post on the northern edge you see the rough circle, fifteen hundred feet in diameter. It is very like a vast funnel, sloping down for nearly three hundred feet to the dizzy pathway (where you will never find me) round the rocky vertical pipe.

Such a dramatic scene has a sinister influence on some people. There have been accidental deaths, suicides and rescues. All through the years the bodies have been found ; one man, with his jacket on inside out, appeared to have been murdered ; another victim of the mine was a soldier in uniform.

Trees grow in the ' Big Hole ' today, masses of shale have fallen in, and the steep walls have become a bird sanctuary. I shudder when I think of it. A gloomy place.

If it is not haunted it should be; haunted by the ghosts of '71 and after, adventurous spirits who hurried from the far corners of the world, toiled feverishly for a time and scattered again, some rich and some broken.

In my youth, and long afterwards, the diamond-bearing 'blue ground' brought up from the Kimberley mines was spread out on 'floors' for a year so that the weather might break up the rock. When I returned to Kimberley between the wars, however, I found a new system at work. The 'blue ground' came to the surface and was tipped and fed slowly on to long conveyor-belts. Lines of intelligent natives were picking by hand, leaving the rough 'blue ground' with its glittering mica particles and taking off the smooth and useless rock. Hand picking is one of the most popular jobs on the mines. There is a reward for every diamond found by a De Beers employee; and although diamonds are seldom found until the final concentration, the chance is always present. A native convict labourer once handed in a stone of 268 carats.

Convicts are no longer employed on the Kimberley diamond mines. In the old days I was always amused to see incorrigible thieves in red-striped jerseys working so close to wealth in a form which might be regarded as exquisitely transportable. Even in the pulsator-house, where the diamonds come to light at last, the convicts were moving about happily amid the machinery. They valued their tobacco rations far more highly than the diamonds under their noses. You could smoke the tobacco, but a diamond was absolutely useless when there was no chance of smuggling it out.

I found it reassuring to note that the pulsator, most spectacular of the diamond recovery processes, had remained unchanged since my childhood. This is simply a table covered with grease and shaken steadily as the gravel washes over it with a stream of water. Diamonds are caught in the grease while the worthless gravel passes on. No one has ever really understood why the device makes this selection; not even the De Beers employee who invented it many years ago. But it works. Every two hours the tables are scraped clear of grease. The whole thick mess is placed in perforated cylinders and boiled. The grease floats out and the diamonds are left in the locked cylinders. And it takes about seventy thousand tons of 'blue ground' to produce diamonds weighing ten pounds.

When I was last in Kimberley they were using dogs to guard the 'blue ground' lying out in the open and still containing a fortune in diamonds. Barbed-wire entanglements enclosed this private treasure-house. In the old days, when the whole output of De Beers had to be exposed to the weather, fifty men patrolled the area.

All the most important places on the mines had their dog sentries at night: the pulsator house and the Kimberley offices. At each spot a dog was chained to a picket-line about a hundred yards long. If it heard any suspicious sound it barked, and up came a 'fighting dog', which had been roaming the area free. Sometimes the dogs found a raider wearing knee and elbow pads, crawling over the ground in search of diamonds. If the man tried to escape the dog would hang on to his arm, but it would never fly at his throat.

When you drive northwards from Kimberley, all the way to Christiana, you see the river diggings. On the red veld beside the Vaal River stand the hovels of the diggers and the heaps of gravel, the sieves and the washing-machines, just as they did when I was a child. Here are true gamblers, men who expose themselves and their families to a degrading life in the hope of sudden wealth. Some of them have sold farms to live in filth.

Yet I would be a hypocrite if I denied feeling the temptation of the river diggings myself. I asked for a scraper so that I could recapture my childhood memories. They brought the gravel from the washer, and showed me how to sweep away the mass of garnets and moonstones, cats'-eyes, carbon, agates and olivine and crystalloids. I went on flicking at the rubbish on the sorting-table until I found a glittering stone at last. In that moment I saw with startling clarity the whole charm of a life that does not even provide three meals a day for most of those who follow it. I wanted to take a partner who knew the game, buy the outfit and sort my own wash. Failure seemed out of the question. A flick of the wrist could turn up a stone large enough to make me rich. After all, it had happened again and again. That is the curse of the river diggings— it can happen. Only when you think of the thousands who have lost everything does common sense prevail. The old river diggings are almost finished. It is a lamentable end to a romantic industry.

Now come with me to the wild, surf-beaten shore where some of the world's greatest diamond discoveries were made.

South Africa's diamond coast begins about a hundred miles north of Saldanha Bay, and from that point to the Orange River every mile is patrolled by police troopers every day. All the richest deposits are so well protected that the gangs which once dashed to the coast by night and returned with sacks of rich gravel would stand no chance at the present time. There are patches of ground on that coast where, in ten minutes, a man might collect diamonds worth thousands. Such places are fenced in and never left alone.

Small camps are in charge of two or more young constables, who carry out the daily patrols north and south of their stations, always at low tide. At high water the cold South Atlantic surf protects the diamonds, and the police may rest. You may call on these lonely policemen if you wish, and stand on beaches where unsuspected wealth lay hidden for centuries. But there are strange crimes in Namaqualand, and many things are forbidden. "You must not carry a spade or even pick up a pebble," a constable explained to me. "When the farmers come and camp out with their families on these beaches at New Year, we have to warn them that their children cannot play as other seaside children do, with spades and buckets."

Police are always on the alert for pot-holes and signs of digging. They play the cat-and-mouse game. When they find a newly-dug hole in the ground they wait under cover at night. Sooner or later the diamond poachers return. Then the law pounces on them. No need to prove they are in possession of diamonds. Their spades and sheepskin shoes (used to deaden the sound of footsteps) mark them as law-breakers.

But all the coastal diamond deposits I have shown you so far have been mere pot-holes, hardly worth guarding. Now, less than fifty miles north of Hondeklip Bay, the fabulously rich diamond crater of Kleinzee opens out before you. Kleinzee stands beside one of those dry and sandy river-beds which are typical of the whole west coast. This is the Buffels River, but you may have to wait for years to see water in it. Long ago, however, the flowing river must have brought down diamonds. The Kleinzee treasure was revealed by accident. There was a farm school near the river mouth in charge of a teacher named De Villiers. He had been there for sixteen years; his heart was in his work, and while others were eagerly prospecting along the coast, De Villiers was building a new school.

It was a simple house of sun-dried bricks, and De Villiers intended to whitewash the walls. He walked across the veld one day with Alberts, the mason, in search of lime. De Villiers kicked the earth in every promising spot. By chance he kicked up a diamond.

Alberts, who had a brother-in-law who was a lawyer, drove swiftly to the little town of Springbok with the news. A syndicate was formed. Alberts and De Villiers found ten more diamonds within sixteen days; a week later they had registered six hundred carats and sold them for £6,000. Then a large company bought the claims for £35,000. I hope the hard-working schoolmaster, the mason and the lawyer were satisfied. Only a week after they had sold out, the famous Kleinzee crater was opened, and the first haul (insignificant compared with later finds) was valued at £120,000. The farm which could not have grazed a hundred sheep for a week had become a treasure-house.

They put barbed-wire round it then, and police guarded the gate. Kleinzee became a little Kimberley, with a huge crushing, washing and pulsator plant dealing with a thousand tons of gravel a day. There are neat electric-lit homes, messes for the single men, barracks for the native labourers.

The manager of this costly enterprise at the time of my visit was Jack Carstens. He was the first man to discover diamonds in Namaqualand. One day in 1925 I had watched old Mr William Carstens and his son Jack at work on their claims six miles south of Port Nolloth. In my mind there was no inkling of the sensational discoveries that would soon follow ; and I am not going to be wise after the event. In those days anyone could become a prospector, go where he wished with spade and sieve, turn up a fortune—or return to Port Nolloth empty-handed. I simply looked at the discoverers, saw them washing their gravel, and thought what a dreary and unprofitable business it was. Yet this was the prelude to the sensational Alexander Bay discovery ; here on the barren shore was the key to a treasure-house that has yielded millions and will reveal millions more. It should have rung a bell in my bored mind. Instead, I walked away feeling thankful that I had booked my passage to Cape Town in the coasting steamer *Pemba*. I went back to the hotel and drank a glass of beer.

Long afterwards Mr Carstens told me the whole story. (He was eighty-four then, and nearly a centenarian when he died.) He said that he had heard of gravel to the south of Port Nolloth before World War I. A farmer had brought him samples, and they looked promising. But his sons went away to the war, and he thought no more of it for ten years. Not until 1925 did they open up the deposit. Jack Carstens was the first of the family to pick a diamond out of the wash. It was not a rich deposit, but their finds more than covered expenses and they discussed further prospecting.

Jack Carstens wanted to go north, to Alexander Bay. " It's a wash-out," declared his old father. Thus the Carstens family lost the chance of millions. Dr Hans Merensky, a geologist who had long believed in the presence of diamonds at the Orange River mouth, heard of the small finds made by the Carstens family and set out to test his own theory. Early in 1927 he opened up the famous fossil oyster terraces at Alexander Bay. In six weeks diamonds worth £150,000 were recovered.

Such a secret could not be kept for long. The great Namaqualand diamond rush started—and the Union Government, to save the diamond market from collapse, stepped in and banned further prospecting. Moreover, the Government took up its mineral rights in the whole neighbourhood beyond the Merensky claims, and soon revealed wealth far greater than Merensky's wildest dreams. Two labourers in official employment at seven and sixpence a day moved a small boulder aside and found diamonds valued at half a million. This was Aladdin's Cave indeed. The rush became a drama.

To understand the difficulties and the final victory of the law over the diamond gangs you must visualise the coast of Namaqualand as it was just after Dr Merensky had patiently followed the scientific trail to the main diamond deposit at Alexander Bay. Even then prospecting was still permitted all along the coast to the south, and on the beaches where every tide washed diamonds on to the rocks. Alexander Bay itself was wired and guarded, but there was nothing to prevent men from creeping up to the fence at night and receiving diamonds flung to them in tins filled with porridge to prevent the tell-tale rattle.

White labourers employed on the State diggings were searched when they left; but a hundred clever devices were used, and for every man caught a score escaped with their loot. Some of the boldest swallowed their diamonds; one man was found by the police with twenty-five diamonds of fair sizes in his stomach, diamonds worth £8,000. It was a trick that was not so dangerous as it appears and there were no deaths. Others hid their diamonds in deep cuts in their legs. Even when the bandages were removed the diamonds were well concealed by the flesh.

Thus it was necessary first to guard the long stretch of diamondiferous coast, besides rich pot-holes farther inland. Equally important was the prevention of all leakages from the State diamond diggings at Alexander Bay.

If the police had failed in this enormous task, the control of the diamond output would have broken down. State and illicit dealers alike would have been left in possession of worthless stones as a result of a glutted market. Indeed, the illicit trade in Namaqualand actually depressed the price of diamonds before the police precautions became effective.

In Port Nolloth I learnt from police officers how the barricade against invaders had been thrown up and maintained. Port Nolloth is the headquarters of the Diamond Detective Department—the 'D.D.D.', which started in the old days at Kimberley and spread its quiet activities wherever diamonds were found afterwards. I do not suppose the Gestapo ever knew more about suspects than the plain-clothes men of the 'D.D.D.' know about the people in the huge diamond area of Namaqualand.

At first the police were hampered by the law, which banned prospecting along the coast but did not make illegal the presence of hordes of diggers close to the sources of the diamonds. A test case established the fact that it was not illegal to prospect in the sea or between high- and low-water mark, and the law had to be altered before this large loophole could be closed. It was said at that time that more diamonds were being sold in Port Nolloth than in Hatton Garden. Every dark night, when the tide was low, men worked in the ice-cold water, filled sacks with gravel, and dashed away in fast cars to wash their finds. Sore legs were the marks of the raider. The game of hide-and-seek in the sand dunes was played for months before the police, reinforced and supported by new laws, were able to make these night raids too dangerous for profit.

Alexander Bay is now a self-contained town, hemmed in by twelve miles of barbed-wire entanglements, and protected further by a no-man's-land stretching to the outer fence. Hundreds of diggers are employed there by the Government. The size of the police force is a secret, but I am sure it is large enough to hold the fort against an attacking army. ' Little London ' they call Alexander Bay, for at night the electric display and the searchlights throw into the sky a white glare that can be seen many miles away. And that is all the ordinary citizens can see of the State diggings. Nothing but a letter signed by the Minister of Mines will procure admission, even into no-man's-land.

When a digger enters Alexander Bay for the six months' period of work he is searched. A man arriving with a large sum of money would have to explain it : money buys diamonds. The pick-and-shovel men working in the gravel trenches are not permitted to touch a diamond. Everything must go into the cocopans, which transport the gravel to the washing-plant. The men wear a special pocketless uniform, which they must leave in the changing room while they walk naked to the bathrooms. These and other precautions have eliminated nearly every risk of loss. The well-known Kimberley method of detecting thefts by swallowing would not be tolerated by white diggers, so for some years past an X-ray plant has been in use. Every digger passing out on leave is photographed.

Sometimes the exiles of Alexander Bay amuse themselves by suggesting undiscovered methods of diamond smuggling. The carrier-pigeon idea was a good one, except that no man would stand a chance of entering the gates with a pigeon in his luggage. One carpenter applied for leave to take his tools away with him, as he might have some odd jobs to do during his holiday. The tools were examined minutely, and diamonds worth £15,000 were found, not inside the wooden handles, but in the hollowed-out metal of the tools. I believe the X-ray specialist played a part in that episode.

One of the best Alexander Bay stories in recent years arose out of the visit of an official to the camp. He travelled in his own motor-car, and while he was attending to his duties someone hid a parcel of diamonds in the petrol-tank. After a few days the official left the camp without being searched and drove back to Pretoria. The unorthodox smuggler secured leave, went to Pretoria, stole the man's car and extracted the diamonds. Steps have been taken to close that sort of loophole, but I have no doubt that from time to time human ingenuity will find ways of defeating the system, though it will not be easy.

Famous diamonds have a way of appearing and vanishing, only to shine again in all sorts of dramas, all too often of the tragic sort. I am thinking now of the Cullinan, the greatest diamond of all (or rather the lost half of the Cullinan), and the last words of a murderer in the condemned cell of Kimberley prison.

All the great diamonds of the world seem to have carried a curse during some part of their careers. One owner of the Hope diamond went to the guillotine, another was torn to pieces by dogs. The slave who slashed his thigh to hide a huge diamond he had stolen, known later as the Regent, was thrown to the sharks. For six hundred years the story of the Koh-i-Noor has been recorded, and there was a time when it left a trail of blood across the East.

Perhaps the Cullinan has lost its sting. The man who was bold enough to split this giant collapsed and spent three months in a sanatorium. Since then the nine stones cut from it have gleamed serenely as the brightest gems in the British crown jewels.

But what of the lost half? Nearly everyone knows that the stone was found in the Premier Mine near Pretoria by Captain Fred Wells nearly sixty years ago. Wells had to climb a vertical face in the open mine to investigate the dazzling sparkle of a huge object reflecting the rays of the setting sun. He levered the blue-white monster out of the soil with his pocket knife and fell, almost breaking his neck in the excitement, with by far the largest diamond ever found.

Yet it was obviously only half the diamond, possibly less than half. There was a 'cleavage face,' and experts declared immediately that this mighty diamond was only a part of a larger octohedral stone. Yet the part measured four inches by two by two. It weighed one pound six ounces; more than three thousand English carats. This meant that the diamond (named Cullinan after the discoverer of the mine) was three times the size of any other diamond known at that period.

Were the experts right in searching feverishly for the 'lost half' of the Cullinan? The theory was supported by some of the leading authorities on the diamond. Among them were Dr G. A. F. Molengraaf, former state geologist in the Transvaal Republic, and Sir William Crookes, President of the Royal Society.

This is not a romantic legend, but something very close to a geological fact. The missing portion may have been stolen; or broken up unnoticed in the crushing machinery;

or it may still rest in the blue clay pipe leading to unknown depths in the bowels of the earth.

In an evil moment the mine manager, McHardy, showed the Cullinan with innocent pride to one Johannes Faurie, a poor farmer living near the Premier Mine. By this time the rumour had gone round that the missing half had been stolen by a mine labourer. Faurie became obsessed with the idea of finding it.

Faurie was really a dangerous criminal, with convictions for robbery and other crimes. He spread a report in the Pretoria underworld that he was willing to pay one thousand gold sovereigns for a very large diamond. There was no immediate response, but in 1907 the offer brought him into touch with a native named Paulus, who had worked on the mine.

At this stage Faurie entered into an agreement with a Dr D. J. van Wyk, who financed the venture. Dr van Wyk, it should be mentioned, intended to return the 'missing half' to the mine authorities and claim a substantial reward. The queer agreement read as follows:

'We the undersigned Johannes Hendrik Hermanus Faurie and Dr Daniel Jacobus van Wyk hereby guarantee and bind ourselves, persons and property to Johannes Paulus that he will not get into any trouble, and that he will not be prosecuted by law in any way whatsoever if he secure and hand over to us certain two parcels of diamonds of which one is a special big one, the whereabouts of which is known to him, and to pay to him his share of cash as agreed by us for his services in this business, on receipt of such cash by us.'

It seems that the agreement was drawn up to reassure Paulus, who feared prosecution. A meeting was arranged, and Dr van Wyk insisted on a detective being present. Detective Hill, who had been stationed at the Premier Mine, accompanied Dr van Wyk and Faurie to the meeting-place on the veld near Pretoria at night.

Faurie, far from sane and crooked to the marrow, hoped to hand Paulus a bag containing metal washers, with a top layer of genuine sovereigns, in exchange for the great diamond. Paulus appears to have discovered the trick, for he fled into the darkness. The three white men never saw him again, though Detective Hill heard in 1927 that he was still alive.

Hill declared that he never saw the stone. He was some distance from the others, probably hidden. Van Wyk and Faurie caught a glimpse of something that looked like an enormous diamond. It was a momentary flash, revealed in the light of a lamp which Faurie had lit to show Paulus the sovereigns.

Faurie was now more determined than ever to carry on the search. He questioned hundreds of natives, until information came to him that the missing half was in the possession of Chief Mathibe in a tribal area near Pretoria. Faurie played a leading part in the intrigues of the tribe—always with the diamond at the back of his mind—and finally he gave the chief a glass of poisoned brandy. As the chief was dying, one of the tribesmen asked Faurie to sign his name. The crazy Faurie did so.

Detective Hill secured the evidence that sent Faurie to the gallows. Faurie's last words in the condemned cell were : " I alone know who the man is who has the other half of the great diamond. He is a man in Mathibe's tribe. If it was not for the diamond I would not be here. And now that I must die, I know where the diamond is."

Faurie was hanged, but the search for the lost half of the

Cullinan went on. Several of South Africa's most experienced diamond detectives were involved in a number of episodes—Major S. R. Brink, his brother S. J. H. Brink and Captain MacIntosh.

Again and again the detectives went out at night with bags of gold to meet natives who were supposed to have the diamond. Major Brink made one appointment at Moselikatse's Nek, above Hartbeespoort dam. He had a leather hand-bag filled with sovereigns, and a revolver in each trouser pocket. So dense were the trees at the spot that he took other precautions against attack. Another detective was hidden in the neighbourhood, ready to rush out if he heard a shot.

Andries Molife, the native Brink had come to meet, appeared and examined the sovereigns. Molife then pointed to a farm in the valley. " It is buried there—I will fetch it," he said.

" How big is this diamond ? " inquired Brink.

Molife clenched his fist. " As big as that," he said. Then he went away. And like Paulus, he never returned.

It is difficult to explain these episodes. The natives must have known that they would never have received any money unless they had something to offer. Perhaps they distrusted the police and feared arrest.

When the Jonker diamond, described as the world's fourth largest diamond, was found in 1934, many people said that this pure white, flawless gem was the ' missing half.' The diggings where the seven-hundred-carat Jonker stone appeared are only three miles from the Premier Mine. Experts did not agree with the theory. The ' missing half ' should be much larger than the Jonker.

Strange to say, the owners of the Premier were not altogether enthusiastic about the large diamonds which came out of that mine. No one knew what to do with the magnificent Cullinan until General Louis Botha thought of presenting it to King Edward VII. After all, how many people could afford half a million pounds sterling for one diamond ?

[July 1962

13

GOLD BRICKS AT BADULLA

P. H. Fawcett

This, the second Ceylon story * from the random
papers of the lost explorer, Colonel P. H. Fawcett,
for obvious reasons demands the precautionary
measure of discretion regarding the exact locations
of the treasures, which are fully explained in the
original notes. The episode of the Gold Bricks is
in the form of a comprehensive synthesis, as though
written with the idea of producing a full-length
account which in fact never materialised. The
Galla-pita-Galla and Hingaray Galla treasure notes
are contained in a leather-bound octavo ledger, fitted
with a lock, in which P. H. F. recorded in great
detail a number of treasure clues in Ceylon, South
America and elsewhere. He was a rabid treasure-
hunter and his ' Treasure Book ' is proof of this.
In it are to be found even extracts concerning the
Cocos Islands treasure, culled from *Blackwood's
Magazine* of January 1873!

Brian Fawcett

Judge Paterson of Galle, whose daughter I subsequently
wedded, showed me a cypher letter sent him in 1875 from
the deathbed of an old Sinhalese village headman—a *Ralamahatma*. It was accompanied by the following note, which
the dying man must have dictated : ' This I promised the
Master many years ago when I said that the kindness he
did me would one day be repaid a hundredfold '.

---

* The first was ' The Passing of Time ', *Blackwood's Magazine*,
February 1959.

"As a matter of fact," Judge Paterson remarked to me, "I couldn't at first recall the occasion. In my position of District Judge I have dealings with so many people—and I have been in Ceylon nearly thirty years, remember. I had no time to pay much attention to the matter; but there did finally come to mind a vague idea of having done a good turn many years ago to a *Ralamahatma* over some ground for coffee sheds."

I fingered the dirty, crumpled sheet of cheap notepaper with its carefully-written script in strange characters. The Chinese ink, rubbed from the stick, had gone a light sepia in many places, or may never have been thickly applied. The sheet itself had suffered somewhat from the destructive boring of termites. The Judge continued:

"A few days afterwards a messenger from the headman's household brought me another paper. He thrust it into my hands and made off without a word. On the paper was written in English: 'Key to Cypher'.

"I threw the whole thing into a drawer of the desk in my study, and there it lay for some time. Then one day, when I was going through old papers, I came across it. The old headman's valedictory note was pinned to it, and my curiosity was aroused; so by means of the key I deciphered it, and here is the result. Read it, Percy."

These were the words I read in the Judge's neat hand-writing:

'At the city of Badulla is a house built upon a hill for the residence of the commissioner. At the foot of this hill is the road which goes to Nuwara Eliya. On the opposite side of that road is a mountain. On the top of the mountain is a nearly level plain. At one end of this plain, and clearly visible from all sides, great rocks are piled. The place is called in the Sinhalese language *Galla-*

pita-Galla. The meaning is in the English tongue ' Rock upon Rock '. Beneath these rocks is a cave, once easy to enter, but now difficult of approach as the entrance is obscured by stones, jungle and long grass. Leopards are sometimes found there. In that cave is a treasure, the existence of which is known to me and to me alone. I acquired this knowledge in a singular way which it would take too long to narrate now. I am a dying man and trace these lines with difficulty. I use symbols in case of this letter falling into the hands of others. By a trustworthy servant I send the key to the cypher, which I dare not trust to the ordinary post. You did me unconsciously a great service once and I am now showing gratitude by making you rich. Enter the cave and when arrived as far as man can go—[the explicit directions are omitted by me. B. F.]—dig six feet deep . . . and you will come upon a great flat slab of rock. Raise this and in a vault below you will find uncut jewels and gold to an extent greater than that possessed of many kings.

'Another method is to take the last letter of the ancient inscription on the rock and measure nine feet north and west of it. . . .'

"And you never had any desire to look for the treasure ? " I inquired.

" My life has been far too busy," the Judge replied. " Besides, this sort of thing really doesn't have much interest for me. But I am aware of your predilection for treasures, Percy ; and that's why I've shown you the documents. If you have any inclination to do any investigating, take them and welcome."

" Do you personally place any credence in this ? Was your headman one whose—er—integrity you could feel confident of ? In other words, do you think it's genuine ? "

" If I were you, Percy, I should be far too cautious to approach such a matter with much optimism. I don't remember the headman at all, and I certainly didn't know him well. But in ancient Lanka (Ceylon) the ground was the wealthy man's bank, and many private hoards were buried for safe keeping. It was the general practice, too, to kill the workers who concealed the treasure. There may well be considerable amounts of precious stones and gold still lying hidden, their owners having been liquidated in a rebellion or raid. It was an age of violence and sudden death in Ceylon, for all the gentle doctrines of the *Hinayana*. But I'm not really competent to form any opinion about the authenticity of this particular story. I know a man who probably could tell you something. His name is Jumna Das, and he is the headman of a village not far from Badulla. He's a highly intelligent man—educated at an English public school—and should you ever go down there to look for this treasure, I can give you a letter to him."

We junior officers in Fort Frederick had been working very hard, and when a stand-easy became possible my Commanding Officer had no objections to granting me a month's leave. This was a heaven-sent opportunity to take a look at Galla-pita-Galla. I wrote Judge Paterson in Galle, and by return he sent me a letter of introduction to Jumna Das, whose village—which must, I'm afraid, be nameless—was some thirty miles out of Badulla. The year was 1888, and I was just twenty-one.

I arranged for a passage down the coast in a native lugger, any discomfort to be found aboard such a craft being more than offset by the delight of sailing those glorious waters from the exquisite and neglected harbour of Trincomalee to Batticaloa. The distance was in any case less than a hundred miles. There was far more discomfort in making the almost incredibly slow seventy-mile journey by bullock cart from Batticaloa to Badulla, capital of the Central Province.

I did not seek out Jumna Das at once. I wanted first to have a look at the place; and with this intention made discreet inquiries in town as to the whereabouts of the rocks. No one seemed to know the name; but one old bazaar man with whom I made friends thought Gallapita-Galla might be near the 'King's Bath', which was on the hill above Mr Dickson's plantation. "There are some rocks," he said; "but my people do not like to go there. They are very silly, Master. They say the place is haunted."

I felt sure I was on the right track, and paid a call on Dickson, the planter. There was now tea where not long ago was only forest, but Dickson's estate scarcely appeared to be flourishing. Dickson himself was red-faced and looked as if he liked the bottle—a small, flabby man and a stertorous mouth breather. His 'wife' was a native, his progeny numerous and none too clean. I made no secret of my mission, and he for his part was not averse to speaking on the subject of nearby treasure; for of course the stories of such were familiar to him. He told me two surprising things. One was that he recollected having attended the bedside of a dying headman who stated that he had disclosed the secret of a large buried treasure to a friend who had done him a good turn. The other was that, when he was planting tea one day, the crowbar for making holes slipped from a coolie's hands and disappeared into the ground. When opened up, a pit was disclosed at the bottom of which was a cave whose walls were brilliant with crystals of mica. On the floor of the cave Dickson picked up a ruby which he subsequently sold for sixty pounds. He never investigated the matter further.

"I'm concerned only with what's above ground," he told me; "not with what's under it. But if you like I'll show you the place."

It was not far from the shabby house. The sides of the pit had fallen in. It may by now be filled in completely, and if so would be very difficult, if not impossible, to find. The position of it was about halfway between the track and the bungalow on the hillside.

"As to this place you're looking for—Galla-pita-Galla did you call it?—I'm afraid I can't tell you anything," said Dickson. "There's a ruin up there they call the 'King's Bath', which may once have been a tank or something, but as for rocks—why, dammit, it's all rocks! Farther along, well outside the bounds of my place, there's a sort of isolated pile of them, with a small *dagoba* on top —that's a shrine—but the name isn't Galla-pita-Galla—it's Hingaray Galla. There's thick jungle there too. One of them archae—what-d'you-call-'ems—archaeologist blokes —that's right—he was a German and his name was Gold-smid—died long ago—found an inscription or something on the rock under the *dagoba* and deciphered it. Gave it to me in exchange for something or other—don't remember what—and I've still got it somewhere. You can make a copy of it if you like. All about some treasure or other underneath. I can't be bothered. As I told you, what I'm interested in is my tea, and I don't give a tinker's damn for all this treasure stuff they say is buried in these parts. Besides, it's unlucky. You mark my words: it's unlucky—best leave it alone. This is Ceylon—it isn't England. When you've lived here as long as I have you'll realise there's things—funny things—you don't find at home."

"You may be right," was my reply; "but there's more to it than just treasure. I'll go and have a look at this inscription at Hingaray Galla, if you'll explain exactly how to find the spot. And then I'm off to visit a local *Ralamahatma* called Jumna Das. I've a letter to him from the friend who gave me the Galla-pita-Galla document."

"Well, you don't have to leave town. You're in luck. I know Jumna Das well. He's here in Badulla on a visit. Saw him only yesterday. And if anyone can tell you where Galla-pita-Galla is, it's him. He's a Kandyan— schooled in England—fine chap—getting on in age a bit now, but still a big man in these parts—descendant of the Kandyan kings, so they say—real gent, if ever there was one. You go off and meet him, and meanwhile I'll look out that old Hingaray Galla paper for you to copy."

Dickson told me where I might find Jumna Das, and that evening I sought him out. He proved to be rather a big man for a Sinhalese, white-bearded and erect, and his English was clipped so slightly as to be virtually perfect. He received me most courteously and beamed upon me when he had read the Judge's letter of introduction.

"I'm delighted to meet you, Lieutenant Fawcett," he said. "Judge Paterson says here that you wish to ask me certain questions concerning the topography and history of this district. Rather than answer you now—if, indeed, I'm able to—why not come to my village and give me the pleasure of your company for a few days? I have to return home first thing tomorrow. My humble house can scarcely offer you the comfort to which you are doubtless accustomed, but if you don't mind roughing it a little it would be conferring a distinct pleasure on me, and we would have plenty of time to discuss all the points on which you may wish to question me. Have you the time available?"

I accepted his invitation like a shot, and set off with him next day after dispatching a note to Dickson informing him of my going and promising to call on him as soon as I returned to Badulla. Jumna Das was a most interesting travelling companion, prolific of information such as one does not ordinarily meet with in this most beautiful of islands, the Ophir of Solomon. Among other things, he told me:

" This region was once the centre of a principality called Rahuna. Gold was mined locally, and the whole hill country was rich in gems. The headmen and princes hereabouts were frequently possessed of great wealth, and such a hoard as you mention might have been buried pending a raid—probably by Tamils—or an uprising. Many such finds of great or small importance have been made by native peoples from time to time, but I do not think the really great hoards have been disturbed. The treasure of the Kandyan kings is known to have been buried here, and has never been found. There is no doubt that archaeological remains and mineral deposits may be found in or near the foothills to the south-east of Badulla, or between a point east of the town and the village of Wellawaya to the south. This region is not well known and has certainly not been widely prospected."

I asked him if he knew the whereabouts of Galla-pita-Galla, and told him why.

" I could take you and show you the place, but it's difficult to explain. I certainly know it, and I have also heard that there were, possibly still are, passages under it.

There are white peoples and native peoples still living in Badulla who can remember a tunnel from the top of the hill, at what is called the ' King's Bath ', to the foot. But this passage has disappeared now in mould. Mould collects very rapidly and obliterates landmarks, you know. I also know that no systematic search has been made at Galla-pita-Galla ; though it is possible there may have been sporadic attempts. My people have a profound respect for the ancient things, which may be called superstition perhaps. It was the custom of the people of old, when hiding their possessions, to protect them with a curse upon anyone who should lay hands on them. You may regard this as nonsense, but we of Ceylon do not ; for we believe that the ancients had powers that have now been forgotten. There are few native peoples who would defy such a curse."

Jumna Das's apologies for his house were superfluous. He made me very comfortable there and was the soul of hospitality. It was only the myriads of hungry fleas that suggested any sense of martyrdom ; but one gets accustomed to these things in the tropics.

On the day after our arrival we were seated on the veranda after a *chota hazri* of fruit and coffee when three Veddahs appeared in the compound. The Veddahs are the bush folk of the Ceylon forests, pure-blooded specimens rarely being met with these days. They live as naked hunters without shelter, are dark-skinned and have very black hair and beards—a people small of stature and shy by nature, speaking a language of their own—the remnants of some race that has vanished into myth even as the fabled giants of Lanka have vanished. I had always wanted to meet some of them, and had never hitherto been successful.

Jumna Das knew these Veddahs well and hailed them by name. He knew enough of their language to inquire what they were bringing. Each was carrying two black bricks about two inches by three by four in size. Jumna Das subsequently translated for my benefit the conversation he exchanged with them.

The bricks, they said, were lumps of iron which from their weight would make very good spear and arrow heads. Would the *Ralamahatma* be kind enough to have these weapons prepared for them? My host told them to deposit the bricks on the veranda and come back in about a fortnight's time with skins in exchange, and all would be ready for them. They salaamed low and retired to the back of the bungalow, where Jumna Das ordered a meal to be given them before they departed.

Later that day, we were again seated on the veranda when Jumna Das rose from his chair and went over to the pile of six iron bricks. He picked one up and hefted it. Then he turned and brought it to me.

" What do you think of this, Lieutenant? It is extraordinarily heavy for its size. Can it really be iron? "

I took the brick from him. Its weight was considerable, and it was thickly coated with a black crust that seemed to me of vegetable origin rather than oxide. I took out my pocket-knife and scratched the crust away until the metal was exposed. It gleamed yellow.

My heart was racing with excitement but I forced my voice to remain steady and asked Jumna Das if by any chance he could obtain any nitric acid. By a stroke of luck he was able to and with it we tested the scratched surface of the brick. Beyond any doubt it was gold. We similarly tested the other bricks. All responded in the same way. Each one weighed approximately fifteen pounds;

so the value of the six must have been about seven thousand pounds sterling.

"You came here seeking treasure, Lieutenant," Jumna Das remarked; "and a by-no-means inconsiderable one has been laid at our feet. Where did they find these gold bricks? Obviously, they have no idea what they are. The Veddahs are very simple people, and iron is worth more to them than gold because with it tools and weapons can be made. We shall have to possess ourselves in patience for two weeks until they return for their arrow and spear heads. Until then we can learn nothing more."

"Would it not be possible to trace them?"

"A Veddah! Oh no, Lieutenant; it would be impossible. They move in the forest as furtively as the wild animals. Only a Veddah could track a Veddah. Myself, I have not the least idea where they live. From time to time they come to me for spear heads and arrow tips which I have made for them in exchange for skins, and afterwards they vanish into the jungle as though they had never been."

"I would dearly love to see the end of this," I remarked; "but I shall be gone before they return. Might I ask you to write and tell me the outcome?"

"But why? Why not stay? There will still be time for you to return to Trincomalee; and perhaps you can postpone your investigations at Badulla for another occasion. This is something quite extraordinary and worth waiting for. Stay here, I beg you, until the Veddahs return. They never fail to appear when they say they will."

I needed little persuasion to accept. The ensuing days were enlivened by the outings we took together, and the fascinating talks on the ancient history of the region which Jumna Das untiringly provided. It was difficult for me to contain my excitement when, on the twelfth day, the Veddahs reappeared salaaming in the compound. A pile of well-polished weapons lay on the veranda ready for them. For their part, they each bore a heavy load of animal skins on their backs, which they laid down in front of us.

My host told them that the metal they had brought was so good that it was easy to work up, and if they brought more of it he was quite prepared to make the weapons free in return for one out of every four bricks for himself. Where, he inquired, did they find it?

The Veddahs salaamed, and their spokesman replied that they had discovered a hole in the ground where the surface had apparently fallen in, and at the bottom of the pit were many, many of these bricks. So heavy were they that only six had been taken. They were not sure if they could find it again. Near this pit, carved stones lay scattered on the ground, as of old buildings, he said. It was far away in the lower forest, but they would instantly go to look for the place and bring the *Ralamahatma* more of the good iron.

Jumna Das translated all this to me before questioning the spokesman further. But no more could be got from the man. He had said his say, and any insistence might have aroused his suspicions. My host directed them to go round to the back of the house, where a meal would be provided for them; the Veddahs salaamed again and withdrew after taking up the arrow heads and spear tips, apparently well satisfied.

"I shall have to leave you tomorrow," I said; "so I won't know what transpires next time they come, unless you write and tell me."

Jumna Das replied:

" If they bring more gold bricks I shall be in a quandary. It has struck me that it may be difficult to dispose of these six without questions being asked ; and I am ignorant of the law of treasure-trove, or even if such a law exists in Ceylon. Certainly I shall write to tell you if the Veddahs succeed in finding their gold pit. I am only sorry you cannot stay longer with me, for your presence has bestowed great honour on my humble house. But I realise you have no choice but to return to Trincomalee without delay. Consider my house as yours, my friend, and give me the pleasure of another visit next time you come this way."

On the following morning I returned to Badulla, made arrangements for the journey back to Trincomalee, and called on Dickson. The planter was a little the worse for liquor, but he had found the Hingaray Galla inscription and the translation by the German archaeologist Goldsmid, of which he had told me ; and I took a copy of both before taking leave of him. I told him that Jumna Das had offered to show me the location of Galla-pita-Galla, but not one word did I say about the Veddahs' gold bricks.

I received a letter from Jumna Das about three months after my return to Trincomalee. The Veddahs had been at his house again with skins, and had informed him that they were unable to find the pit with the iron bricks.

' I cannot tell if what they say is true, or whether they are suspicious of the interest I have expressed. It would seem unlikely that jungle men of their sort cannot retrace steps to any place where they have found something useful to them.

' When they left my house this time, I sent the village tracker, a very good man, to follow and find out where they went. But the tracker failed lamentably, and I now fear I did a foolish thing, making Veddahs suspect I am spying on them. Alas, they may now never return!

'I can do nothing with six ingots of iron still in my house until law is clarified to me. I think that if you, sir, will do a great good kindness by consulting honourable Judge Paterson on matter as purely hypothetical case, not mentioning my name or the indisposable iron in my house, much help will result. I am thinking of it in case you should ask him, suppose you find something valuable in Galla-pit-Galla, how would you be able to dispose of it legally and above board, without resorting to a criminal act against the law, and at same time not having the Government take it all away in confiscation.

'Before Veddahs came with that iron I was a happy man with no cares except for my village. I now worry all the time. I beseech you to learn from my case the moral of this before you make a search at Galla-pita-Galla. These things bring always bad luck.'

In the meantime, my interest was focusing more upon that fascinating site, Hingaray Galla. If Goldsmid's translation of the inscription were correct, *that* should be the starting point for any systematic search. I say 'starting point' because no less than three separate hoards were indicated in the inscription, and Hingaray Galla appeared to offer the best chances of initial success. Galla-pita-Galla was probably the location of the second of these hoards—there was certainly something there, if the Judge's old headman was speaking the truth—and the third might reasonably be supposed to lie still undisturbed at the bottom of Dickson's ruby pit.

The first and most obvious thing for me to do was to authenticate Goldsmid's translation. This took time. By diverse means I was at last enabled to contact the expert H, who took the copy of the inscription for study. He returned it with the remark that it was merely a list of temple properties. This was disappointing; for H was reputed to possess an encyclopaedic knowledge of the languages of ancient Lanka. A fellow officer in Fort Frederick, with whom I was on very friendly terms at the time, then suggested that he send it to the Indian scholar W, who had the chair of Eastern Archaeology at Oxford. He knew W well enough to solicit that eminent man's opinion.

"And what's more, old chap," he said to me, "I'd suggest you let me have Goldsmid's translation to go with the copy of the inscription. It isn't signed or anything. If I ask old W to say if the translation is correct, there's far more likelihood of getting an opinion out of him than if I ask him to decipher the damned inscription itself. To vet Goldsmid's version probably wouldn't take long; but to work out the meaning of the inscription from scratch might be a formidable enough undertaking to make him reply to me that he just hadn't time. See what I mean?"

I thought the idea a sound one and gave him both copies to send off to his friend W. A reply in less than six months was unlikely; but there was plenty of time. I invited him to join forces with me for the work at Badulla when the opportunity should occur for getting down to it; but he lacked my own enthusiasm, and was in any case not sanguine about the chances of us both being able to obtain the necessary amount of long leave at the same time.

When I next saw Judge Paterson I sounded him out on Jumna Das's behalf. But I was dealing with a man of rigid judicial integrity, and there could be but one answer:

"My dear boy: if by any chance you were to unearth anything of value at Badulla, it would be obligatory on your part to place it in the hands of the authorities, *at once*."

For the first time I began to appreciate Jumna Das's predicament. Next moment I was asking myself if the actual discovery of the Hingaray Galla hoard would be accompanied by an overwhelming sense of triumph or the feeling of something like anticlimax. Did the hound find its greatest pleasure in the chase or in the killing of its quarry? Cats spend hours over the capture of a bird or mouse, and lose interest in the dead body. Were I to discover a considerable treasure, could I be sure that it would not cause me so much embarrassment and worry as to make me rue the day I found it? But I was too young to harbour such thoughts for long. That particular bridge could be crossed when I came to it. First I must find the treasure. In any case, even if under the law of treasure-trove the whole thing were handed over to the authorities, there was always a comfortable percentage of its value returned to the finder. Perhaps it would be the best plan for Jumna Das to declare his gold bricks and take what was returned to him—better than keeping them hidden away in his house, where they could do no good to him or to anyone else.

The return of the Hingaray Galla papers from W in Oxford washed from my mind all traces of doubt and left me boiling over with renewed enthusiasm. The translation of the inscription, said the scholar, was substantially correct. As far as he could judge, the inscription did indeed refer to a large treasure buried under the rock with the *dagoba* on top.

Five years passed before I was able to be in Badulla once more, with enough time—and only just enough—

for a search at Hingaray Galla. Dickson had gone. His estate, such as it was, had been sold to a Sinhalese. But Jumna Das was still in his village. The *Ralamahatma* came to Badulla to meet me. He conducted me personally to Galla-pita-Galla. Someone had been digging there. I saw no cave, such as the headman's document had mentioned, but there were some traces of fairly recent activity at one end of the piled rocks—the work of a single man, by the look of it. Dickson must have changed his mind about being interested only in his tea. But was it Dickson who had dug there, or the present owner? Jumna Das remarked:

"Whoever it was, my young friend, it does not appear that he succeeded in finding anything. The digging is not extensive and does not go beneath the rock—unless it has been carefully filled in and the earth arranged to hide the truth. But if he had carried away whole vast treasure of the Kandyan kings I would feel only sorrow for him! I have had no peace of mind since those accursed gold bricks were brought by the Veddahs—who, by the way, I have not seen since I foolishly sent my village tracker on their trail. The six bricks are still in my house. However, I do think that at last—after all this time—a solution to the problem is presenting. More I cannot yet say. . . ."

I spoke to him of my plans for the work at Hingaray Galla. He had already seen the translation of the rock inscription. He feared that procuring labour might be my biggest problem.

"The peoples who live here fear these ancient places very much. You will call me foolish perhaps, but I too would not dare defy the warning in that inscription, and I beg you to think again before you do. Ceylon is a very old country, and ancient peoples had more wisdom than we of today know of. I do not like the idea of disturbing what they buried for safe keeping. If you find what you seek and take it away from a centuries-old resting place, very bad things might happen to you. Leave treasure alone, I pray you, and study instead other remains ancient peoples left—as I do. These jungles cover traces of civilisations far older than those of Anaradhapura and other places which tourists go to see. I would prefer to know more of those ruins the Veddahs tell me about than all the black bricks at the bottom of the pit they found!"

So should I—now. But in 1893, as an impecunious Artillery lieutenant, the idea of treasure was too attractive to abandon. Moreover, there was now promise of an exciting climax to my searches in this region. The immediate need was for labour. Jumna Das shrugged his shoulders in a gesture of resignation at my obstinacy, but promised what help he could give in procuring that labour.

In the little-trodden jungle surrounding Hingaray Galla there was a tiny village whose inhabitants, half Veddahs, visited the place in fear and trembling (so bad was its reputation, even in daylight) to gather up from time to time the coins kicked out from under the rock by the porcupines. Jumna Das paid a visit to the headman of this village on my behalf; a parley was held with the elders of the community; and a flat refusal to disturb the earth in any way near the rock was almost immediately forthcoming. A more generous offer in the matter of payment caused some of the men to think again. There was much argument and wagging of heads. A further increase in the offer resulted finally in a reluctant acceptance by eight men and the headman to constitute my labour force. The estimated cost of the work was now greater than I had anticipated, which meant that I would be forced to cut it short if there was not immediate success.

With everything ready for the work to commence I moved into a lonely camp in the jungle near the rock. The village was far enough away to be out of earshot, and when darkness had fallen my sense of isolation in this haunted spot was pronounced. I did in fact have a peculiar and somewhat terrifying experience there, which I don't propose to relate here; but it served in some measure as corroborative evidence to convince me, if that were still necessary, that the treasure hoard of Hingaray Galla might be unearthed relatively easily—and certainly that it was there for the taking.

My men displayed clear signs of nervousness when, next morning, they arrived on the scene carrying picks and shovels. I indicated to the headman where to start digging, choosing a likely-looking spot under a slight overhang of the rock face, on the same side as the partially-eroded inscription. There was no spirit in the way they handled their tools. Obviously, it would take little to discourage them altogether.

The ground was banked up to a height of several feet all round the rock. After shifting some of this soil we discovered a layer of river stones, and beneath that, more soil followed by another layer of river stones. The small holes and animal burrows pockmarking the earth at the foot of the rock must be quite extensive, I thought, if through them coins were ejected from a deposit in a pit or cave beneath. I was impatient to complete the penetration, urging the headman to order his coolies to put their backs into it. But it was useless. Two or three would peck at the ground with their shovels while the rest argued among themselves vociferously in a language I could not understand.

Slowly, slowly our hole increased in depth as the sun moved towards the west. At this rate it might be a couple of days before we won through; but the picks were now turning up scraps of broken pottery, bricks and bits of rusty iron. My excitement was intense. About two hours before sunset I went to my tent for a drink of water. Suddenly there came startled cries from the coolies. I rushed out in time to see them hurling their tools aside and stampeding for the jungle, led by the headman. Something white, or nearly white, caught my eye in the digging —something that swayed to and fro in the midst of the raw red earth and tumbled stones. Receding yells and crashes from the scrub told me that my coolie gang was in full flight for their village.

The cause of their panic was a white cobra. It was quite a large specimen of its kind, and without doubt the scraping and thumping of tools had disturbed it in its lair somewhere deep under the rock. It had emerged from one of the many burrows. Probably blinded by the unaccustomed light, it lifted its head with its extended hood of a sickly, pale colour about two feet off the ground and remained in that position swaying gently from side to side. I could see its flickering tongue, but the spectacle marks on the hood were so bleached as to be scarcely perceptible. It was clearly a creature of the dark, living on the insects and rodents that found their way to its vicinity. The daylight must have caused it discomfort; for in a short while it dropped into a coil, quested about with its head, and slowly re-entered the hole from which it had crept. The end of its ghostly white tail remained outside for an appreciable interval before being drawn within.

I was not eager to pass another night in my tent in that weird place; so, leaving the camping equipment to be collected next day, I set off for Badulla. I knew nothing would induce those men to return and resume work. They were frightened enough of the place anyway, and I was aware of the general superstitious dread of white cobras among people of their kind. They would consider it a warning to keep away—a warning by the guardian spirits.

Jumna Das went further than merely agreeing with me on that point. He even congratulated me on my own 'escape'.

" You young men are so impetuous," he said. " You will not accept the warnings of us old ones who have the experience. I am glad your work at Hingaray Galla has been stopped ; for you are my friend, and it would distress me for you to suffer the penalties had you been successful in reaching the treasure. Try no more, I beg you. Let sleeping dogs lie. So far you have lost nothing but your time, and a little money, which is of no importance. Had you gone on and taken away what may be there under Hingaray Galla, death in some horrible form might have come to you ! "

I let Jumna Das have his say, but without abandoning the idea of some day completing the investigations interrupted in such a frustrating manner. It was obviously impossible to do any more on this occasion. Apart from the labour problem, my funds were too limited.

I never managed to get back there at all. The year 1895 found me at Shoeburyness on the ' Long Course ' of gunnery, followed by a spell at Falmouth. When I eventually returned to Ceylon it was as a married man. I can now abandon any thought of treasure hunting at Badulla without regret ; but by the look of it, my little son Jack is going to pass through the same phase as I did when he reaches early manhood. Already he is fascinated by the stories we tell him of Galla-pita-Galla and Jumna Das's gold bricks. He frequently demands as a bedtime story ' Daddy's adventure at Hingaray Galla ', and this is never complete for him without a reading of the inscription carved on the rock under the ruined shrine—the words that Goldsmid penned so long ago. But those words would thrill anyone with an ounce of romance in him, let alone a small boy. Judge for yourself :

' There were years of famine in the land during which there was no rain. Consequently the population lay down to die. The King and his subjects after a time brought all their wealth and possessions and buried them in a cave under this rock and blocked up the passage, building a large embankment all round. There was buried an image of Buddha of the height of a man, made of *Maharatrang* (ancient gold) worth an immense fortune, besides which even elephant chains were buried here, and everything in the land of any value. This inscription was made and a *dagoba* was built over the rock to mark the spot.

' Three different lots of treasure were buried in this place—one belonging to the King ; one to the temples ; and one to the subjects.

' Beware—a curse will fall on whoever dares disturb what has been placed here.'

[March 1965

TALES from 'BLACKWOOD' ★

The following books are uniform with this volume:

FLYING TALES (*Second Series*)

TALES OF THE FIGHTING NAVY

SOLDIERS' BATTLE TALES

MEDICAL TALES

GREAT ESCAPE TALES

GHOST TALES

Price 21s per volume

★BLACKWOOD'S MAGAZINE

The doyen of short story magazines. Founded in 1817, it provides original stories of work and play, adventure and humour, and honest and intelligent comment on world affairs. For a sample copy, send a sixpenny stamp to 6 Buckingham Street, London WC2.